The School Mathema

G000150790

When the SMP was founded in 1961, its main objective was to devise radically new secondary school mathematics courses to reflect, more adequately than did the traditional syllabuses, the up-to-date nature and usages of mathematics. The first texts produced embodied new courses for O-level and A-level, and SMP GCE examinations were set up, available to schools through any of the GCE examining boards.

Since its beginning the SMP has continued to develop new materials and approaches to the teaching of mathematics. Further series of texts have been produced to meet new needs, and the original books are revised or replaced in the light of changing circumstances and experience in the classroom.

The SMP A-level course is now covered by *Revised Advanced Mathematics Books 1, 2* and *3*. Five shorter texts cover the material of the various sections of the A-level examination SMP Further Mathematics. The SMP Additional Mathematics syllabus has been revised and a new text replaces the original two books at this level.

The six Units of *SMP 7–13*, designed for pupils in that age-range, provide a course which is widely used in primary schools, middle schools and the first two years of secondary schools. A useful preliminary to Unit 1 of *SMP 7–13* is *Pointers*, a booklet for teachers which offers suggestions for mathematical activities with young children.

There is now a range of SMP materials for the eleven to sixteen age-range. The SMP O-level course is covered by *Books 1, 2* and *New Books 3, 4, 5. Books A–G* and *X, Y, Z*, together with the booklets of the *SMP Calculator Series*, also cover the O-level course, while *Books A–H* provide a CSE course for which most CSE boards offer a suitable examination.

SMP 11–16, designed to cater for about the top 85% of the ability range, is the newest SMP secondary school course, providing varied materials which facilitate the provision of a differentiated curriculum to match the varying abilities of pupils. Publication of this course began in 1983 and will be complete in 1988.

Teacher's Guides accompany all these series.

The SMP has produced many other texts, and teachers are encouraged to obtain each year from Cambridge University Press, The Edinburgh Building, Shaftesbury Road, Cambridge CB2 2RU, the full list of SMP publications currently available. In the same way, help and advice may always be sought by

THE LITTLEHAMPTON SCHOOL

teachers from The School Mathematics Project, The University of Southampton, Southampton SO9 5NH. SMP syllabuses and other information may be obtained from the same address.

The SMP is continually evaluating old work and preparing for new. The effectiveness of the SMP's work depends, as it always has done, on the comments and reactions received from a wide variety of teachers – and also from pupils – using SMP materials. Readers of the texts can, therefore, send their comments to the SMP in the knowledge that they will be valued and carefully studied.

THE
SCHOOL
MATHEMATICS
PROJECT
New Book 3: Part 2

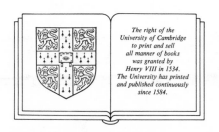

*The right of the
University of Cambridge
to print and sell
all manner of books
was granted by
Henry VIII in 1534.
The University has printed
and published continuously
since 1584.*

CAMBRIDGE UNIVERSITY PRESS

Cambridge

London   New York   New Rochelle
Melbourne   Sydney

Published by the Press Syndicate of the University of Cambridge
The Pitt Building, Trumpington Street, Cambridge CB2 1RP
32 East 57th Street, New York, NY 10022, USA
10 Stamford Road, Oakleigh, Melbourne 3166, Australia

First published 1982
Sixth printing 1986

Printed in Great Britain at the
University Press, Cambridge

British Library cataloguing in publication data

School Mathematics Project
The School Mathematics Project.
New Book 3
Part 2
1. Mathematics—1961–
I. Title
510   QA39.2
ISBN 0 521 28626 3

Contents

Preface   *page* vii

11 Circles   1

12 Proportion and graphs   23

    Revision exercises 11, 12   43

13 The right-angled triangle   44

14 Matrices   69

15 Statistics   84

    Revision exercises 13–15   101

16 Can you convince me?   103

17 Transformations and matrices   122

    Revision exercises 16, 17   136

18 Graphs and inequalities   138

19 Configurations   150

20 Probability   — PRAC -ENT)   168

    Revision exercises 18–20   180

    Answers   182

    Index   195

Preface

SMP Books 1–5 were published in the early sixties and have remained as the basic SMP O-level course, unchanged except for metrication. The revision of *Books 3, 4* and *5* draws on the experience of teaching with the original texts and incorporates other material developed by the SMP during the intervening years. While the mathematical content remains fundamentally unchanged the order of presentation of the material has been modified; the TEC Level I mathematics objectives have been borne in mind throughout the writing. The aim has been to make the texts accessible to a wider range of pupils, with clearer explanations and more carefully graded exercises, giving attention both to the practice of the necessary technical skills and to the use of the concepts in a variety of contexts. The electronic calculator is seen as the primary calculating aid throughout the books. Suggestions for ways in which pupils can use computers as an aid to learning mathematics are made at appropriate points in the latter half of the course. Each chapter concludes with a 'Summary exercise' and a 'Miscellaneous exercise'. Answers to about half the questions in exercises other than summary, miscellaneous and revision are provided at the end of each book; other answers are to be found in the accompanying *Teacher's Guides*.

The new books, like their predecessors, provide opportunities for the teacher to develop topics beyond the O-level examination syllabuses, both of which are fully covered in the texts.

The 'two books per year' arrangement of the 'lettered' books has proved convenient and economical. It is hoped that, presenting the last three years' work in five volumes rather than three will give schools the flexibility to allow for the different paces at which pupils work through the course. There is a range of SMP material designed for the first two years of the secondary school. Besides *Books 1* and *2*, *Books A–D*, *Cards I* and *II* and *Units 5* and *6* of *SMP 7–13* can be used. *SMP New Book 3* has been written to follow from any of these alternatives; in addition it contains sufficient material for pupils who transfer to the SMP course at this stage.

The authors of the original books, on whose contributions this series is based, are named in *The School Mathematics Project: The First Ten Years*, published by Cambridge University Press.

SMP New Books 3, 4 and *5* have been produced by

David Cundy	Timothy Lewis
Giles Dickins	Charles Parker
Colin Goldsmith	Alan Tammadge
Katie Hairs	Nigel Webb
John Hersee	Lynette Weekley

and edited by David Cundy.

Many others have helped with advice and criticism, particularly the teachers and pupils who have tested the material in draft form.

11

Circles

1. WHAT IS A CIRCLE?

Figure 1

Look at Figure 1. The human eye is quite good at recognising circles, whether seen 'straight on' as in (*a*), or from an angle as in (*b*). Were you deceived by (*c*)? The background should make it clear that this is an elliptical light-fitting; the angle from which the photograph has been taken was chosen to make it appear circular.

Make a tracing of the essential parts of Figure 1(*a*) and (*c*) and use your compasses to see whether the outlines are circular. Why does a pair of compasses produce a circle?

Your answer to this last question will have led you to something like a definition of a circle. The point of your compasses is fixed, and the pencil point is held at a fixed distance from the compasses' point. We define a circle to be the set of all points in a plane at a fixed distance from a fixed point. Why do we say 'in a plane'?

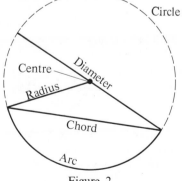

Figure 2

Figure 2 reminds you of the various technical words relating to a circle. Strictly the word radius (plural, radii) means a line from the centre to a point of the circle. But we can say 'this circle has a radius of one metre', meaning that its radii all have length one metre. There is no confusion in practice. This also applies to the word diameter. What is the connection between the lengths of a diameter and a radius of a circle?

Our definition of a circle means that a physical model of a circle is a carefully bent thin wire, not a circular disc (although the edge of a disc is a circle). An *arc* is any part of a circle. By common usage, 'the area of a circle' means the area of the region bounded by it.

2. THE CIRCUMFERENCE OF A CIRCLE

Discuss how you would measure the distance round the circles in: (*a*) a penny; (*b*) a bicycle wheel; (*c*) a cocoa tin; (*d*) a traffic roundabout; (*e*) a pencil. Take care to specify exactly what you will be measuring. This distance, or length, is called the *circumference* of the circle.

Measure the circumference and the radius or diameter of a number of objects. Draw up a list as follows:

Name of object	Circumference	Radius	$\dfrac{\text{Circumference}}{\text{Radius}}$
10p piece	89 mm	14 mm	6.4

Is the accuracy the same for all the objects you measured? Tick the measurements of which you are most confident. Is it a good idea to find the average of all the entries in the fourth column? What do you obtain? You will find that in each case the fraction works out at about 6, probably slightly greater. We can express the result in an approximate formula. If we let C and r stand for the number of units of length in the circumference and radius respectively, then

$$C/r \approx 6 \quad \text{or} \quad C \approx 6r.$$

Exercise A

(Use the approximate formula $C \approx 6r$ throughout. Do not use a calculator in this exercise.)
*1   Find the approximate circumferences of:
     (*a*) a plate, radius 11 cm;
     (*b*) the big wheel at a fair, radius 8 m;
     (*c*) a circular layout of model railway track, radius 1 m;
     (*d*) the circle traced out by a conker whirled on a 70 cm string.

 2   Find out the actual dimensions of a '65-centimetre bicycle wheel'. How far forward (in metres) does the cycle travel with one revolution of its wheels?

*3   Find the approximate radii of:
     (*a*) a steering wheel 125 cm in circumference;
     (*b*) the trunk of the 'tree of 100 horses' in Sicily, of girth about 51 m;
     (*c*) the circular wall of a city which is 4 km round;
     (*d*) the neck of a man whose collar size is 40 cm.

4 Rope is usually graded by its circumference. Calculate the approximate diameter of
    (a) a 5-centimetre rope;   (b) a 15-centimetre rope.
   What size rope would you expect to use for a clothes line?

5 A drill bit of diameter 6 mm is rotating at a rate of 900 revolutions per minute. Find
   the speed of a point on the edge of the bit in metres per second.

3. THE NUMBER CALLED π

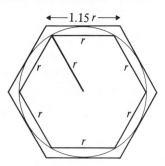

Figure 3

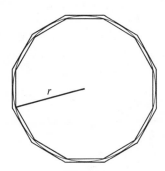

Figure 4

Figure 3 shows a circle and two regular hexagons. One hexagon has its vertices
on the circle, and so its perimeter is less than the circumference of the circle.
The other hexagon has been drawn so that its sides touch the circle; its perimeter is greater than the circumference of the circle.

Perimeter of inner hexagon		Circumference of circle		Perimeter of outer hexagon
	$<$		$<$	
$6r$	$<$	C	$<$	$6.9r$

Figure 4 shows the result of using the same idea with regular dodecagons.
This time we find that the circumference is between about $6.2r$ and $6.4r$. So the
formula for the circumference of the circle should really be:

   $C = 6\text{-and-a-bit} \times r$.

If d is the number of units of length in the diameter, then $d = 2r$ and so:

   $C = 3\text{-and-a-bit} \times d$ (half the previous 'bit'!).

We now look at this 3-and-a-bit more closely.

The Babylonians and the ancient Jews thought that the bit did not matter. They used 3 as the multiplier. It is interesting to look this up in the Bible. Read the First Book of Kings, Chapter 7 Verse 23.

The ancient Egyptians, as can be seen from the Rhind Papyrus, used the fraction $\left(\dfrac{16}{9}\right)^2$ as the multiplier. This works out at about 3.16.

The ancient Greeks worked very hard to find more accurate versions of this important number. Archimedes gave various ones, among them $3\frac{1}{7}$ and $3\frac{10}{71}$. In the end he said that the true number lay between them, that is, between 3.1429 and 3.1408.

The Chinese were also aware of $3\frac{1}{7}$. This is not too bad an approximation for many purposes and is often used today. Tsu Chung Chieh (about AD 430) gave the number as $\dfrac{355}{113} = 3.141\ 592\ 92\ldots$, a much more accurate approximation.

Modern mathematicians using computers can work out the same number to many thousands of decimal places. This number, however, is still an approximation. They have proved that none of the fractional values is exact; indeed, it is impossible to find an exact fraction for this number. To 20 decimal places we obtain 3.141 592 653 589 793 238 46.

It is no wonder that it is convenient to have a special name (pi) and a special symbol (π) for so troublesome a number. π is the Greek letter p. You will see later why it is better to use the special letter to denote 3-and-a-bit, rather than 6-and-a-bit.

We can now write the circumference formula as
$$C = 2\pi r, \quad \text{or} \quad C = \pi d.$$
We shall take the value of π to be 3,

$$\text{or } 3.1$$
$$\text{or } 3.14$$
$$\text{or } 3.142$$
$$\text{or } 3.1416$$

according to the accuracy of the data and the required accuracy of the answer. Remember that the value of π will always be an approximation.

Is there a special key for π on your calculator? If so, what does the calculator display for π?

Example 1

Calculate the circumference of a circle of radius 3.92 m.

The circumference is $2\pi \times 3.92$ m $= 24.633\ 28$ m (if we take π to be 3.142) $\boxed{\text{C}}$
$$= 24.6 \text{ m (to 3 s.f.).}$$

Example 2

Calculate the radius of a circle of circumference 2.175 m.

The radius is r metres where $2\pi r = 2.175$

$$\Leftrightarrow r = \frac{2.175}{2\pi}$$

$$= 0.346\,161\,19 \text{ (if we take } \pi \text{ to be 3.1416).} \quad \boxed{C}$$

The radius is 0.3462 m (to 4 s.f.).

Exercise B

In this exercise, give answers to an appropriate number of significant figures. If you do not have a π key on your calculator, you are advised to enter π to an accuracy of one more significant figure than the data of the question.

*1   Use your calculator to help you to calculate the circumferences of circles with the following radii:
   (a) 6.1 cm;   (b) 29.4 cm;   (c) 18.64 m;   (d) 0.045 cm.

2   Calculate the circumferences of circles with the following diameters:
   (a) 2.35 cm;   (b) 4.97 m;   (c) 2.5 mm;   (d) 1.28×10^6 m.

*3   Calculate the radii of circles with the following circumferences:
   (a) 4090 km;   (b) 3.558 m;   (c) 6 cm;   (d) 89 mm.

4   Calculate the diameters of circles with the following circumferences:
   (a) 3.875 mm;   (b) 3.142 m;   (c) 40 0001 km;   (d) 9.4×10^{11} m.

*5   'A 500-metre length running track is circular. Its radius is roughly twice the length of a cricket pitch (approx. 20 m).'
   Is this true or false? State what value of π you will use and why.

6   Cotton is wound on a cotton reel of radius 1 cm. There are said to be 1000 turns and the length is given as 54 m. Is this reasonable?

*7   The minute hand of Big Ben is 3.3 m long. How far does the tip move in an hour?

8   A tricycle has wheels whose diameter including the tyres is 42 cm. What is their circumference? How far, in metres, does a wheel go forward in 80 revolutions? What is the forward speed, in metres per second, of the tricycle when the wheels are rotating at 80 revolutions per minute?

*9   The radius of the cylinder on the winch at the top of a well is 10 cm. How many times must the handle be turned to draw up a bucket of water through 4.8 m?

10   A flywheel is rotating at 450 revolutions per minute. If it is 1 m in diameter, how fast would Frank the fly, sitting on the edge, be travelling in metres per second? Could Frank possibly sit on such a flywheel?

*11   Taking the radius of the earth to be 6400 km and the time for a rotation to be 24 h, find, in km/h, the speed of rotation about the earth's axis of a man standing on the equator. Is a man in London travelling at the same speed?

12   A circular cycle track has an inside radius of 75 m and a width of 7.5 m (see Figure 5). How much further does a cyclist go in one lap if he cycles round the outside rather than the inside?

*13   Figure 6 shows the inner boundary of the inner lane of a running track. The ends are semicircles of radius 50.0 m.
   (a) How long are the straights if one lap is 500 m?
   (b) There are three lanes, each 1 m wide. They are marked by lines parallel to the track shown. If three competitors, running one lap, start and finish level, and

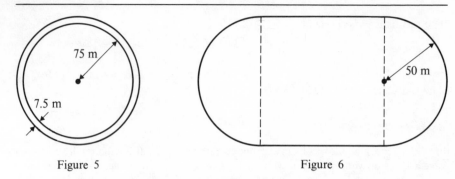

Figure 5   Figure 6

run along the inner boundaries of their lanes, find out how far each has run.
How is this compensated for in practice?

14 (a) Explain how the formula $C = 2\pi r$ can be rearranged in the form $r = \dfrac{C}{2\pi}$.

  (b) Similarly, make d the subject of the formula $C = \pi d$.
    Use the rearranged formulae to help you find:
      (i)   the radius of a circle of circumference 2.35 m;
      (ii)   the radius of a circle of circumference 2.35×10^{-12} m;
      (iii) the diameter of a circle of circumference 3.74 m;
      (iv)   the diameter of a circle of circumference 3.74×10^8 km.

4. THE AREA BOUNDED BY A CIRCLE

Figure 7(a) shows a disc of radius 2 cm. What is its circumference? The region it
bounds has been divided into four equal parts, one of which is split into two
halves. These parts have been re-assembled in Figure 7(b).

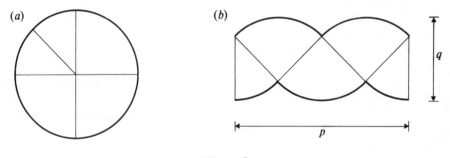

Figure 7

Describe the shape of (b) as clearly as you can. Discuss the distances p and q.
What light does (b) throw on the area of the disc?
    Figure 8(a) shows a congruent disc divided into eight equal parts, one of which
is again split into two halves. The parts have again been re-assembled and the
result is shown in Figure 8(b).

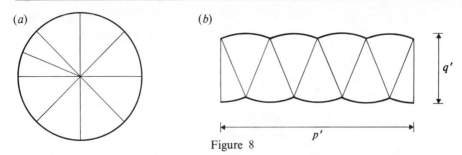

Figure 8

Estimate p' and q'. Use your answers to make a better estimate of the area of the disc. Sketch the shape of the re-assembled figure if the disc were divided into sixteen equal parts.

If a disc of radius r units were split into a very large number of equal parts, what would be the dimensions of the figure into which it could be re-assembled? What would be its area?

The area of a disc of radius r units is given by the formula:
$$A = \pi r^2,$$
where A is the area in square units. This formula can be proved to be exact for any disc.

Example 3
    Calculate the area of a circle of radius 3.92 m.

The area is $\pi \times 3.92^2$ m^2 = 48.281 229 m^2 (if we take π to be 3.142).   ☐C
(If a π key is used, you will have 48.274 969 at this stage.)
The area is 48.3 m^2 (to 3 s.f.).

Example 4
    Calculate the radius of a circle of area 1.27 m^2.

Let r metres be the radius. Then
$$\pi r^2 = 1.27$$
$$\Leftrightarrow \quad r^2 = \frac{1.27}{\pi}$$
$$\Leftrightarrow \quad r = \pm \sqrt{\left(\frac{1.27}{\pi}\right)} = \pm 0.635\ 768\ 15 \quad \text{(if we take } \pi \text{ to be 3.142).}\quad \boxed{C}$$

(If a π key is used, you will have 0.635 809 37 at this stage.)
The radius is 0.636 m (to 3 s.f.).

Exercise C

In questions 1–6, do not use your calculator.
*1   Taking the value of π to be 3, estimate the areas enclosed by the circles whose radii are:
        (a) 4 cm;   (b) 100 m;   (c) 20 m;   (d) 30 mm.
        Be careful to include the units in your answers.

2 A circle encloses an area of about 75 cm². Taking the value of π to be 3, what will be the square of its radius? In what units? What will be the actual radius, approximately, and in what units?

*3 Taking the value of π to be 3, estimate the radii of circles which enclose areas of:
(*a*) 300 km²;   (*b*) 12 m²;   (*c*) 150 cm²;   (*d*) 240 mm².

4 A brake disc has a diameter of 8 cm. What is its approximate area?

*5 Find the area of the sports ground shown in Figure 9.

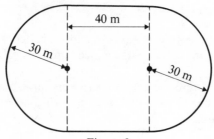

Figure 9

6 A circular cattle enclosure has to enclose about 120 m². What should its radius be? Justify the accuracy you use.

In questions 7–21, use your calculator in those questions where it is helpful and give answers to an appropriate number of significant figures. Use a suitable approximation for π.

*7 (*a*) Calculate the area of a circle of diameter 3.79 m.
(*b*) Calculate the diameter of a circle of area 16.35 cm².

8 A radar screen is circular and has a diameter of 42 cm. About 10% of its area is ineffective. Find its effective area.

*9 Find the radii of circles whose areas are:
(*a*) 4050 cm²;   (*b*) 12 000 m²;   (*c*) 2.85 m²;   (*d*) 123 km².

10 Find:
(*a*) the side of a square of area 345 m² ;
(*b*) the diameter of a circle of area 345 m².

*11 A farmer needs some hurdles, each 2 m long, to enclose a circular area of about 55 m². How many will he need?

12 A circular pond of diameter 22 m is to be surrounded by a path of width 1 m costing £3.50 per square metre to lay. Calculate the cost of laying the path.

*13 The end face of a casting is to be square, with four circles of radius 1.5 cm cut from it. (See Figure 10.) If the shaded area is to be 80 cm², find the length of the side of the square.

Figure 10

14 It can be shown that the area of an equilateral triangle, the sides of which are of length s metres, is $\dfrac{s^2\sqrt{3}}{4}$ m² .

(a) Calculate the perimeter of an equilateral triangle of area 1.00 m².

(b) Calculate the perimeter of a square of area 1.00 m².

(c) Calculate the perimeter of a regular hexagon of area 1.00 m².
(N.B. If opposite vertices of a regular hexagon are joined, the hexagon is split into six equilateral triangles).

(d) Calculate the perimeter of a circle of area 1.00 m².

(e) What do your answers to (a)–(d) suggest?

15 Show that the circumference and area of a circle of radius 2 units are numerically the same. Why can you not therefore say that, for such a circle, the circumference and the area are equal?

16 A mirror manufacturer is considering the possibility of saving money on the silvering process by no longer silvering the edge of the mirror which will be covered by a frame. In silvering a circular mirror of diameter 25.0 cm, he could leave the silvering of a strip of width 0.5 cm all round the edge. What is the area that would then be unsilvered? Express this area as a percentage of the area of the mirror.

17 (a) Rearrange the formula $A = \pi r^2$ in the form $r = \dots$

(b) Use your result to help you calculate:
  (i) the radius of a circle of area 8.75 cm²;
  (ii) the radius of a circle of area 8.75×10^{-6} cm².

(c) Show that, if the diameter of a circle is d units, the area, A, enclosed by it is $\frac{1}{4}\pi d^2$.

(d) Make d the subject of the formula $A = \frac{1}{4}\pi d^2$. Does your result 'agree' with the formula you obtained in part (a)?

(e) Use these formulae to help you calculate:
  (i) the area of a disc of diameter 4.11 cm;
  (ii) the diameter of a disc of area 4.11 cm².

18 The length of a radius of a circle is measured as 8.8 cm.

(a) What is the lower bound for the radius (i.e. the smallest it could be)?

(b) What is the lower bound for the area of the circle?

(c) What is the upper bound for the radius?

(d) What is the upper bound for the area of the circle?

(e) Give the area of the circle in the form:
  lower bound < area < upper bound.

(f) Give the area of the circle, calculated as $\pi \times 8.8^2$, accurate to an appropriate number of significant figures.

5. SECTORS OF A CIRCLE

A sector of a circle is a region bounded by part of the circle and two radii. Note that there are two sectors corresponding to any two radii. The larger is called the major sector and the smaller the minor sector. The simplest way of defining the size of a sector is to give its radius and the angle between the radii. Measure the angles of the two sectors in Figure 11. What relation is there between these angles?

Figure 11

Example 5

Calculate the perimeter of a sector of angle 201° cut from a circle of radius 3.45 cm. (See Figure 12.)

The perimeter consists of the arc (the curved line) and the two radii.

201° corresponds to $\dfrac{201}{360}$ of a complete

turn. The length of arc, therefore, is

$\dfrac{201}{360}$ × circumference

$= \dfrac{201}{360}$ × 2π × 3.45 cm

$= 12.102\,986$ cm   (using a π key) ⓒ

$= 12.10$ cm (to 4 s.f.).

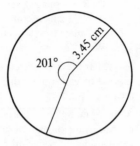

Figure 12

The perimeter, then, is $(12.10 + 2 × 3.45)$ cm

$= 19.0$ cm (to 3 s.f.).

Example 6

Find the area of a 35° sector of a circle of radius 5.2 cm.

The area of the sector is $\dfrac{35}{360}$ of the area

enclosed by the circle

$= \dfrac{35}{360}$ × π × 5.2² cm²

$= 8.258\,898$ cm²   ⓒ

$= 8.3$ cm² (to 2 s.f.).

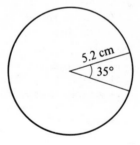

Figure 13

Exercise D

*1   Find the perimeter of an 81° sector cut from a circle of radius 7.5 cm.

2   Find the perimeter of a sector of angle 143° cut from a circle of radius 4.7 cm.

*3   Find the areas of sectors cut from a circle of radius 13.7 cm by radii at angles of:
   (a) 31°;   (b) 310°;   (c) 124°;   (d) 50°.
   What area should the sum of your answers to (b) and (d) give you?

*4   Taking the value of π to be 3, estimate the angle between two radii which cut off an arc of length 9 cm from a circle of radius 6 cm.

5   Taking the value of π to be 3.14, find the angle of a sector of a circle of radius 1.0 m whose curved boundary is of length 1.0 m.

*6   A sector of a circle of radius 47 mm has an area of 771 mm². Find the angle of the sector.

7 In Figure 14 the area of the sector and the area of the square are equal. Find the angle of the sector.

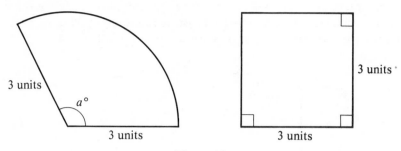

Figure 14

8 The radius of each of the circular sectors shaded in Figure 15 (*a*) is 1.0 cm. If the triangle in Figure 15 (*a*) is equilateral calculate the total shaded area.

If the radius of each of the circular sectors shaded in Figure 15 (*b*) is also 1.0 cm, explain why the total shaded area is the same as for Figure 15 (*a*) even though the triangle is not equilateral.

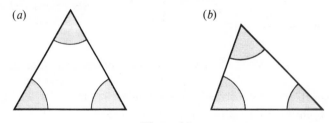

Figure 15

6. CYLINDERS

Take a rectangle of paper, measuring 15 cm by 10 cm, as shown in Figure 16. Bend it so that *AB* touches *DC*, and so that the ends are circles. The object formed is called a circular cylinder. If you bend it so that the ends are ellipses (or ovals) it is called an elliptical cylinder, and other shapes are also possible. You must bend the paper carefully so that the ends are exactly the same shape and size. What is the approximate radius of the end-circles in your model?

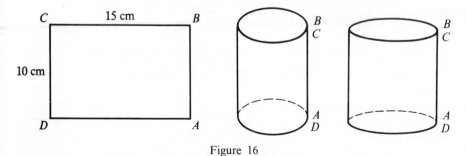

Figure 16

Now make a second cylinder with height 10 cm and base radius 4 cm approximately. What shape and size of paper will you need for its net?

In general terms, if the radius of the base is r units, and the height is h units, then we shall require a piece of paper measuring $2\pi r$ units by h units. (See Figure 17). This gives us the formula for the curved surface area, A, in square units:

$$A = 2\pi rh.$$

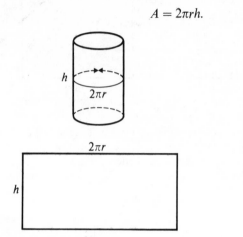

Figure 17   Figure 18

The area of the base is πr^2 square units. Think of these as the small squares of millimetre graph paper. If each of these is the base of a wooden match of height h units, then they will form a solid of volume $\pi r^2 h$ cubic units. The smaller the square units chosen to cover the base, the more nearly will the bundle of matches form a circular cylinder. (See Figure 18.) It is therefore reasonable to express the volume V, in cubic units, by the formula:

$$V = \pi r^2 h.$$

Example 7

Calculate the surface area and volume of a cylinder of base radius 1.25 cm and height 3.75 cm.

Surface area of curved side of cylinder is $2\pi \times 1.25 \times 3.75$ cm^2
$$= 29.45... \text{ cm}^2.$$ C

Area of the two circular ends is $2 \times \pi \times 1.25^2$ cm$^2 = 9.817 ...$ cm^2.   C

Total surface area is the sum of these and is $39.26...$ cm$^2 = 39.3$ cm^2 (to 3 s.f.). (N.B. The figures given were obtained using a calculator with a π key. If 3.142 is used as an approximation for π, the fourth significant figure is different in some parts of the calculation but the final answer, to an accuracy of three significant figures, is the same.)

If you have a memory on your calculator, you can store the area of the curved side while working out the area of the ends, and finally add the two together.

Volume of the cylinder is $\pi \times 1.25^2 \times 3.75$ cm^3
$$= 18.407... \text{ cm}^3 = 18.4 \text{ cm}^3 \text{ (to 3 s.f.)}.$$

Example 8

Calculate, to the nearest centimetre, the height of a cylindrical can required to hold 1 litre (1000 cm³) if the diameter of the base is to be one-third of the height.

Let h cm be the height of the can. Then the base diameter is $\frac{1}{3}h$ cm and the base radius is

$$\tfrac{1}{2} \times \tfrac{1}{3}h \text{ cm} = \tfrac{1}{6}h \text{ cm}.$$

The area of the base is $\pi(\tfrac{1}{6}h)^2 \text{ cm}^2 = \dfrac{\pi h^2}{36} \text{ cm}^2.$

The volume of the can is the base area multiplied by the height

$$= \frac{\pi h^2}{36} \times h \text{ cm}^3 = \frac{\pi h^3}{36} \text{ cm}^3.$$

So $\dfrac{\pi h^3}{36} = 1000 \Leftrightarrow \pi h^3 = 36 \times 1000 = 36\,000$

$$\Leftrightarrow h^3 = \frac{36\,000}{\pi}$$

$$\Leftrightarrow h = \sqrt[3]{\left(\frac{36\,000}{\pi}\right)} \approx \sqrt[3]{11\,459}$$

which, by decimal search, gives $h \approx 23$.
So the height of the can should be about 23 cm.

Exercise E

*1   Taking the value of π to be 3, find the areas of the curved surfaces of the cylinders with the following dimensions:
(a) radius 4 m, height 3 m;   (b) radius 3 m, height 4 m.
Did you expect them to be equal? Say why.

2   Find the volumes of the cylinders in question 1. Did you expect them to be equal? Explain your findings.

*3   Taking the value of π to be 3.14, calculate the area of the curved surface and the volume of a cylinder of height 2.45 cm and base radius 0.55 cm.

4   (a) Starting with the formula $A = 2\pi rh$, show that $r = \dfrac{A}{2\pi h}$ and find a formula for h in terms of A and r.
(b) Calculate the radius of a cylinder of height 11.2 cm whose curved surface area is 493 cm².
(c) Calculate the height of a cylinder of diameter 6.9 m whose curved surface area is 23 m².

*5   (a) Starting with the formula $V = \pi r^2 h$, show that

$$r = \sqrt{\left(\frac{V}{\pi h}\right)}$$

and find a formula for h in terms of V and r.
(b) Calculate the radius of a cylinder of height 99 cm and volume 3600 cm³.
(c) Calculate the height, in centimetres, of a cylinder of diameter 6.47 cm and volume 235 cm³.

6   The area of the curved surface of a cylinder is 18 m². Taking the value of π to be 3, make a statement about its height and base radius. Give two possible sets of dimensions. How many possible sets are there in all?

*7   120 g of seaside rock has a volume of about 200 cm³. If the radius of the cylindrical rock is 1.5 cm, about how long must the stick be?

8   A down-pipe on the side of a house has a radius of 4.5 cm and a length of 4 m. You have a tin of paint that will cover 2 m². Is this enough to paint the pipe? If it is more than enough, will you have enough left over to paint another pipe of the same size? If not, what fraction of one would you expect to be able to paint?

9   Measure the diameters of a 10p piece and a 5p piece, and the height of a pile of, say, ten of each of these coins. Hence find the volume of a 10p piece and of a 5p piece, as accurately as you can, in cubic millimetres. What is the ratio of their volumes? Find out how banks 'count' their silver.

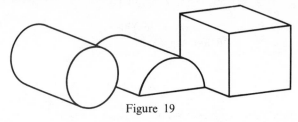

Figure 19

10   Figure 19 shows three of the bricks in a child's building set: a cylinder, a half-cylinder and a cube. They all have a volume of 1.00 cm³ and are 1.00 cm long.
   (a) Find their other dimensions.
   (b) Which do you think has the largest, and which the smallest, surface area? Calculate the areas to check your guess.

*11   Water flows steadily at 2.35 m/s through a pipe of internal diameter 5.00 cm. How long, to the nearest minute, will it take to fill a cylindrical tank having internal base diameter 1.85 m and internal height 3.15 m?

12   1000 m of paper of thickness 0.025 cm is wound onto a roll of diameter 7.5 cm. Calculate the diameter of the whole roll. If the paper strip is 15.0 cm wide, calculate the volume of paper in the roll.

7. CONES

The following investigation can be carried out individually or in groups.
On paper, draw accurately three identical diagrams like the one in Figure 20 (which is not to scale). Allow for a depth of 16 cm.

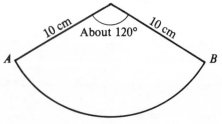

Figure 20

(1) Cut the first one of them out with an tab on *AC* as in Figure 21.

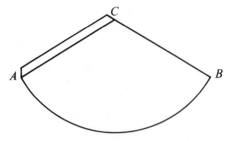

Figure 21

(2) On the second diagram, join *AB* with a straight line, and cut out the tri-angle with a tab on *AC* as in Figure 22.

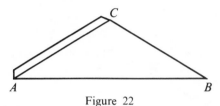

Figure 22

(3) On the third diagram, draw in the radius which bisects angle *ACB* and find the point *D* half-way along it. With centre *D* and radius *DA*, draw a new arc *AB* and cut out the shape indicated with continuous lines in Figure 23.

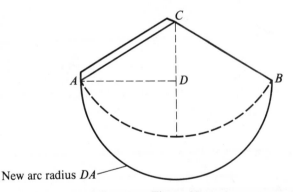

New arc radius *DA*

Figure 23

Label the three shapes you have cut out (1), (2) and (3) respectively. Fold each of the cut out shapes so that *CA* lies as accurately as possible along *CB* and glue these edges together using the tabs. Smooth the join so that the open end of the conical shape formed is as nearly circular as possible.

Which of the three nets that you have cut out forms a 'right circular cone', i.e. a cone in which the vertex lies on the perpendicular to the circular base which passes through the centre of the circle? (See Figure 24.) In what ways do the other two shapes differ from the right circular cone and from each other?

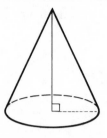

Figure 24

In a right circular cone, the vertex is the same distance from all points on the circular base. This distance is called the slant height. Why, then, are the other two shapes not right circular cones?

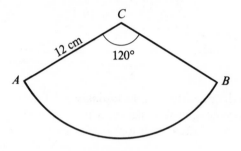

Figure 25

Example 9

   (*a*) In Figure 25, what is the length of arc *AB*, expressed as a multiple of π?
   (*b*) If this shape is cut out and folded into a cone, what does *AB* become? What, therefore, is the radius of the base of the cone?

(*a*) The length of the arc *AB* is $\dfrac{120}{360} \times 2\pi \times 12$ cm $= 8\pi$ cm.

(*b*) The arc *AB* becomes the whole circumference of the base of the cone. If the radius of the base is *r* cm, we have

$$2\pi r = 8\pi \Leftrightarrow r = 4.$$

The radius of the base is 4 cm.

Surface area of a cone

If a right circular cone of base radius *r* and slant height *s* (see Figure 26), made of thin card, is cut along a slant height and flattened out (see Figure 27) the arc length *AB* has length $2\pi r$ because it previously formed the whole circumference of the base of the cone.

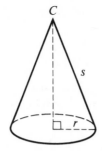

Figure 26

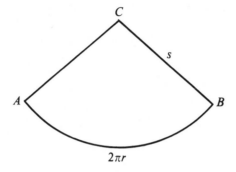

Figure 27

The sector CAB is part of a disc of radius s which has circumference $2\pi s$ and area πs^2. The area of the sector CAB is therefore

$$\frac{2\pi r}{2\pi s} \times \pi s^2 = \pi r s.$$

Example 10

A right circular cone has base diameter 3.6 cm and slant height 9.4 cm. Calculate the area of its curved surface.

The base radius of the cone is $\dfrac{3.6}{2}$ cm = 1.8 cm.

The surface area is $\pi \times 1.8 \times 9.4$ cm^2 = 53.155 747 cm^2 = 53 cm^2 (to 2 s.f.).   [C]

Exercise F

*1 Calculate the area of the curved surface of a cone with base radius 24 cm and slant height 52 cm.

2 (*a*) Calculate the total surface area of a cone which has both slant height and diameter equal to 3.5 m.

   (*b*) A cone with total surface area 24 m^2 has its base diameter equal to its slant height. Calculate its base diameter.

*3 A sector of a disc of radius 25 cm, with angle 135° at the centre, forms the net of a cone. Find:

  (a) the slant height of the cone;
  (b) the circumference of the base of the cone;
  (c) the base diameter of the cone;
  (d) the area of the curved surface of the cone.

4 Four identical cones are made from the four quadrants of a circular disc of diameter 15 cm. Calculate:

  (a) the base diameter of each cone;
  (b) the total surface area of the curved sides of all four cones.

*5 A child's covered paddling pool consists of (i) a circular inflatable pool of outer diameter 2.0 m and height 20 cm, and (ii) a conical tent, attached round the bottom to the top edge of the pool, and supported by a central pole of height 2.0 m. (See Figure 28.)

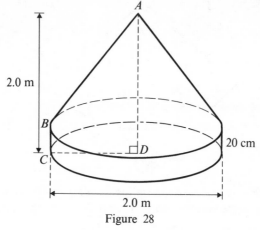

Figure 28

  (a) Make a scale drawing of the trapezium $ABCD$ and measure the length of AB.
  (b) Assuming it to be possible to close the tent completely, without overlap, design the net for the piece of material out of which the tent is to be made.
  (c) Suggest a suitable simple way of providing an entrance.

6 A circular theatre is designed with a conical roof of diameter 64 m, sloping at 40° to the horizontal. Make a scale drawing of triangle VAB in Figure 29, and measure AV.

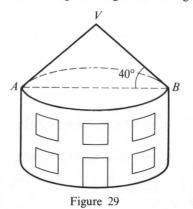

Figure 29

Calculate the area of the roof and hence find the approximate cost of covering it with roofing felt at £8.50 per square metre.

*7 The net for a container for a Luxury Choc-nut Sundae is made from a 21 cm square sheet of appropriate material as shown in Figure 30, which is not to scale. Before joining by welding, the base of the container should be 0.5 cm greater in diameter than the diameter of the bottom of the container wall.

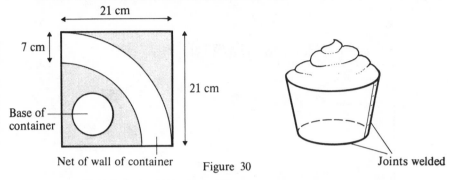

Net of wall of container   Figure 30   Joints welded

(a) Calculate the necessary base diameter and show with a scale drawing that it is possible to cut the base out of the card as suggested in Figure 30.

(b) What is the diameter of the top of the container?

8 A lampshade, in the shape of a truncated right circular cone (i.e. with the top of the cone cut off) is illustrated in Figure 31.

(a) Make a 1 :10 scale drawing of the net of the lampshade.

(b) The lampshade fabric is sold in 1 m widths. What is the least length of material needed to make
  (i) one lampshade;
  (ii) five similar lampshades?

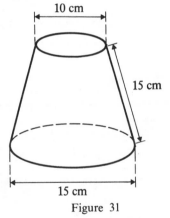

Figure 31

SUMMARY

A circle is the set of all points in a plane at a fixed distance from a fixed point (the centre). The various technical words relating to circles are illustrated by Figure 32.

(Section 1)

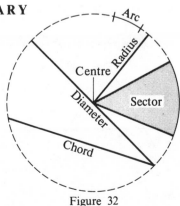

Figure 32

Circumference of a circle, of radius r : $C = 2\pi r$ (Sections 2, 3)

$\pi = 3.141\ 5926\dots$ (Section 3)

Area enclosed by a circle: $A = \pi r^2$ (Section 4)

The area of a sector of a circle is $\dfrac{a}{360} \times$ (area enclosed by the circle), where $a°$ is the angle of the sector.   (Section 5)

The area of the curved surface of a cylinder with radius r and height h is $2\pi rh$; the volume of the cylinder is $\pi r^2 h$.   (Section 6)

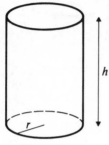

Figure 33

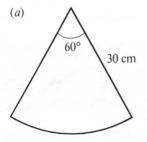

Figure 34

The net of the curved surface of a right circular cone is a sector of a circle. Its area is πrs, where r is the radius of the base of the cone and s is its slant height.   (Section 7)

Summary exercise

1 (a) Estimate the circumference of a circle of radius 3m.
   (b) Calculate the circumferences of circles of radii:
      (i) 2.97 m;   (ii) 3.07×10^3m.

2 (a) Estimate the area of a circle of radius 10 m.
   (b) Calculate the area of a circle of radius 11.9 m.
   (c) Calculate the area of a circle of diameter 20.79 cm.

3 Calculate the radii of circles of circumferences:
      (a) 462m;   (b) 1350 m.

4 Calculate the radii of circles of areas:
      (a) 40.1 cm^2;   (b) 401 m^2.

5 Estimate the lengths of the arcs illustrated in Figure 35.

(a)
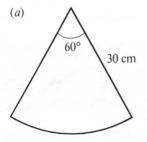

60°

30 cm

(b)
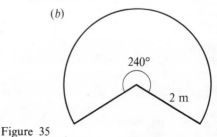

240°

2 m

Figure 35

6 Calculate the areas of sectors:
  (a) of 48° from a circle of radius 4.55 cm;
  (b) of 240° from a circle of radius 2.03 m.

7 Calculate the total surface area of a cylindrical tin of radius 4.3 cm and height 14.1 cm.

8 Calculate the mass of 10 m of lead piping having an internal diameter of 2.54 cm and thickness 5.0 mm if the density of lead is 11 300 kg/m³.

9 A Nkosi hut is basically a cylinder of diameter 4.0 m and height 2.0 m with a conical roof of slant height 2.8 m. The walls and roof require re-thatching with leaves of the kosi tree. Neglecting the area of the doorway and window, estimate the surface area of the hut to be re-thatched.

Miscellaneous exercise

1 Express $\frac{22}{7}$ as a decimal correct to four decimal places. To the same accuracy $\pi = 3.1416$.

To how many places is $\frac{22}{7}$ a correct approximation to π? If you worked out, to an accuracy of four significant figures, the area enclosed by a circle of radius 10 cm taking $\pi = \frac{22}{7}$, estimate the size of your error. Express this as a percentage of the better approximation.

2 The front wheel of a penny-farthing bicycle has three times the radius of the back wheel. How many times does the back wheel rotate while the front wheel is turning twice? (You do not need to use the value of π.)

3 The diameter of a 10p piece is 28 mm. Ten 10p pieces are melted down and made into a new monster coin of the same thickness. What will be its diameter? (You do not need to use the value of π.)

4 Two circles have radii of 2 m and 3 m respectively.
  (a) Write down expressions for: (i) their circumferences and (ii) their areas, but do not work them out. Write down the ratio of their circumferences and the ratio of their areas.
  (b) A third circle has a radius of 5 m. Write down the ratios of: (i) its circumference and (ii) its area, to those of the 2 m circle.

5 Two radii of a circle of radius 18 cm make an angle of 135°. What is the ratio of the areas of the two sectors? Is any of the information superfluous?

6 A cyclist is travelling at 8 m/s. His bicycle wheels have a diameter of 65 cm. What is their circumference in metres? Find the approximate number of revolutions per minute made by the wheels.

7 Members of the Ukosi tribe live on the slopes of Mount Tikosi where they grow kosi nuts which have very high protein content. The mountain is an extinct volcano, approximately the shape of a cone, of base diameter 40 km and an average slope of 8°.
  (a) Make a scale drawing of the mountain viewed from the side and find its slant height.
  (b) Calculate the area of the mountain slopes in hectares. (1 ha $= 10^4$ m².)
  (c) There are about 100 kosi nut trees per hectare, and each family owns, on average, 350 trees. If all the mountain slopes are covered with kosi nut trees, approximately how many families live on the mountain?

8 Water is flowing through a cylindrical pipe of radius 1.5 cm at the rate of roughly 1 m³ every 4 minutes. At what speed is the water moving in the pipe in cm/s?

9 1 litre (1000 cm³) of water is used to fill a cylindrical jug of radius 5 cm and height 8 cm; the remainder is poured into a measuring cylinder of cross-sectional area 10 cm². How far up will it come?

10 A circle of radius 10 cm is drawn completely inside one of radius 20 cm on graph paper with a 0.2 cm grid. Estimate the ratio of the number of grid points inside the smaller circle to the number between the two circles.

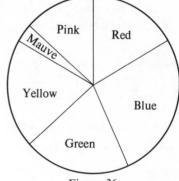

11 Figure 36 shows a pie chart representing the favourite colours of 30 children at a party. Measure the angles of the appropriate sectors, and find the number of children who liked:
  (*a*) the most popular colour;
  (*b*) the least popular colour.

Figure 36

12 A witch's hat is required for a Hallowe'en Party. It is proposed to make it out of cardboard sheets measuring 65 cm by 50 cm, and it has to be a cone, with a broad rim made separately. Design such a hat to fit a head of circumference 50 cm, showing on a clear sketch what shapes need to be cut out of the cardboard. Label all lengths clearly. How would you fix the pieces together?

13 In the third century, Pappus discovered a simple formula for the volume of the solid formed by rotating a circle through 360° about a line in its plane. The solid shown in Figure 37 has the shape of a car inner tube. The shaded circle is the 'generating' circle. Where is the axis of rotation? Describe the locus of the centre of the circle. Pappus showed that the volume is the product of the area of the generating circle and the length of the locus of its centre. Write down a formula to express this, giving suitable letters to the lengths that have to be known. Calculate the volume of the inner tube in Figure 37, given that the diametric distances are $AD = 24$ cm and $AB = 7$ cm.

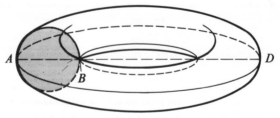

Figure 37

14 Pappus showed that the result of question 13 could also be applied to solids formed by rotating figures other than circles. Describe the solid formed by rotating the rectangle with vertices $A(3, {}^-10)$, $B(4, {}^-10)$, $C(4, 10)$ and $D(3, 10)$ about the y-axis. Write down the coordinates of the centre of the rectangle $ABCD$. Find the volume of the solid formed.

12

Proportion and graphs

1. COMPARING

An aircraft flying at a steady speed travels 400 kilometres in 80 minutes. How far does it travel in 36 minutes? How far does it travel in 62 minutes?

The speed of the aircraft is $\dfrac{400}{80}$ km/min = 5 km/min, so in 36 minutes it travels 36×5 km = 180 km; in 62 minutes it travels 62×5 km = 310 km. Table 1 shows these answers and the original information.

Time in minutes	(t)	80	36	62
Distance flown in kilometres	(d)	400	180	310

Table 1

Each value of d is five times the corresponding value of t, so we can write $d = 5t$. The number 5 corresponds to the speed of 5 km/min and is the scale factor for the mapping $t \rightarrow d$.

Sets of numbers like these, for which there is a scale factor mapping one set to the other, are said to be *proportional*. The scale factor is often called *the constant of proportionality*.

Example 1

A bank exchanged £25 for 285.25 francs, before deducting commission.

(a) At the same rate of exchange, for how many francs would £30 be exchanged?

(b) At the same rate of exchange, how many pounds would have to be exchanged to obtain 700 francs?

The rate of exchange was $\dfrac{285.25}{25}$ francs per pound = 11.41 fr/£.

(a) £30 will therefore be exchanged for 30×11.41 francs = 342.30 francs.

(b) To map the number of pounds to the number of francs we multiply by 11.41; to reverse the process, we divide by 11.41. To obtain 700 francs, £$\dfrac{700}{11.41}$ = £61.35 (to the nearest penny above) will have to be exchanged.

Notice that we could write $F = 11.41 L$, where F is the number of francs equivalent to £L.

23

Exercise A

*1 A greengrocer is selling three oranges for 12 pence.
  (*a*) Find the cost of: (i) seven oranges;   (ii) seventeen oranges.
  (*b*) How many oranges could be bought for: (i) 32 pence;   (ii) 88 pence?
  (*c*) Write down a formula for the cost in pence, *C*, of *n* oranges.

2 A ship cruising at a steady speed travels 50 km in 2 hours.
  (*a*) How far would it travel in: (i) 3 hours;   (ii) 11 hours?
  (*b*) At what speed is it cruising?
  (*c*) At the same speed, how long would it take to travel: (i) 175 km;   (ii) 350 km?
  (*d*) Write down a formula for *d*, the distance in kilometres travelled in *t* hours.

*3 Today's rate of exchange for the obol is 6.30 obols to the pound. Copy and complete the following table:

Number of pounds	(*P*)	1	2	7		
Number of obols	(*B*)	6.30			100.80	189.00

Write down a formula for *B* in terms of *P*.

4 In 1978 gasoline cost 59 cents a gallon at Art's Service Station. Copy and complete the following table:

Number of gallons	(*n*)	1	2.1	11.0	
Cost in dollars	(*C*)	0.59	1.00	4.0	

Write down a formula for *C* in terms of *n*.

*5 The current, *I*, in amperes (A) flowing through a resistor is proportional to the potential difference, *P*, in volts (V) across the resistor. If a current of 0.15 A flows when the potential difference is 2.5 V, what current will flow when the potential difference is 4.7 V?

6 A peanut of mass 0.41 g is found to contain 16.9 kilojoules (kJ) of energy. Assuming this to be a typical peanut, find the energy stored in one kilogram of peanuts.

*7 The mass of 2.5×10^{-6} m^3 of mercury is found to be 0.034 kg.
  (*a*) Calculate the density of mercury in kg/m^3.
  (*b*) Calculate the mass of 3.1×10^{-5} m^3 of mercury.
  (*c*) What volume of mercury has a mass of 1.0 kg?

8 A gas cylinder contains gas at a temperature of 288 K and pressure of 1.80×10^5 N/m^2. What will the pressure be if the gas is heated to 303 K, assuming that the pressure is proportional to the temperature?

2. MULTIPLIERS AND RATES

A ship which sails 50 km in 3 hours would, at the same speed, travel 200 km in 12 hours. Notice that we do not need to calculate the speed of the ship in order to make such a deduction: in four times the time, the ship will travel four times as far. The number 4 is acting as a *multiplier* between members of the same set.

Example 2
  On Bolesian Railways the cost of a ticket is proportional to the distance travelled. If a ticket for a journey of 75 km is 155 obols, find the cost of tickets for journeys of 15 km and 120 km.

15 is $\frac{1}{5}$ of 75, so the journey of 15 km will cost $\frac{1}{5} \times 155$ obols $= 31$ obols.
120 is 8×15, so the journey of 120 km will cost 8×31 obols $= 248$ obols.
The solution can also be set out in a single table, as shown in Table 2.

Distance in kilometres	75	$\xrightarrow{\times \frac{1}{5}}$	15	$\xrightarrow{\times 8}$	120
Cost in obols	155	$\xrightarrow[\times \frac{1}{5}]{}$	31	$\xrightarrow[\times 8]{}$	248

Table 2

Example 3
An aircraft is travelling at 5 km/min. Write this speed in
(*a*) km/h; (*b*) m/s.

Table 3 shows the information given and required, and the multipliers we could use.

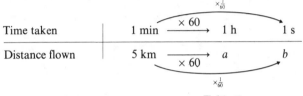

Table 3

(*a*) In 1 hour the aircraft would fly 60×5 km $= 300$ km. Its speed is 300 km/h.

(*b*) In 1 second the aircraft would fly $\frac{1}{60} \times 5$ km $= \dfrac{5000}{60}$ m ≈ 83 m. Its speed is 83 m/s to 2 s.f.

If *y* is proportional to *x* (abbreviated to $y \propto x$) we can either
(1) use one pair of values of *y* and *x* to find the scale factor and use the scale factor to find other corresponding pairs of values, or
(2) use multipliers to obtain directly from one pair of values other corresponding pairs.

Exercise B

*1 Copy and complete the following tables, using multipliers:

(*a*) $d \propto t$

t	2	4		12	24
d	7		28		

(*b*) $p \propto r$

r	3	6	30	10	
p	51				255

(*c*) $y \propto x$

x	15	30	60	10	
y	9				0.6

(*d*) $z \propto P$

P	6	60	20	5	
z	5.7				11.4

2 Copy and complete the following tables, using multipliers:

(a) $y \propto x$

x	3	12	60	5	
y	8.1				135

(b) $P \propto T$

T	300	30	240	270	
P	1.1				3.3

(c) $v \propto t$

t	1.5	3	15	5	
v	14.7				9.8

(d) $C \propto n$

n	20	60	240	80	
C	3.65				73

*3 A car uses 9.5 litres of petrol in travelling 100 kilometres. How much petrol will it use in travelling:

(a) 300 km; (b) 270 km?

4 If 500 kg of coal cost 1355 Ruritanian ruples, how much would 800 kg of coal cost?

*5 If 150 litres of heating oil cost 1330 Ruritanian ruples, how much would:

(a) 900 litres, (b) 1200 litres, cost?

6 If a supersonic airliner travels 4800 km in 2 hours, how far would it travel in:

(a) $\frac{1}{2}$ hour; (b) 3 hours?

How long would it take to fly non-stop:

(c) from London to Buenos Aires (about 10 000 km);

(d) round the world (40 000 km)?

*7 A train takes 66 minutes to travel 91 km. What is its average speed in:

(a) km/min; (b) km/h; (c) m/s?

8 A gold bar of volume 27 cm^3 has a mass of 521 g. Find its density in:

(a) g/cm^3; (b) kg/m^3.

*9 A bank exchanged £25 for DM 119. What was the exchange rate:

(a) in Deutschmark per pound; (b) in pence per Deutschmark?

10 A train takes 2 hours and 42 minutes to travel (non-stop) from London to Darlington, a distance of 373 kilometres.

(a) What is its average speed in: (i) km/min; (ii) km/h; (iii) m/s?

(b) At this speed, how far would it travel in: (i) 25 minutes; (ii) 2 hours?

(c) Doncaster is 251 kilometres from London and on the railway route from London to Darlington. If the train left London at 8.00 a.m., when would you expect it to pass through Doncaster?

*11 A spring stretches 32 mm when a load of 12 N is applied. It is thought that the extension of the spring is proportional to the load applied.

(a) How much will the spring stretch for loads of: (i) 60 N; (ii) 15 N?

(b) What would the load be if the spring stretched: (i) 64 mm; (ii) 72 mm?

12 The pointer on a weighing machine turns through 190° when a 3.2-kilogram parcel is placed on the pan.

(a) Through what angle would it turn for parcels of the following masses:

(i) 0.8 kg; (ii) 0.2 kg; (iii) 1.0 kg?

(b) What mass would cause the pointer to turn through:

(i) 19°; (ii) 10°; (iii) 350°?

3. GRAPHS OF PROPORTIONAL SETS

A train is travelling at a steady speed and the distance travelled in various times is shown in the table below.

Time in minutes	(t)	4	7	12	15
Distance in kilometres	(d)	8	14	24	30

How fast is the train travelling? What is the scale factor of the mapping $t \longrightarrow d$? What is the equation connecting d and t?

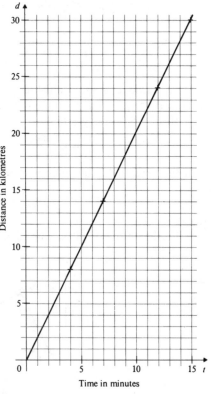

Figure 1 shows a graph of the information. Notice that since we are concerned with the mapping $t \longrightarrow d$, t has been plotted across the page. The points plotted from the table have been joined by a straight line so that other values can be read from the graph.

Why should the line go through the origin?

What is d when $t = 5$? when $t = 6$?
What is d when $t = 13$? when $t = 14$?

Figure 1

Increasing t by 1 increases d by 2: every minute the train goes a further 2 km. This is shown on the graph by how steeply it rises. (See Figure 2.)
The fraction

$$\frac{\text{increase in } d}{\text{increase in } t}$$

is the *gradient* of the graph.

In this case the gradient is 2. Notice that it is the same as the scale factor of the mapping $t \longrightarrow d$ and that $d = 2t$.

In general if $y \propto x$ the graph of $x \longrightarrow y$ is a straight line through the origin. The gradient of the line is equal to the scale factor.

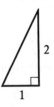

Figure 2

Figure 3 shows the distance–time graph for a slow freight train. What is its speed?

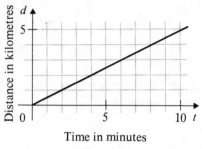

Figure 3

The gradient of a straight-line graph can be found by considering any two points on the graph. In Figure 3, for example, when $t = 6, d = 3$, and when $t = 10, d = 5$, so the gradient is

$$\frac{\text{increase in } d}{\text{increase in } t} = \frac{5 - 3}{10 - 6} = \frac{2}{4} = \frac{1}{2}.$$

For the freight train, $d = \frac{1}{2}t$, corresponding to its speed of $\frac{1}{2}$ km/min.

Example 4

Find the gradients of the line segments AB, BC and AC in Figure 4.

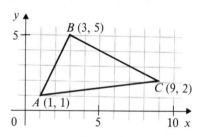

Figure 4

$$\text{Gradient of } AB = \frac{\text{increase in } y}{\text{increase in } x} = \frac{5 - 1}{3 - 1} = \frac{4}{2} = 2$$

$$\text{Gradient of } BC = \frac{\text{increase in } y}{\text{increase in } x} = \frac{2 - 5}{9 - 3} = \frac{^{-}3}{6} = \frac{^{-}1}{2}$$

$$\text{Gradient of } AC = \frac{\text{increase in } y}{\text{increase in } x} = \frac{2 - 1}{9 - 1} = \frac{1}{8}$$

Notice that, since y decreases as x increases along BC, the gradient is negative.

Example 5

Find the equation connecting y and x for the graph of Figure 5.

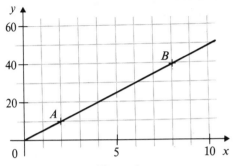

Figure 5

Since the graph is a straight line through the origin, $y \propto x$. Notice that different scales have been used on the two axes.

The gradient is $\dfrac{40 - 10}{8 - 2} = \dfrac{30}{6} = 5$ (using points A and B on the graph).

The scale factor is 5 and $y = 5x$.

Exercise C

*1 Find the gradients of the graphs in Figure 6, leaving your answers as fractions in their lowest terms (or as integers).

(a)

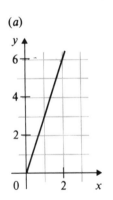

(b)

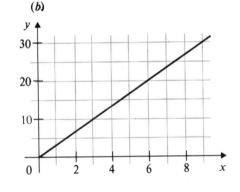

(c)

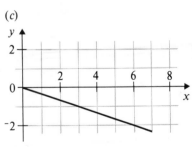

(d)

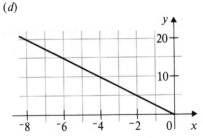

Figure 6

*2 Write down the equations connecting y and x for each of the graphs in Figure 6.

3　Find the gradients of the graphs in Figure 7, leaving your answers as fractions in their lowest terms (or as integers).

(a)

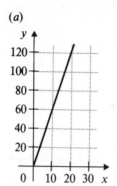

(b)

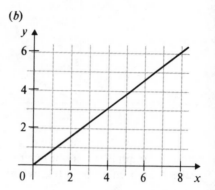

(c)

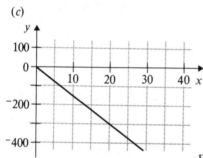

(d)

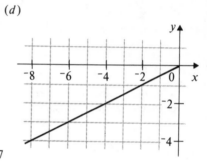

Figure 7

4　Write down the equations connecting y and x for each of the graphs in Figure 7.

*5　Find the gradients of the lines joining:
    (a) (1, 3) to (5, 15);　　(b) ($^-$1, 3) to (3, 10);
    (c) (4, 10) to (6, 4);　　(d) ($^-$2, $^-$3) to ($^-$1, 5).

6　Find the gradients of the lines joining:
    (a) (2, 5) to (6, 15);　　(b) (3, $^-$2) to (5, 2);
    (c) (3, 2) to ($^-$5, 6);　　(d) (2, $^-$5) to ($^-$3, 10).

*7　Find the gradients of the lines joining:
    (a) ($^-$5, $^-$7) to ($^-$1, $^-$5);　　(b) ($^-$3, 2) to (5, 2);
    (c) (2, 5.2) to (5, 8.5);　　(d) (2, 6.7) to (6, 4.3).

8　Find the gradients of the lines joining:
    (a) (2.1, 3.2) to (3.6, 4.7);　　(b) (3.4, 1.3) to (4.6, 3.1);
    (c) (3.7, 1.6) to (3.2, 3.7);　　(d) ($^-$2.3, 1.2) to (0.2, 3.1).

*9　Find the gradients of the lines joining:
    (a) (p, p^2) to $(2p, p^2 + p)$;　　(b) (1, 3) to $(p, 3p)$;
    (c) (^-2p, 0) to $(2p, p + 1)$;　　(d) $(p + 4, 2p + 1)$ to $(p + 7, 1 - p)$.
    Simplify your answers wherever possible.

10　Find the gradients of the lines joining:
    (a) (p, q) to (q, p);　　(b) $(p + 2, q - 2)$ to $(p + 5, q + 7)$;
    (c) (q, q) to $(1, q)$;　　(d) $(q, 4)$ to $(1, 4q)$.
    Simplify your answers wherever possible.

*11 Write down the gradients of the graphs of:
   (a) $y = 3x$;   (b) $y = ^-\frac{2}{3}x$;   (c) $x = ^-2y$;   (d) $x + y = 0$.

12 Write down the gradients of the graphs of:
   (a) $y = ^-4x$;   (b) $2y = 5x$;   (c) $y = 2$;   (d) $3x + 5y = 0$.

*13 The extension of a spring for different loads was measured, with these results:

Load in newtons	(L)	10	15	20	25	30	35	40
Extension in cm	(E)	2.9	4.6	6.0	7.6	8.8	10.5	12.1

   (a) Plot these results on a graph of $L \longrightarrow E$. Do the points you have plotted lie on a straight line?
   (b) Draw a straight line to pass through the origin and as close to the plotted points as you can. Find the gradient of the line, and write down an approximate equation connecting E and L.

14 The volume of a fixed mass of gas was measured at various temperatures, with these results:

Temperature in K (T)	273	283	288	302	328	351	373
Volume in m³ (V)	8.0×10^{-6}	8.3×10^{-6}	8.4×10^{-6}	8.8×10^{-6}	9.6×10^{-6}	10.3×10^{-6}	10.9×10^{-6}

   (a) Plot these results on a graph of $T \longrightarrow V$ and draw a straight line to pass through the origin and as near to the plotted points as possible.
   (b) Find the gradient of the straight line and write down an equation connecting V and T.

*15 A boy tries to read the scale on a petrol pump every 15 seconds while a car's petrol tank is being filled. These are his readings:

Time in seconds	0	15	30	45	60	75	90	105
Pump readings in litres	0	8	12	18	25	31	37	43

   (a) Plot these results on a graph. (Take the time scale across the page.) Which reading did he get badly wrong?
   (b) Draw a straight line to pass through the origin and as close to the plotted points as you can.
   (c) What was the reading on the pump 100 seconds after the start?
   (d) (i) What is the gradient of your line?
       (ii) How fast (in litres per second) was the tank being filled?

16 In an experiment with a trolley coasting down a slope, the speed of the trolley was measured every second with the following results:

No. of seconds after trolley starts	(t)	0	1	2	3	4	5
Speed of trolley in m/s	(v)	0	3.8×10^{-2}	7.7×10^{-2}	11.5×10^{-2}	15.1×10^{-2}	18.9×10^{-2}

   (a) Plot these results on a graph of $t \rightarrow v$ and draw a straight line to fit the points as closely as possible.
   (b) (i) What is the gradient of your line?
       (ii) What was the acceleration of the trolley?

4. STRAIGHT-LINE GRAPHS

We have seen that if $y \propto x$ then $y = kx$ for some number k (the scale factor), and the graph of $x \longrightarrow y$ is a straight line through the origin with gradient k. In this section we consider some equations whose graphs are straight lines that do not pass through the origin.

For example, we can plot the graph of $y = 2x - 3$ by using the table of values shown in Table 4. The points obtained from this are plotted in Figure 8 and joined by a straight line.

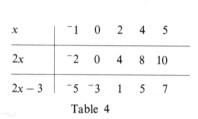

x	$^-1$	0	2	4	5
$2x$	$^-2$	0	4	8	10
$2x - 3$	$^-5$	$^-3$	1	5	7

Table 4

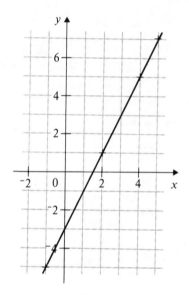

Figure 8

Using the points (2, 1) and (5, 7) on the line, we find that the gradient of the line is $\dfrac{7 - 1}{5 - 2} = \dfrac{6}{3} = 2$.

Exercise D

*1 (a) Copy and complete the following table:

x	0	2	4	6	8
$\frac{1}{2}x$	1				
$\frac{1}{2}x + 3$	4				

(b) On the same diagram plot the graphs of $y = \frac{1}{2}x$ and $y = \frac{1}{2}x + 3$ for values of x between 0 and 8.

(c) What is the gradient of the graph of $y = \frac{1}{2}x + 3$?

(d) Where does the graph of $y = \frac{1}{2}x + 3$ cross the y-axis?

2 (*a*) Copy and complete the following table:

x	$^{-}1$	0	1	2	4
$3x$				6	
$3x - 2$				4	

(*b*) On the same diagram plot the graphs of $y = 3x$ and $y = 3x - 2$ for values of x between $^{-}1$ and 4.

(*c*) What is the gradient of the graph of $y = 3x - 2$?

(*d*) Where does the graph of $y = 3x - 2$ cross the y-axis?

*3 (*a*) On the same diagram plot the graphs of $y = {}^{-}2x$ and $y = 5 - 2x$ for values of x between $^{-}1$ and 4.

(*b*) What is the gradient of the graph of $y = 5 - 2x$?

(*c*) Where does the graph of $y = 5 - 2x$ cross the y-axis?

4 (*a*) On the same diagram plot the graphs of $y = {}^{-}\frac{2}{3}x$ and $y = 4 - \frac{2}{3}x$ for values of x between $^{-}3$ and 6.

(*b*) What is the gradient of the graph of $y = 4 - \frac{2}{3}x$?

(*c*) Where does the graph of $y = 4 - \frac{2}{3}x$ cross the y-axis?

*5 (*a*) Plot the graphs of:

(i) $y = 2(x - 3)$;   (ii) $y = 2(x + 1)$

for values of x between $^{-}1$ and 5.

(*b*) What are the gradients of the graphs?

(*c*) Where do the graphs cross the x-axis?

6 (*a*) Plot the graphs of:

(i) $y = -\frac{1}{2}(x - 4)$;   (ii) $y = -\frac{1}{2}(x - 6)$

for values of x between $^{-}8$ and 8.

(*b*) What are the gradients of the graphs?

(*c*) Where do the graphs cross the x-axis?

5. EQUATIONS OF STRAIGHT LINES

The results of the previous exercise suggest that, for example:

(1) the graph of $y = 4x + 3$ is a straight line with gradient 4 crossing the y-axis at $(0, 3)$;

(2) the graph of $y = 4(x - 3)$ is a straight line with gradient 4 crossing the x-axis at $(3, 0)$.

More generally,

(1) the graph of $y = kx + c$ is a straight line with gradient k crossing the y-axis at $(0, c)$;

(2) the graph of $y = k(x - a)$ is a straight line with gradient k crossing the x-axis at $(a, 0)$.

These results can be used to write down the equations of straight-line graphs. For example, the line in Figure 9 has gradient 2 and crosses the y-axis at $(0, 1)$, and so it has equation $y = 2x + 1$. The line in Figure 10 has gradient $\frac{1}{2}$ and crosses the x-axis at $(3, 0)$, and so it has equation $y = \frac{1}{2}(x - 3)$.

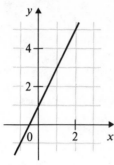

Figure 9

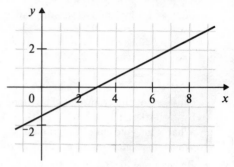

Figure 10

Exercise E

In questions 1–8 write down the equations of the lines shown in the corresponding diagram.

*1
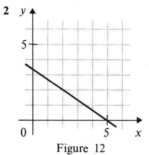

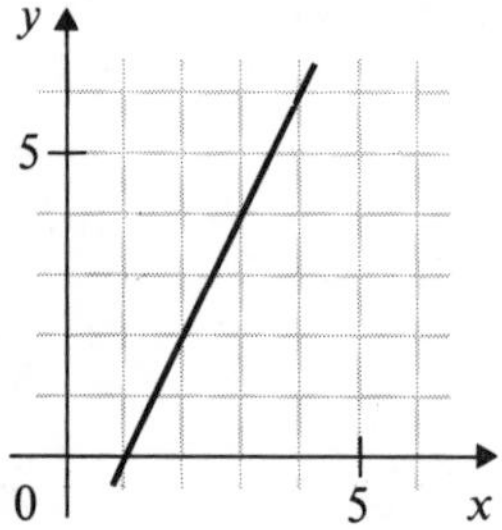

Figure 11

2

Figure 12

*3
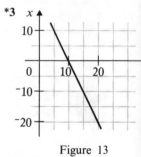

Figure 13

4

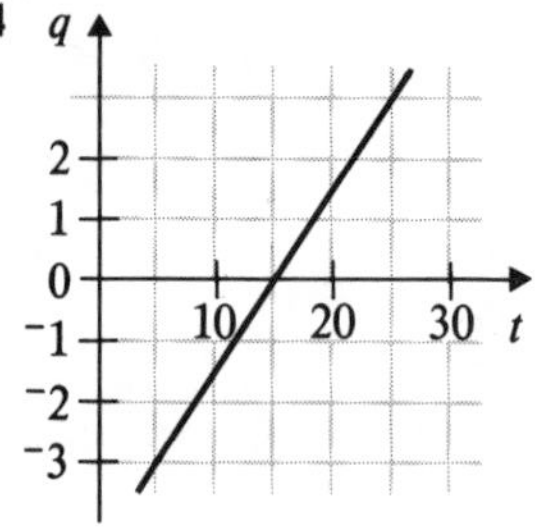

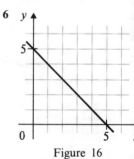

Figure 14

*5

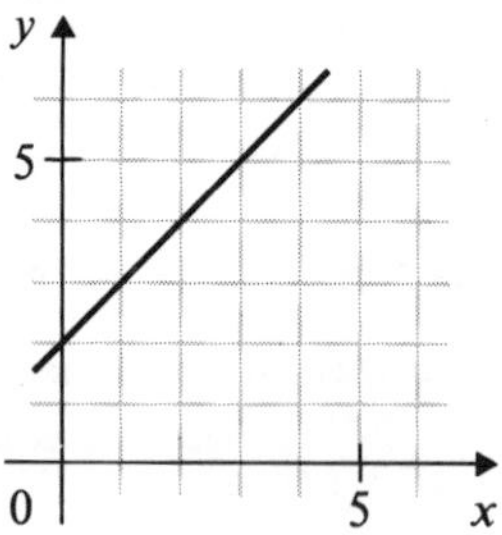

Figure 15

6

Figure 16

*7
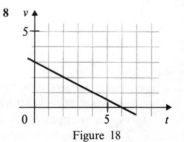

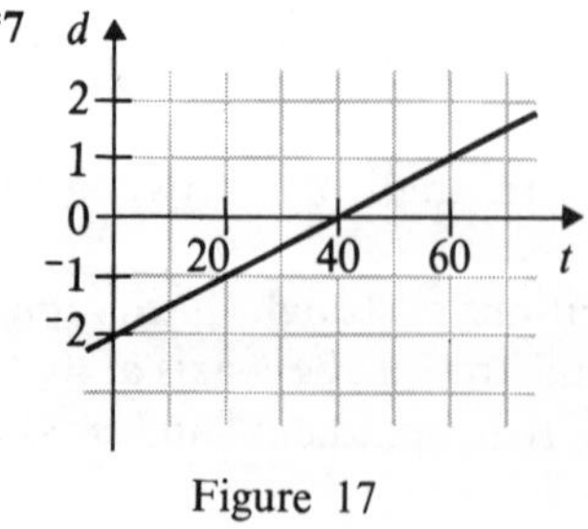

Figure 17

8

Figure 18

6. AVERAGE GRADIENTS

Figure 19 is a map on a scale of 1 : 25 000 of part of a mountain in south-eastern France. Look at the last stretch of road rising from the north-west to the Pas de la Graille. The distance on the map between the hairpin bends at grid references 781 088 and 798 076 is about 8.8 cm and so the horizontal distance between the corresponding points on the road is approximately 25 000 × 8.8 cm = 220 000 cm = 2200 m. These points are 1457 m and 1597 m above sea-level, and so the road has risen 140 m. The average gradient of this section of the road is

$$\frac{1597 - 1457}{2200} = \frac{140}{2200} \approx 0.064.$$

(This gradient would be shown on a road sign as 6%.)

The road does not rise steadily between the two points, so this is only an average gradient; some stretches of the road are steeper than this and some are less steep, as sketched in Figure 20.

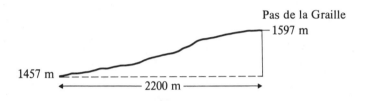

Figure 20

Exercise F

*1 Take measurements from the map in Figure 19 to find the average gradients between:
   (a) the hairpin bend at 781 088 and spot height 1508 at 788 084;
   (b) spot height 1508 at 788 084 and spot height 1539 at 791 081.

2 Find the average gradients of the stretches of road between:
   (a) the hairpin bends at 797 081 and 781 088;
   (b) the hairpin bends at 780 093 and 797 081.

*3 What is the average gradient of the footpath called 'Chemin de Frère Jean' between spot height 1123 at 782 096 and the Pas de la Graille?

4 A walker approaches the summit from the south, using the forestry tracks. What is the average gradient of his route between spot height 1370 at 771 065 and the point where he crosses the road (spot height 1736 at 771 081)? Where is the steepest part of his route?

*5 Figure 21 is a distance–time graph for a car-journey.
   (a) (i) How far did the car travel between 9 a.m. and noon?
      (ii) What was the average speed for those three hours?
   (b) (i) How far did the car travel between 10 a.m. and 11 a.m.?
      (ii) What was the average speed for that hour?
   (c) Find the average speeds between:
      (i) 9.30 a.m. and 10 a.m.;   (ii) 10.30 a.m. and 10.45 a.m.
   (d) Find the average speeds between:
      (i) 9.45 a.m. and 10.15 a.m.;   (ii) 11.15 a.m. and 12 noon.

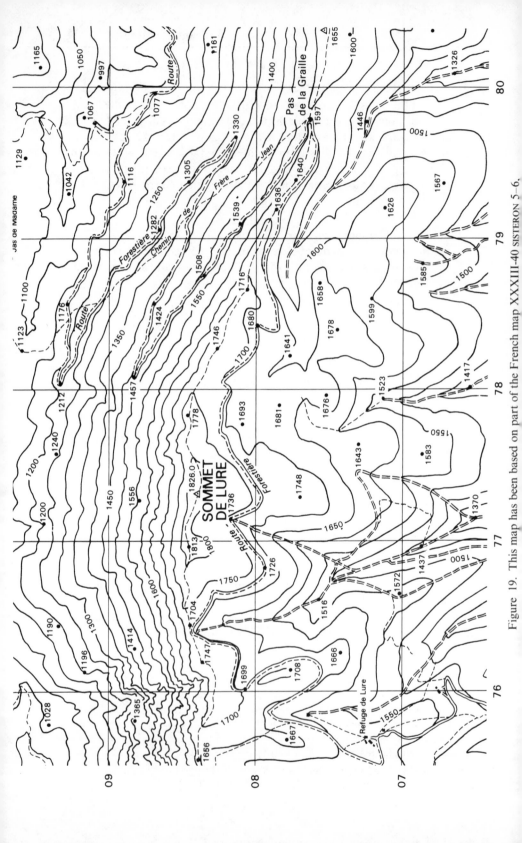

Figure 19. This map has been based on part of the French map XXXIII-40 SISTERON 5-6.

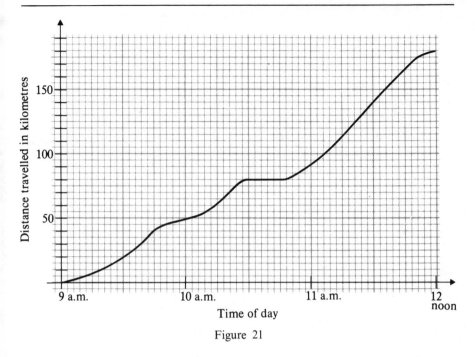

Figure 21

6 Table 5 is part of a timetable for a train travelling from London to Hereford. The left-hand column gives the distances in kilometres from London.

0	Paddington	dep.	1500
58	Reading	arr.	1532
102	Oxford	arr.	1603
124	Charlbury	arr.	1620
136	Kingham	arr.	1629
148	Moreton-in-Marsh	arr.	1641
172	Evesham	arr.	1659
194	Worcester (Shrub Hill)	arr.	1718
		dep.	1720
241	Hereford	arr.	1808

Table 5

(a) What was the average speed for the complete journey:
   (i) in km/min;   (ii) in km/h?
(b) Draw a graph of time $\longrightarrow$ distance from London
(c) Use your graph to find:
   (i) the average speed of the train between 1500 and 1600;
   (ii) its average speed between 1700 and 1800.
   Can you suggest a reason for the difference between your answers to (i) and (ii)?

*7 Find the average gradient between A and B in each of the graphs in Figure 22. What does the gradient represent in each case?

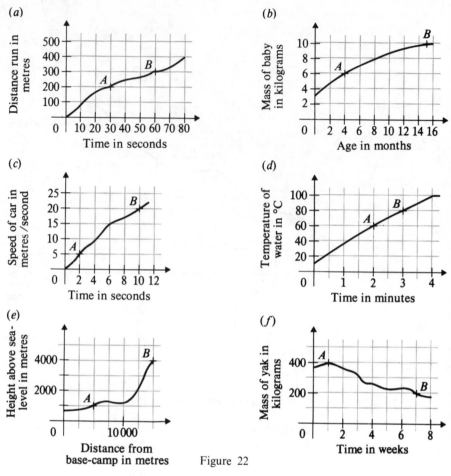

Figure 22

8   Figure 23 shows a graph of the volume of water in a bath. Describe what you think was happening, giving rates where appropriate.

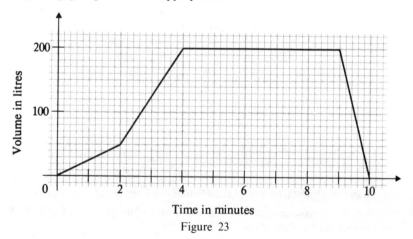

Figure 23

9 Figure 24 shows the volume of water in a reservoir during one day.
   (*a*) What was the average rate of increase of the volume of water between
       (i) 9 a.m. and 11 a.m;   (ii) 6 a.m. and 6 p.m.?
   (*b*) During which half-hour was the volume decreasing fastest? What was the
       average rate of decrease then?

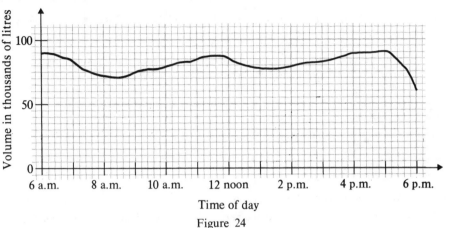

Time of day

Figure 24

SUMMARY

If $y \propto x$ then

(1) $y = kx$, where k is the scale factor or constant of proportionality;

(Section 1)

(2) corresponding values of x and y can be found by using the same multiplier;

(Section 2)

(3) the graph of $x \longrightarrow y$ is a straight line through the origin with gradient k.

(Section 3)

   The gradient of a line joining two points on a graph of $x \longrightarrow y$ is the fraction

$$\frac{\text{increase in } y}{\text{increase in } x}.$$

(Section 3)

   The graph of $y = kx + c$ is a straight line with gradient k which crosses the
y-axis at $(0, c)$. (See Figure 25.)

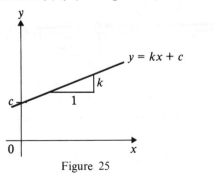

Figure 25

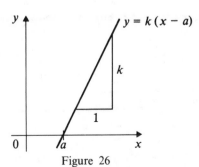

Figure 26

The graph of $y = k(x - a)$ is a straight line with gradient k which crosses the x-axis at $(a, 0)$. (See Figure 26.)   (Sections 4, 5)

In working with examples involving measurements,
(1) the gradient is associated with a rate;   (Section 2)

(2) a 'best-fit' straight line may have to be drawn because of errors of measurement;   (Section 3)

(3) when the graph is not a straight line the gradient of the line joining two points on the graph gives information about average rates.   (Section 6)

Summary exercise

1 (a) Copy and complete this table if $Z \propto p$:

p	2.0	7.0	8.0	40
Z		9.1		67

(b) Write down an equation connecting Z and p.

2 (a) An observer hears the sound of an explosion 1.3 seconds after he sees the flash from it. If the explosion took place 430 m from him, what was the speed of the sound wave (i) in m/s;   (ii) in km/h?
  (b) In a thunderstorm 12 seconds elapse between seeing a lightning flash and hearing the thunder. How far away was the storm?

3 Find the gradients of the sides of the triangle ABC if A, B and C have coordinates $(1, 3), (^-2, ^-5)$ and $(3, ^-1)$ respectively.

4 For a fixed mass of gas at constant pressure, the volume is proportional to the temperature (measured in K). A hot-air balloon contains a volume of 597 m³ of air when the temperature is 288 K. If we assume no air escapes from the balloon, what volume would it contain if heated through 10 degrees?

5 If 1 m³ of copper has a mass of 8.8 tonne, and 1 m³ of aluminium has a mass of 2.7 tonne, how much should the mass of a copper saucepan be, if an aluminium one of the same shape and size has a mass of 1.5 kg?

(a)

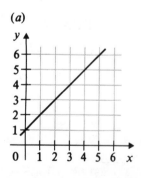

(b)

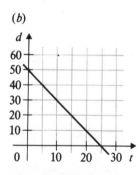

(c)

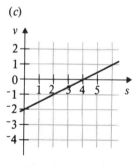

Figure 27

6 Write down the equations of the lines in Figure 27.

7 The following sets of values of x and y were obtained from an experiment. It is thought that $y \propto x$.

x	1.1	3.4	5.8	6.7	8.4
y	0.028	0.085	0.15	0.17	0.24

Draw the best straight-line graph to pass through these points and the origin, and find its equation.

8 Figure 28 shows the air temperature out of doors in England on one afternoon and evening.
   (*a*) What time of year do you think it was?
   (*b*) What were the average rates of change of temperature:
        (i)   between noon and 6 p.m.;
        (ii) between 6 p.m. and 8 p.m.;
        (iii) between noon and 10 p.m.?

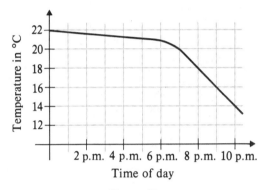

Figure 28

Miscellaneous exercise

1 A car uses 16.3 litres of petrol in travelling 182 km. The petrol cost 550 L\$ (Lilliputian dollars) for 20 litres.
   (*a*) What is the petrol consumption in litres per 100 km?
   (*b*) What is the cost of petrol in L\$ per litre?
   (*c*) How much does petrol for a 100 km journey cost?
   (*d*) How much will a motorist driving 15 000 km in a year spend on petrol?

2 How long will a kettle at 90°C take to cool to 80°C if the average cooling rate is 4.8°C per minute?

3 A silver coin has a diameter of 2.8 cm and a thickness of 2.0 mm.
   (*a*) Calculate its volume and its mass. (Density of silver = 10.5×10^3 kg/m³.)
   (*b*) If the price of silver is 42 Ruritanian ruples per gram, find the value of the silver in the coin.

4 0.485 kg of paraffin absorbs 13 100 joules of heat energy when its temperature is raised by 11.4°C.
   (*a*) Calculate the amount of energy required to raise the temperature of 0.485 kg of paraffin by 1°C.

(b) Calculate the amount of energy required to raise the temperature of 1 kg of paraffin by 1°C.

5 Pierre plans to walk along the summit ridge of the Montagne de Lure, starting at the 1704 spot height (grid reference 764 084) and ending at the Pas de la Graille (798 076). Use measurements from Figure 19 to draw a graph of horizontal distance travelled ⟶ height above sea-level. Find the average gradients for the principal stages of the route.

6 A survey of weekly earnings among plaice-farmers in Atlantis produced the following information:

Hours worked	16	27	30	33	39	42	49	51
Earnings in cowries	5.92	9.99	11.10	12.21	14.43	15.90	19.75	20.85

(a) Show this information on a graph of earnings against hours.
(b) After how many hours are the farmers paid overtime rates?
(c) (i) What is the normal wage-rate (in cowries per hour?)
    (ii) What is the overtime wage-rate?

7 The quarterly electricity bills for a small house for two years were as follows:

Date of bill	Jan.	April	July	Oct.	Jan.	April	July	Oct.
Number of units	964	1148	446	380	808	1050	326	298
Cost	£34.01	£39.80	£17.69	£15.61	£29.09	£36.72	£13.91	£13.03

(a) Show this information on a graph of cost in pounds against number of units.
(b) Find the gradient of the graph.
(c) The cost is calculated from a fixed quarterly charge and a charge per unit. Find these.

REVISION EXERCISE 11

1 Calculate $(1.8 \times 10^5) \div (6 \times 10^8)$, writing your answer in standard form.

2 On copies of the Venn diagram shown in
   Figure 1, show clearly the following sets:
   (a) $A \cup B'$;   (b) $A' \cap B'$;   (c) $A' \cap B$.

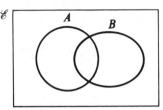

Figure 1

3 Write 0.004 827 6
   (a) correct to 3 decimal places;
   (b) correct to 3 s.f.;
   (c) in standard form.

4 Estimate, to an accuracy of one significant figure, the values of:
   (a) $497 \div 2340$;   (b) 4072^2;   (c) 0.072×42.

5 (a) Find the result of increasing £13 by 12%.
   (b) £x, when increased by 12%, becomes £13. Find x.

6 Write without brackets and collect terms together:
   (a) $7(p + 2) + 3(p - 4)$;
   (b) $8(m - 3) + 4(6 - m)$;
   (c) $2a - 3(a - 1)$.

7 Find the images of $(2, 7)$ under rotations of 90° about:
   (a) $(0, 0)$;   (b) $(2, 0)$;   (c) $(4, 3)$.

8 Construct, using ruler and compasses, a triangle ABC in which $AB = 10.0$ cm, $BC = 12.0$ cm and $CA = 15.0$ cm. Construct the bisector of angle BAC and mark the point D where it meets BC. Measure the length of BD.

REVISION EXERCISE 12

1 Find the value of $2p^3 - q^2$ when $p = {}^-3$ and $q = {}^-2$.

2 If $\dfrac{7000 \times 800}{0.001} = 5.6 \times 10^n$, what is the value of n?

3 Write $\dfrac{\frac{1}{4} - \frac{1}{5}}{\frac{1}{4} + \frac{1}{5}}$ as a simple fraction.

4 Solve the equation $\dfrac{24}{6 - 5x} = 3$.

5 Divide £444 in the ratio $2 : 3 : 7$.

6 If $\mathbf{T}$ is the translation with vector $\begin{bmatrix} 3 \\ -4 \end{bmatrix}$ and $\mathbf{E}$ is enlargement with centre $(0, 0)$ and scale factor 2, draw a diagram to show f, $\mathbf{T}(f)$, $\mathbf{E}(f)$, and $\mathbf{TE}(f)$ where f is the line segment joining $(3, 1)$ and $(2, 4)$. (Allow enough space in your diagram for values of x and y between $^-5$ and 10.) Describe precisely the single transformation equivalent to $\mathbf{TE}$.

7 A train travels 119 km in 46 min. Calculate its average speed in km/h. Find the upper and lower bounds for your answer, assuming that both measurements have been given to the nearest whole number.

8 Find the height of a cylinder which has a volume of 1217 cm³ and a radius of 11.2 cm.

13

The right-angled triangle

1. PROBLEMS AND TRIANGLES

An orienteer planned a route through a belt of thick wood to reach a straight track on the eastern boundary. His shortest route would be due east, but after going 200 m he discovers that he has been misreading his compass. If he actually travelled 30° north of his intended direction, how much 'useful' progress has he made?

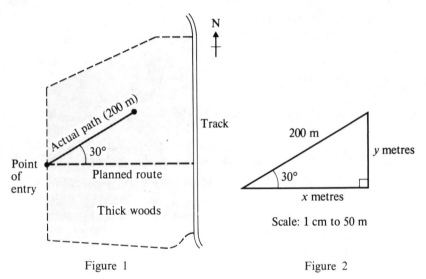

Figure 1   Figure 2

One method of solving the problem is to make a scale drawing, such as the one in Figure 2. This is a mathematical model and, like all such models, it is simpler than the real situation. Compare Figure 2 with Figure 1 and see what has been omitted.

By measuring the side marked x metres in Figure 2 we find that the orienteer has made about 170 m progress in his intended direction. The length marked y metres might also be of interest: he is about 50 m off his planned path.

Many different problems in the real world can be tackled by using right-angled triangle models such as Figure 2. We do not want to have to make a new scale drawing every time; this can be slow and is unlikely to be very accurate.

We compare all our triangles with 'standard' triangles in which the hypotenuse (the side opposite the right angle) is one unit long. We need to know one other angle; then the drawing can be completed, and the other sides measured. Figure 3 shows the standard triangle for an angle of 30°.

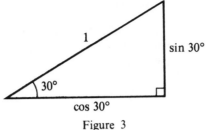

Figure 3

In such a standard triangle the length alongside the angle depends just on the angle; it is a function of the angle. This function is called the *cosine* function, usually abbreviated to cos. Similarly the *sine* function, abbreviated to sin, gives the side opposite the angle. The sine and cosine of any angle can be found using accurate drawings such as Figure 3, or from tables or a calculator with *trigonometric* functions (the general name given to functions such as cos and sin).

Exercise A

1 Make your own accurate copy of Figure 3, using 10 cm for the unit. Use your drawing to find cos 30° and sin 30° to as many figures as you think are justified by your drawing.

2 Repeat question 1, but this time draw the standard triangle for 40° and hence find cos 40° and sin 40°.

3 Draw a quarter-circle, as in Figure 4, using 10 cm as your unit.
   (a) Explain why the coordinates of *P* are (cos 30°, sin 30°) if the angle *xOP* is 30°.
   (b) On your diagram mark in the positions of *P* when the angle *xOP* is 0°, 10°, 30°, ... , 80°, 90°. By reading off the coordinates of these points, make a table of values of the cosines and sines of these angles.

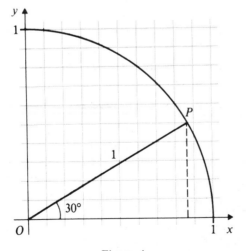

Figure 4

2. USING COSINES

Using the table you constructed in Exercise A, question 3, or printed tables, or a calculator with trigonometric functions, we can solve the orienteer's problem and other problems involving right-angled triangles without using scale drawing.

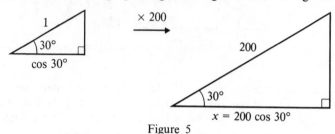

Figure 5

Figure 5 shows how the 30° standard triangle can be enlarged to give the triangle we used (in Figure 2) to model the problem. Since the hypotenuse is required to be 200 the scale factor of the enlargement is 200 and so $x = 200 \cos 30°$.

From tables or calculator, $\cos 30° \approx 0.866$.

$$x \approx 200 \times 0.866 = 173.2$$
$$\approx 170$$

The orienteer has made about 170 m of useful progress.

Example 1

Catherine is sailing a small boat across Eddrachillis Bay. She has sailed 4.1 km from Loch Dhrombaig (grid reference 117 338) on a bearing of 032° and wants to know whether she is far enough north to be able to sail due east to the sheltered anchorage of Calva Bay.

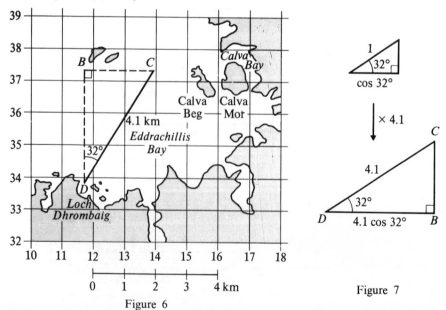

Figure 6

Figure 7

We first draw a simpler diagram to model the part of the situation which concerns us, in this case the triangle *DBC*. We draw it in such a position that we can compare it easily with the 32° standard triangle. (See Figure 7.)

Catherine is 4.1 cos 32° km north of her starting-point.

$$DB = 4.1 \cos 32° = 3.476\,997\,2 \quad \boxed{\text{c}}$$
$$\approx 3.5$$

The grid reference of Loch Dhrombaig gives its coordinates as (11.7, 33.8), where the units are kilometres, so her new northerly coordinate is $33.8 + 3.5 = 37.3$. To sail safely past the northernmost point of Calva Mor on an easterly course this coordinate needs to be at least 37.6, so she is not yet far enough north.

Exercise B

*1 Find the lengths marked with letters in Figure 8. (Give all your answers correct to 2 s.f.; use rough estimates to check your answers.)

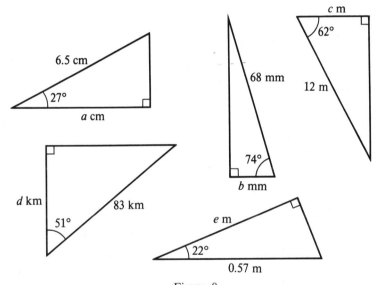

Figure 8

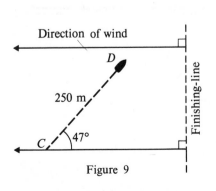

Figure 9

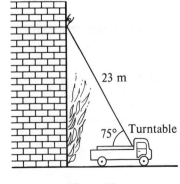

Figure 10

*2   Alison is helming in a dinghy, racing upwind to the finishing-line. She has just sailed 250 m on a tack from C to D as close to the wind as possible but this is 47° off the direction she wants to go. (See Figure 9.) How much closer does this tack bring her to the finishing-line?

3   A mobile fire-escape ladder, mounted on a turntable, can be extended to a length of 23 m, but it is unsafe unless it is at an angle of 75° or more to the horizontal. How close must the turntable be brought to a burning building, if this requires the ladder to be fully extended? (See Figure 10.)

3. USING SINES

Mary is flying a kite and would like to know how high it is. She estimates that she has paid out 50 m of string, and that it makes an angle of about 55° with the horizontal.

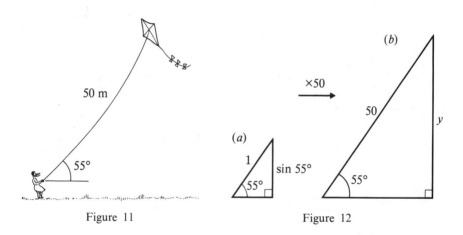

Figure 11   Figure 12

Our first step is to model the situation with a right-angled triangle and to draw the corresponding standard triangle beside it. By using enlargement, we see that

$$y = 50 \sin 55° = 40.957\,602.$$ ©

The kite is about 40 m above the ground. (Our model ignores the height of Mary's hand above the ground, the size of the kite, the sag of the string and the slope of the ground, and the figures were given as estimates, so no more than one significant figure accuracy is justified.)

Notice that, since the required length, y, is opposite the given angle, we use the sine of the angle.

Exercise C

*1 Calculate the lengths marked with letters in Figure 13.

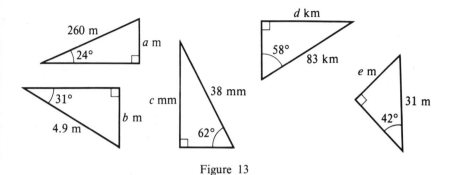

Figure 13

*2 A small aircraft leaves a runway and climbs at an angle of 19°. After flying 800 m, how high is it above the runway?

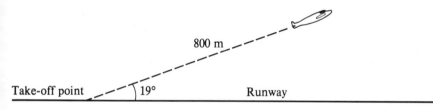

Figure 14

3 An inexperienced orienteer planned to travel due north from the control point to the canal bridge. (See Figure 15.) It is only when he emerges on the canal bank that he realises that misreading his compass has put him 30° off course. He estimates that he has walked 500 m already and is contemplating swimming the canal, but how far would he have to walk along the towpath to the bridge?

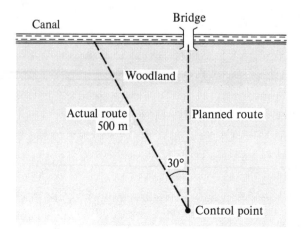

Figure 15

4. COSINE AND SINE MULTIPLIERS

A point has polar coordinates $(9, 37°)$. What are its cartesian coordinates?

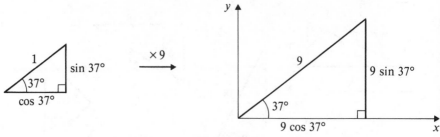

Figure 16

Enlarging the 37° standard triangle we find that
$$x = 9 \cos 37° \approx 7.2 \quad \text{and} \quad y = 9 \sin 37° \approx 5.4.$$
We can set these results out in a table as follows:

Sides of standard triangle	1	$\cos 37°$	$\sin 37°$		scale factor
Sides of enlarged triangle	9	$9 \cos 37°$	$9 \sin 37°$		9

Table 1

However, if we look at the multipliers within these proportional sets, we see that we find x and y by multiplying the hypotenuse by $\cos 37°$ and $\sin 37°$.

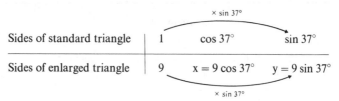

Table 2

This is illustrated for sine in Table 2. Using cosine and sine as multipliers in this way makes it unnecessary to draw the standard triangle. Their use is conveniently illustrated in Figure 17.

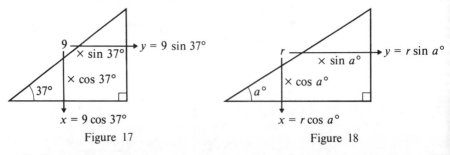

Figure 17   Figure 18

To find x, the length alongside the angle, we multiply the hypotenuse by the cosine of the angle; to find y, the length opposite the angle, we multiply the hypotenuse by the sine of the angle. (See Figure 18.)

Example 2

For a new art block at a school the architect suggests an asymmetrical roof in order to provide a good north light. The best studio lighting requires windows sloping at about 70° above the horizontal, and for structural reasons there is to be a right angle at the roof ridge. The architect wants to know how long each slope will be, if her plans are for a studio 7.50 m wide.

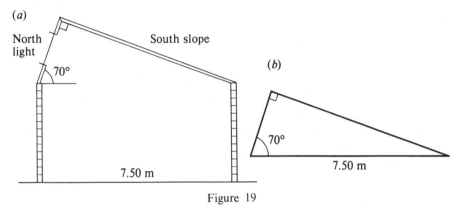

Figure 19

The south slope is opposite the 70° angle in Figure 19(*b*) and we can therefore find its length by multiplying the hypotenuse by sin 70°.

Length of south slope = 7.50 sin 70° m ≈ 7.05 m.

Length of north slope = 7.50 cos 70° m ≈ 2.57 m (since the north slope is alongside the 70° angle).

We can check that we have got these the right way round by using Figure 19(*a*) to make rough estimates of the lengths of the slopes: the north slope is about one-third of the width of the studio, so is about 2.5 m; the south slope is a little less than the width, about 7 m.

Exercise D

*1   Find the lengths marked with letters in Figure 20.

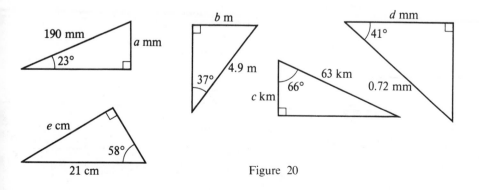

Figure 20

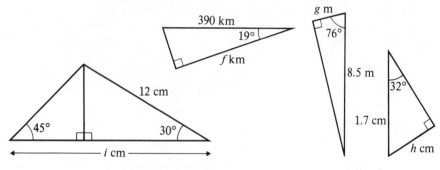

Figure 20 (continued)

2 Find the cartesian coordinates of the points with the following polar coordinates:
$A(8, 22°)$, $B(11, 33°)$, $C(7, 53°)$ and $D(10, 70°)$.
Check your answers by plotting the points on graph paper.

*3 An expedition is making an advance drop of supplies by helicopter into a jungle clearing. Radar at the base-camp gives the distance of the helicopter as 20.7 km in a direction 16.3° above the horizontal. (This is called the angle of elevation of the helicopter.) In order to pin-point the helicopter's position, its horizontal distance from the camp is needed. Calculate this distance.

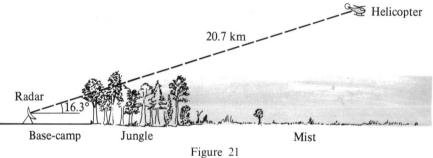

Figure 21

4 A fire-engine has a ladder which can be extended to 23 m and can be raised to an angle of 82° above the horizontal. What is the greatest height it can reach?

*5 An expedition vehicle carries some stout planks 4.5 m long, which can be placed to form a ramp to enable the vehicle to surmount obstacles (see Figure 22). If the vehicle can climb a 12° slope, what is the highest obstacle it can surmount?

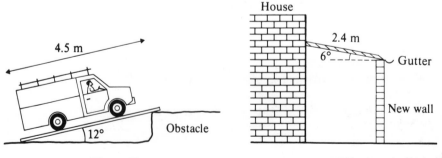

Figure 22   Figure 23

6 A sheet of corrugated plastic to roof a conservatory is 2.4 m long. If a slope of 6° is required to ensure adequate rainwater run-off (see Figure 23), how much higher than the gutter should the other end be fastened to the house?

*7 Andrew is building some shelves and on one he plans to store some LP records which, in their sleeves, are up to 32 cm high. Although they should be stored vertically to avoid warping, he is short of space and thinks they will be safe up to 15° off the vertical. (See Figure 24). How close together can he build the shelves?

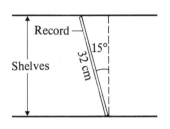

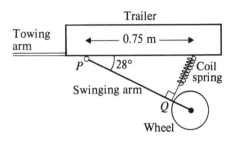

Figure 24   Figure 25

8 Paula is designing the suspension for a light trailer to tow behind a bicycle, as shown in Figure 25. The swinging arm and coil spring are to be mounted 0.75 m apart, and the spring is to be set at right-angles to the arm. If she decides on an angle of 28° below the horizontal for the swinging arm, how long will she have to make it from the pivot P to Q, where it joins the wheel fork?

*9 Starting from a point with grid reference 252 709, a helicopter flies on a bearing of 073° and covers a distance of 42 km before landing. Calculate how far (*a*) east and (*b*) north the helicopter lands from its starting-point and hence give the grid reference of its position. (Recall that grid reference 252 709 means the coordinates are (25.2, 70.9), the units being kilometres.)

10 A crane has a jib 8.3 m long mounted on a platform 1.2 m above the ground. The jib can be raised to an angle of 72° above the horizontal, and the hook can be hoisted to within 0.4 m below the top of the jib. What is the greatest height above the ground to which a small load can be lifted?

11 Captain Polo is nearing the end of his crossing of the Bogi Desert, following the caravan trail to the great bazar of Um, on a bearing of 037°. His camels, however, are sore-footed and refractory, so he is planning to take them due north across country to the shore of Lake Boozi, which is believed to run west from Um. From an ancient stone he knows that he is 120 leagues from Um; how far is he from the lake, by the shortest route?

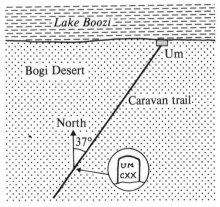

Figure 26

5. FINDING THE HYPOTENUSE

Mark is going to unblock a gutter on his house, using a ladder whose length can be adjusted. He needs it to rest 6.0 m up the wall and he thinks that the safest angle would be 65° above the horizontal. (See Figure 27 (*a*).) How long should he make his ladder?

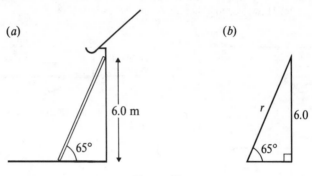

Figure 27

Figure 27(*b*) shows the relevant right-angled triangle. Since the length 6.0 is opposite the 65° angle, it could be obtained from *r* by multiplying by sin 65° (≈ 0.906).

r ——[Multiply by 0.906 >]—— 6.0

Reversing this, we obtain *r* by dividing by 0.906:

r ——[< Divide by 0.906]—— 6.0

$$r = \frac{6.0}{0.906} \approx 6.6.$$

The ladder should be about 6.6 m long.

In general, if we know *r* and the angle $a°$ we find x and y by multiplying *r* by $\cos a°$ and $\sin a°$, as illustrated in Figure 28(*a*). If we know x or y and want to find *r*, then we reverse the process and divide by the appropriate multiplier as shown in Figure 28(*b*).

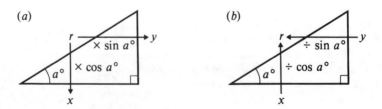

Figure 28

Example 3

A hole is to be drilled through a partition wall to feed a television aerial cable through into the next room. The partition is made of prefabricated sheets 7.0 cm thick. The corner where the hole has to go is hard to reach, and the hole will have to be drilled at an angle of 20° to the horizontal. How long will the drill bit have to be?

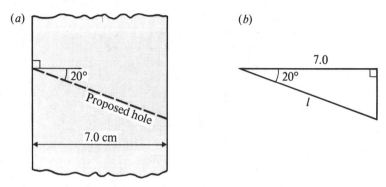

Figure 29

Figure 29 (*b*) shows the relevant right-angled triangle from which we see that

$$l = \frac{7.0}{\cos 20°} \approx 7.4.$$

The drill bit must be at least 7.4 cm long, plus an allowance for the part inserted in the drill chuck.

Exercise E

*1 Find the lengths marked with letters in Figure 30.

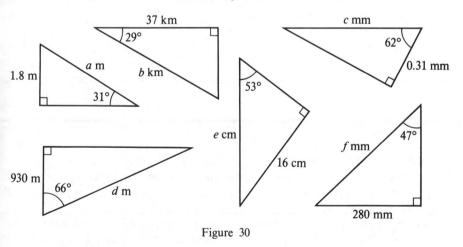

Figure 30

*2 A window-cleaner leans his ladder against a wall at an angle of 70° to the horizontal. If it reaches 6.5 m up the wall, how long is the ladder?

3 An old mine-shaft is cut through a stratum of rock 8.3 m thick. Ladders were used to descend it, so the shaft is not vertical, but at an angle of 12° to the vertical. (See Figure 31.) What is the length of the shaft?

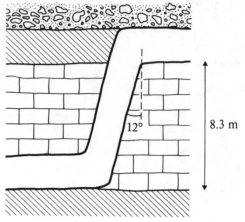

Figure 31

*4 A balloon is to be used to carry the aerial for a home-made radio. It is found that the wind makes the wire slope at an angle of 65° to the horizontal, and it is desirable to reach a height above the ground of 80 m. How long must the wire be?

5 Offshore drilling rigs frequently bore wells off the vertical in order to reach sources of oil. If such a well is drilled at an angle of 34° to the vertical, and the oil-bearing stratum is 320 m below the sea-bed, how far will the drill bit have to cut before striking oil?

6 A yacht at Y is racing for the finishing-line, sailing as close to the wind as possible. If the nearest point, Z is 580 m directly upwind, and the yacht sails at 42° off this direction, to finish at X, how far must it sail?

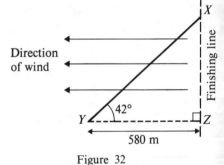

Figure 32

6. TANGENTS

Giant redwood trees in California grow to amazing heights. A forester comes across a new candidate for the record books, and wants to make an estimate of its height – without, of course, being able to climb it or cut it down. Consider how he might do this.

One method which, by using surveying instruments, can be made very accurate, is to measure the 'angle of elevation' of the tree-top seen from a known distance. If the forester estimates this as 35° from a distance of 150 m, let us see how we can find the height.

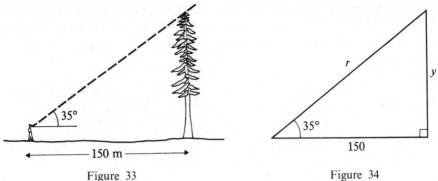

| Figure 33 | Figure 34 |

Figure 34 shows the right-angled triangle, in which we want to calculate y. This can be done in two stages, as follows:

$$r = \frac{150}{\cos 35°} = 183.116\ 19 \qquad \boxed{\text{c}}$$

$$y = r \sin 35° = 105.031\ 13. \qquad \boxed{\text{c}}$$

The tree is about 105 m high.

This slightly clumsy two-stage method involves finding r, which we did not want to find. The process is illustrated as follows:

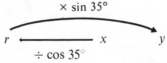

The calculation could be performed in one step if we had a multiplier for obtaining x from y directly. This multiplier is called the *tangent* of the angle and is abbreviated to tan. Its use is illustrated by Figure 35(a). tan 35° ≈ 0.700, so $x = 150 \Rightarrow y = 150 \tan 35° \approx 150 \times 0.700 = 105$, as before.

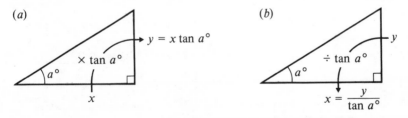

Figure 35

We use tan in problems in which the hypotenuse is unknown and not required. In the above example we were finding y from x and so we multiplied by the tan of the angle. If we want to find x from y, we reverse the process and divide by the tan of the angle. (See Figure 35(b).)

Example 4

A small boat is sailing off a mountainous coast, and the skipper is unsure of her exact position. She recognizes one peak due east of the boat, and finds that its height is given on the map as 2420 m. With a sextant she makes a careful measurement of its angle of elevation as 6.9°. How can she calculate her distance from the mountain, and fix her position?

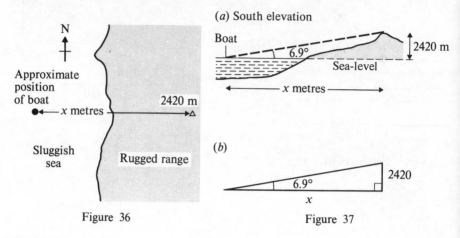

Figure 36   Figure 37

From the right-angled triangle in Figure 37(b) we obtain

$$x = \frac{2420}{\tan 6.9°} \approx 20\,000.$$

She is about 20 000 m, or 20 km, from the mountain.

Exercise F

1   Make your own accurate copy of Figure 38, using 10 cm for the unit. Use your drawing to find tan 30° to as many figures as you think are justified by your drawing.

2   Repeat question 1, but this time use an angle of 20° and find tan 20°.

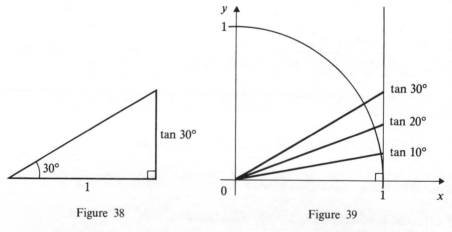

Figure 38   Figure 39

3   Copy Figure 39 onto graph or squared paper, using a convenient length, such as 5 cm, for one unit in each direction. Allow for values of *y* up to at least 3. (The quarter circle

is for comparison with Exercise A, question 3.) Use your protractor to draw standard triangles with one unit length in the x-direction and with angles of 10°, 20°, ... ; you will have to stop well before 90°. Measure the y-coordinate of the top corner of each triangle, recording the results in a table. Compare your results with the printed tangent tables, or values of tan θ from your calculator. (This diagram suggests why the name 'tangent' is given to two apparently unconnected things.)

*4 Calculate the lengths marked with letters in Figure 40.

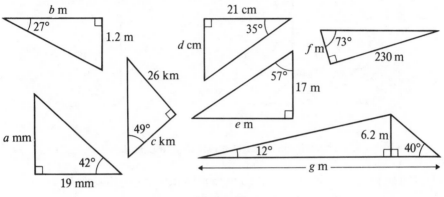

Figure 40

5 From the Staten Island Ferry the angle of elevation of the top of one of the towers of the World Trade Center (411 m tall) is 9.6°. How far is the ferry from the tower?

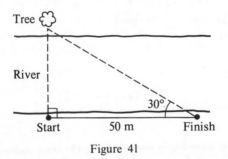

Figure 41

*6 Helen is trying to estimate the width of a river, which has approximately straight and parallel banks. She stands on one bank, directly opposite a tree on the other bank. Then she walks 50 m along the bank, and looks back at the tree. If her line of sight now makes an angle of 30° with the bank, how wide is the river?

7 From a cliff 80 m high Michael looks down on a boat at sea. His line of sight is 9° below the horizontal. (This is called the angle of depression.) How far is the boat from the cliff?

8 From the top of a cliff 80 m high Jill sights a porpoise at an angle of depression of 18°. How far is the porpoise from the foot of the cliff?

7. FINDING ANGLES

One of the stays holding a television mast upright is of length 50 m and attached to the mast at a point 45 m above the ground. In order to design the anchorage for the stay it is necessary to know the angle that the stay makes with the ground. Figure 42(a) illustrates the situation; Figure 42(b) shows the right-angled triangle concerned. The angle marked $\theta°$ is the one we wish to know.

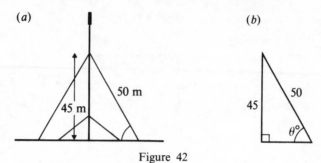

Figure 42

If we knew θ, we should be able to find $\sin \theta°$ and calculate
$$50 \sin \theta° = 45.$$
However, from this equation we can obtain, by dividing both sides by 50,
$$\sin \theta° = \frac{45}{50} = 0.9.$$
So we need to find out which angle has a sine equal to 0.9. We could search through the sine tables, or, using a calculator with trigonometric functions, use trial and error; $\sin 60°$ is too small, $\sin 70°$ is too large, so try $\sin 65°$ next, and so on. To the nearest degree, we obtain $64°$ as the answer.

In the last step of this solution we used the sine tables backwards, looking for the angle that gave 0.9. If we think of sine as a function mapping $64°$ onto 0.9, we were using the inverse function, as shown in this diagram:

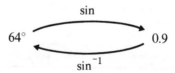

We can write $\sin^{-1} 0.9 \approx 64°$; this is read as the 'inverse sine', or sometimes as the 'arc sine', of 0.9. It is fairly easy, with practice, to use ordinary sine tables 'backwards'; most calculators with trigonometric functions have a separate button for $\sin^{-1}$, or an extra button marked 'inv' or 'arc', so that the trial and error method is unnecessary.

Example 5
A ramp is to be built to give access to a raised warehouse entrance. The ramp has to rise 1.5 m, and 10 m of the loading-bay is available for its construction. Before accepting this design, we wish to check that fork-lift trucks will be able to carry loads up the ramp; their steepest safe operating slope is $10°$.

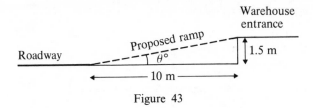

Figure 43

$$1.5 = 10 \tan \theta°$$
$$\tan \theta° = 1.5 \div 10 = 0.15 \quad \text{(dividing both sides by 10)}$$
$$\theta° = \tan^{-1} 0.15$$
$$\approx 8.5°$$

The proposed ramp will slope at about 8.5°, and is therefore suitable for the fork-lift trucks.

Exercise G

*1 Find the angles marked with letters in Figure 44.

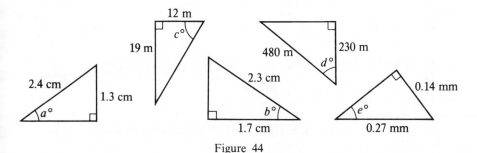

Figure 44

*2 A fragile and valuable old picture is being moved for an exhibition and has to pass through a door which is wide enough, but rather low. It is feared that the canvas may sag, loosening the paint, if the picture is tilted too far from the vertical. Calculate the angle between the picture and the vertical if the frame, which is 2.75 m high, is tilted so that it just passes through the door, which is 2.58 m high. (See Figure 45.)

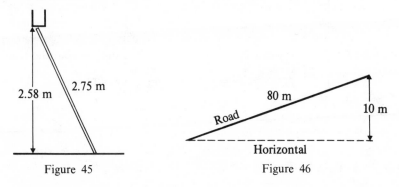

Figure 45   Figure 46

3   Find the angles made with the x-axis by the following:

     (a) the vector $\begin{bmatrix} 4 \\ 7 \end{bmatrix}$;

     (b) the line joining (1, 5) to (6, 7);

     (c) the line with equation $y = 2x + 3$.

*4   In Chapter 12 we met the mathematician's gradient, calculated as

$$\frac{\text{increase in } y}{\text{increase in } x}.$$

     For roads and railways, the surveyor's gradient is more convenient, calculated as

$$\frac{\text{increase in height } (y)}{\text{distance along road } (r)}.$$

In the example in Figure 46, this is $\dfrac{10}{80} = \dfrac{1}{8}$; on some British road signs this appears

as 1:8 or 1 in 8, but more commonly the fraction $\dfrac{1}{8}$ is converted to $\dfrac{12\frac{1}{2}}{100}$, and the sign

shows $12\frac{1}{2}\%$. (For the small gradients found on roads, the difference between mathematician's and surveyor's gradient is slight.)

     Calculate the angle of slope of roads with the following surveyor's gradients:

     (a) 1:6;   (b) 1 in 14;   (c) 6%;   (d) 14%.

*5   Find the bearing of a church at grid reference 076 941 from a hill-top at grid reference 042 815.

6   Find the bearing of a farmhouse at grid reference 798 091 from a mountain summit at 773 084.

7   A rule of thumb used in anchoring dinghies safely says that the length of cable should be at least three times the depth of the water; what is the greatest angle the cable can make with the horizontal if this rule is used?

8. PROBLEMS WITHOUT ANGLES

A flagstaff is made with eyes to attach the guy-wires at a height of 4.30 m, and the lower ends of the wires are to be made fast to stakes 2.70 m from the base. How long will the wires have to be?

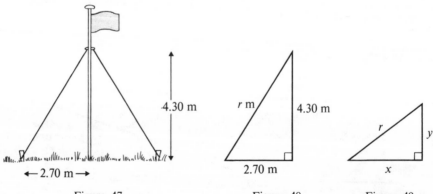

Figure 47   Figure 48   Figure 49

Although we could use the methods of section 7 to find the angle that the wire makes with the horizontal, and then find the length of wire as in section 5, this is unnecessarily tedious. Instead we can use Pythagoras' theorem which states that in a right-angled triangle the square of the hypotenuse is equal to the sum of the squares of the other two sides. In symbols:

$$r^2 = x^2 + y^2.$$

One proof of this result is given later in this section; some other proofs will be considered in Chapter 16.

We can use Pythagoras' theorem to find the length of the guy-wires as follows:

$$r^2 = 2.70^2 + 4.30^2 = 25.78$$ ☐

$$r = \pm \sqrt{25.78} \approx \pm 5.08$$

The guy-wires need to be at least 5.08 m long, plus an allowance for fixing at each end.

Example 6

A ladder 4.8 m long is to be placed against a wall. The foot of the ladder must not be placed in a flower-bed which extends a distance 1.5 m from the foot of the wall. How high up the wall can the ladder reach?

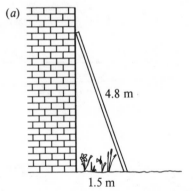

(a) 4.8 m 1.5 m

(b) y m 4.8 m 1.5 m

Figure 50

By Pythagoras' theorem,

$$4.8^2 = 1.5^2 + y^2$$
$$\Leftrightarrow \quad y^2 = 4.8^2 - 1.5^2$$
$$= 20.79$$ ☐
$$\Leftrightarrow \quad y = \pm 4.6 \quad \text{(to 2 s.f.).}$$

The ladder can reach about 4.6 m up the wall.

Proof of Pythagoras' theorem

Figure 51 is constructed by drawing a line from A to meet the hypotenuse BC at right-angles. The angle ACB must be $90° - \theta°$ because the angles of triangle ABC add up to $180°$. The same reasoning applied to triangle ACD tells us that the angle DAC is $\theta°$.

From triangle ABD, BD $\quad = x \cos \theta°$.
From triangle DAC, DC $\quad = y \sin \theta°$.
Adding, $\quad BD + DC = x \cos \theta° + y \sin \theta°$,
so $\quad\quad\quad r \quad\quad = x \cos \theta° + y \sin \theta°$
$\quad\quad\quad\quad\quad\quad\quad$ since $BD + DC = BC = r$.
From triangle ABC, x $\quad = r \cos \theta°$,
$\quad\quad\quad\quad\quad y \quad\quad = r \sin \theta°$
and so $\quad\quad \cos \theta° \quad = \dfrac{x}{r}, \quad \sin \theta° = \dfrac{y}{r}$.

Substituting these in r $\quad = x \cos \theta° + y \sin \theta°$,

we obtain $\quad\quad r \quad\quad = x\dfrac{x}{r} + y\dfrac{y}{r}$.

Multiplying both sides by r,
$$r^2 = x^2 + y^2.$$

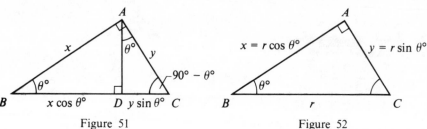

Figure 51   Figure 52

Exercise H

*1 Calculate the lengths marked with letters in Figure 53.

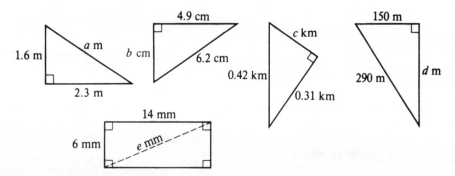

Figure 53

2 Find the distances between the following pairs of points:
  (a) (3, 1) and (7, 4);   (b) (4, 9) and (9, 2);
  (c) (1.2, 2.1) and (4.7, 10.5);   (d) ($^-$1.3, 2.1) and (4.3, $^-$3.5).

*3 A farm gate is to be constructed by welding lengths of steel piping together. If it is to be 1.3 m high and 3.2 m wide, how long a piece should be cut as a diagonal brace?

4 Calculate the distance as the crow flies from a rookery at grid reference 247 108 to a pond at grid reference 281 092.

*5 An orienteer planned to walk through a rectangular patch of woodland parallel to its shortest side, which is marked on his map as 450 m. On reaching the far side he reckons he has walked 500 m; how far from his planned point did he emerge from the wood?

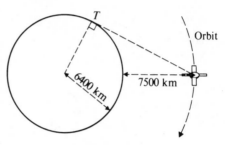

6 Figure 54 shows a satellite in orbit 7500 km above the earth's surface. The tracking station at T is about to lose contact with the satellite. How far away from T is the satellite?

Figure 54

7 When the trapdoor into a loft is open the dimensions of the opening are 81 cm by 89 cm. Will a piece of boarding 1.18 m wide fit through the opening?

SUMMARY

Trigonometry can be used to solve problems in which a right-angled triangle is a suitable model. Figure 55 shows most of the calculations we need for finding sides of a triangle when we know the angle $\theta°$.

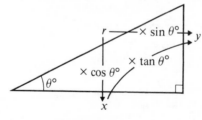

$$x = r \cos \theta°$$
$$y = r \sin \theta°$$
$$y = x \tan \theta°$$

Figure 55

To find angles, we use one of these equations, choosing the one where we know both lengths, and then use the appropriate inverse trigonometric function.

For problems not involving angles at all, we use Pythagoras' theorem:
$$r^2 = x^2 + y^2.$$

When modelling problems from the real world, we should remember the simplification involved in using a perfect right-angled triangle, as well as the inaccuracy of any measurements.

Although accurate scale-drawing is time-consuming, it is worth drawing any triangle approximately the right shape and making a rough estimate of the answer as a check on the calculation.

Summary exercise

1 Calculate the sides and angles marked with letters in Figure 56.

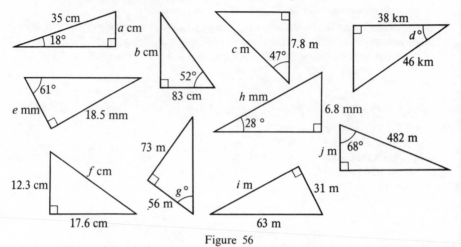

Figure 56

2 Figure 57 shows the track of a repair ship which is checking the repeaters in an underwater communications cable running due south. In difficult conditions it has lost contact with the cable, and the captain decided to sail 2.5 km before searching for it. If his track was on a bearing of 178.5°, how far is he from the nearest point on the cable?

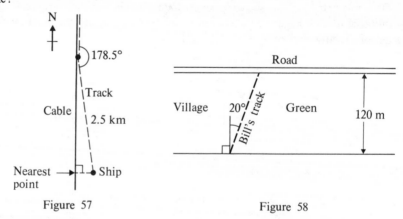

Figure 57   Figure 58

3 Figure 58 shows Bill's track as he runs across the village green to catch the bus. If the green is 120 m wide, how far does Bill run?

4 Calculate the polar coordinates $(r, t°)$ of these points whose cartesian coordinates are given:

   A (5, 2); B (3, 8); C (19, 27); D (5, ⁻3).

5 A chisel is made from steel 8mm thick, and its ground face, when sharpened, is 15 mm wide from the cutting edge. At what angle has it been ground?

Miscellaneous exercise

1 Figure 59 illustrates the cross-section of
   a railway tunnel; the arc is part of a
   circle of radius 5.5 m. Calculate:
   (*a*) the angle *AON*;
   (*b*) the area of the major sector *OAB*;
   (*c*) the area of triangle *OAB*;
   (*d*) the volume of the tunnel, if its
   length is 200 m.

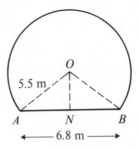

Figure 59

2 An outcrop of ore 2.8 m from top to bottom is discovered in the face of a vertical cliff.
   If the ore seam dips directly into the cliff at 22° below the horizontal, find its true
   thickness. The ore is to be mined from above, but it is not safe to dig less than 50m
   from the cliff edge. If the outcrop was observed 23 m below the top of the cliff, how
   deep will the shortest safe shaft have to be?

3 A helicopter has to fly from its base, grid reference 107 843, to rescue a dinghy in
   difficulties at grid reference 438 951. Visibility is poor; on what bearing should the
   pilot fly, and how far should he go before looking out for the dinghy?

4 Safety regulations limit the height of a children's slide to 3 m, and the angle of slope to
   35°. What length of metal is required for the highest, steepest slide allowed, with a
   2.5 m horizontal section at the bottom?

5 The sloping sides of a bivouac tent are 1.5 metres long, and, to ensure good run-off of
   rainwater, they slope on each side down to the ground at 50° below the horizontal.
   How wide will the floor space be?

6 A range-finder is constructed by mounting the two halves of a pair of binoculars on a
   fixed baseboard 1 m apart. The right-hand one is fixed at 90° to the board, and the
   left-hand one is swivelled until it, too, is pointing straight at the object whose distance
   is to be measured. If the left-hand one is at an angle of 88.9° to the board, what is the
   range? If this angle is measured incorrectly as 89.0°, what is the error in the range?

7 A strip of land 2.5 m wide is available for the construction of a boat shed. If it is hoped
   to sling a 4.9-metre mast diagonally across the ceiling, for winter storage, how long will
   the shed have to be?

8 A poor billiards player miscues a shot at the red, 2.3 m away. If he was 5° off course, how
   close did his ball come? (Note that this is measured at right-angles to the track of the
   ball.) Begin by modelling the balls as points; then allow for their size, where both
   have radius 2.5 cm.

9 If the maximum error in aiming a rifle is 0.2°, how far from the bull may the shots hit
   the target on a 25-metre range?

10 The line of a new gas main crosses a road at an angle of 35° to the direction of the
    road, and a trench must be dug for it. If the road is 8.5 m wide, how long must the
    trench be?

11 A telescope has a 3° field of view, and Anne is looking through it at a power-station
    chimney. If the chimney is 68 m high, and it just fits into the field of view, how far is
    Anne from the chimney?

12 In a pot-holing rescue, a casualty is strapped to a stretcher 2.1 m long. It is planned to

haul this up a shaft only 1.9 m wide, but for medical reasons the stretcher must not be tilted at more than 30° to the horizontal. Is this plan acceptable?

13 A navigator on a ship sailing at 20 km/h knows that his course will take him to a closest approach of 8 km to a lighthouse. If his radar now gives his distance from the lighthouse as 28 km, how long will it be until the ship is at its closest to the lighthouse?

14 The diameter of the earth's orbit round the sun is about 3.0×10^8 km. Light travels at 3.0×10^5 km/s, and takes about 4.3 years to reach us from the nearest star. Over a period of six months, the change in the earth's position makes this starlight reach us from a slightly different angle, which can be measured against the virtually constant direction of light from distant galaxies. Calculate this change in angle, known as the *parallax* of the star.

15 A 15-kilogram mass is supported by two wires as shown in Figure 60. To find T_1 and T_2, the tensions in the wires, a triangle is constructed, with sides proportional to the force vectors involved. (See Figure 61.) Calculate T_1 and T_2.

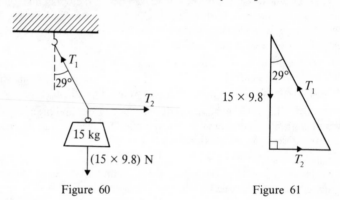

Figure 60   Figure 61

16 Figure 62 shows a ray of light passing from air into glycerine and being refracted towards the line perpendicular to the surface. The angle $i°$ is known as the angle of incidence and the angle $r°$ is known as the angle of refraction. The ratio $\dfrac{\sin i°}{\sin r°}$ is called the refractive index of the liquid.
    (a) In an experiment it is found that when $i = 21.4$, $r = 14.4$. Calculate the refractive index of glycerine.
    (b) Calculate the angle of refraction corresponding to an angle of incidence of 60.0°.
    (c) Calculate the angle of incidence corresponding to an angle of refraction of 30.0°.
    (d) Try to calculate the angle of incidence corresponding to an angle of refraction of 60.0°. Can you explain why it is impossible?

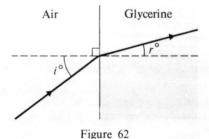

Figure 62

14

Matrices

1. DATA STORAGE

Sharpers, a factory making woodwork tools, supplies several wholesalers regularly. To keep checks on factory stocks, production figures, accounts and so on, a great amount of numerical data must be handled. It helps to arrange this systematically. For example:

| | Week ending 11 February | | | |
	Hammers	Chisels	Screwdrivers	Saws
Order from Whites Ltd	20	30	40	10
Order from Wilsons Ltd	30	50	0	20
Order from Walkers Ltd	20	40	30	30

Table 1

This information may be written $\begin{bmatrix} 20 & 30 & 40 & 10 \\ 30 & 50 & 0 & 20 \\ 20 & 40 & 30 & 30 \end{bmatrix}$

provided that everybody concerned knows that the first column of numbers in this *matrix* refers to numbers of hammers ordered, and so on. In a practical situation there would be many more than 3 rows – representing the many wholesalers supplied – and a separate column for each product made in the factory, and there might be 50 or more of these.

Up-dating and processing the weekly information can be a large chore and that is why firms now use computers for much of this work. Feeding the information into a machine must be done in an appropriate way and this is where matrix ideas are most helpful. To develop these, we shall keep to small matrices like the (3 row, 4 column) one above.

Exercise A

*1

| | | Type of biscuit | | |
	Chocolate	Thin wine	Shortbread	Lincoln cream
Holly Berries	8	10	6	4
Box Sleigh Bells	12	0	15	9
Reindeer Special	16	8	12	10

This matrix might be displayed in the packing department of the Freak Bean Biscuit Factory to help workers assembling Christmas gift boxes.

(*a*) How many shortbread biscuits are there in each Reindeer Special box?

(*b*) How many chocolate biscuits are there in each Holly Berries box?

69

2 Susan, Bridget and Jennifer are making their own dresses for a party. Susan's pattern needs 4.5 m of velvet, 4.0 m of binding, a 35 cm zip and 3 buttons. Bridget's outfit has a separate jacket; her dress and jacket need 1.5 m of velvet, 5.0 m of cotton, 1.5 m of binding, a 20 cm zip and no buttons. For Jennifer's dress 2.5 m of velvet, 2.0 m of binding and no zip or buttons will be needed. State their requirements in matrix form.

3 A firm of manufacturers of radio parts sells a number of 'do-it-yourself' kits for the amateur radio constructor. They market a kit called the Beginner's Bijou with 3 transistors, 2 coils, 1 speaker, 7 resistors and 5 capacitors; another, the Straight Eight, has 8 transistors, 6 coils, 2 speakers, 25 resistors and 24 capacitors, while the Super Sister has 6 transistors, 8 coils, 1 speaker, 23 resistors and 16 capacitors. Tabulate this information in a (3 row, 5 column) matrix.

4 The following information was taken from a cookery book:

Shrewsbury biscuits: 100 g butter, 10 g sugar, 150 g flour, 1 egg.
Shortbread biscuits: 450 g flour, 275 g butter, 150 g sugar, 2 eggs.
Lincoln biscuits: 200 g flour, 200 g sugar, 100 g butter, 1 egg.
Bannocks: 500 g butter, 250 g sugar, 1 kg flour.
Easter biscuits: 100 g sugar, 100 g butter, 200 g flour, 1 egg.
American biscuits: 400 g flour, 75 g butter, 25 g sugar, 2 eggs.

(a) Tabulate this data in a (6 row, 4 column) matrix and add another column to give the total mass of raw materials for each recipe. (Assume that an egg has a mass of 60 g.)

(b) Calculate another (6 row, 4 column) matrix giving the mass of each ingredient in 1 kg of each kind of biscuit.

(N.B. Should you want to make the biscuits, such items as baking powder, salt, ginger and spoonfuls of milk have been omitted.)

2. MATRIX COMBINATION

Sharpers' wholesale prices for their woodwork tools are set out in Table 2.

Hammer	£1.50
Chisel	£1.00
Screwdriver	£0.60
Saw	£2.00

Table 2

The order from Whites Ltd for 20 hammers, 30 chisels, 40 screwdrivers and 10 saws would cost

$20 \times £1.50 + 30 \times £1.00 + 40 \times £0.60 + 10 \times £2.00 = £(30 + 30 + 24 + 20) = £104$.

If we are going to calculate the costs of the orders from all three warehouses, it helps to write them as a matrix combination. We write:

$$
\begin{array}{c}
\text{Tools} \\
\begin{array}{cccc} H & C & D & S \end{array} \\
\text{Warehouses} \begin{array}{c} W_1 \\ W_2 \\ W_3 \end{array} \begin{bmatrix} 20 & 30 & 40 & 10 \\ 30 & 50 & 0 & 20 \\ 20 & 40 & 30 & 30 \end{bmatrix}
\end{array}
\begin{array}{c}
\text{Prices} \\
\begin{bmatrix} 1.50 \\ 1.00 \\ 0.60 \\ 2.00 \end{bmatrix} \begin{array}{c} H \\ C \\ D \\ S \end{array}
\end{array}
\text{Tools} =
\begin{array}{c}
\text{Prices} \\
\begin{array}{c} W_1 \\ W_2 \\ W_3 \end{array} \begin{bmatrix} 104 \\ * \\ * \end{bmatrix}
\end{array}
$$

On the left-hand side of the equation the left matrix represents the orders from the 3 warehouses for the 4 types of tool; the right matrix gives the prices of the 4 tools. Notice the patterns:

(Warehouse\Tool) (Tool\Price) = (Warehouse\Price)
(3 row, 4 column) (4 row, 1 column) = (3 row, 1 column)

Compare the dominoes:

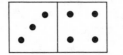 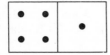 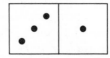

We have seen how the number 104 arises from the first row of the left matrix and the only column of the right matrix. The second and third rows of the left matrix are similarly combined with the right matrix to produce the other two entries. Check that these are 135 and 148.

We can extend this method of combination to situations in which the right matrix has more than one column. For example, if the prices for the 4 tools are increased to £2, £1.50, £0.80 and £2.50, we can arrange all the information as follows:

$$
\begin{bmatrix} 20 & 30 & 40 & 10 \\ 30 & 50 & 0 & 20 \\ 20 & 40 & 30 & 30 \end{bmatrix}
\begin{matrix} \text{Old} & \text{New} \\ \begin{bmatrix} 1.50 & 2.00 \\ 1.00 & 1.50 \\ 0.60 & 0.80 \\ 2.00 & 2.50 \end{bmatrix} \end{matrix}
=
\begin{bmatrix} 104 & * \\ 135 & * \\ 148 & * \end{bmatrix}
$$

(Warehouse\Tool) (Tool\Price) = (Warehouse\Price)
(3 row, 4 column) (4 row, 2 column) = (3 row, 2 column)

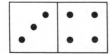 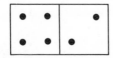 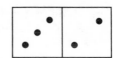

Notice that the third row of the left matrix and the second column of the right matrix combine to give the number in the third row and second column of the final matrix, as illustrated in Figure 1.

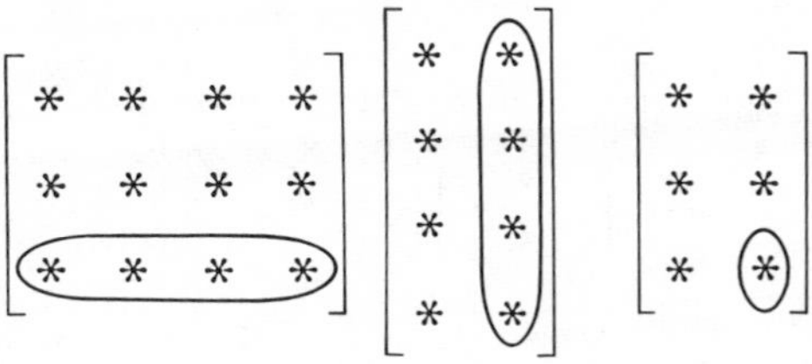

$$
\begin{bmatrix} * & * & * & * \\ * & * & * & * \\ * & * & * & * \end{bmatrix}
\begin{bmatrix} * & * \\ * & * \\ * & * \\ * & * \end{bmatrix}
\begin{bmatrix} * & * \\ * & * \\ * & * \end{bmatrix}
$$

Figure 1

Because we combine rows of the left matrix with columns of the right matrix, there must be the same number of elements in a row of the left matrix as in a column of the right matrix. The left matrix must have as many columns as the right matrix has rows. We can only combine matrices in this way if the numbers of rows and columns fit the 'domino pattern'. The matrices are then said to be *compatible*.

It is because matrices can be combined in this systematic and useful way that they are of such value for data storage. Computers can easily handle large amounts of information when it is arranged in this way. We shall practise the method of combination using some small matrices with simple numbers. If the matrices being combined are called **A** and **B**, we write the combination as **AB**; it is called a *matrix product*. The process of combining matrices in this way is called *matrix multiplication*.

Example 1

Find the matrix product **AB** if $\mathbf{A} = \begin{bmatrix} 3 & 2 & 1 \\ 0 & 2 & 4 \end{bmatrix}$ and $\mathbf{B} = \begin{bmatrix} 6 & 0 & 1 \\ 0 & 2 & 3 \\ 1 & 5 & 1 \end{bmatrix}$.

First we note that (2 row, 3 column) (3 row, 3 column) = (2 row, 3 column) so that **AB** will have 2 rows and 3 columns.

The first row of **A** is combined with each column of **B** in turn to give the first row of **AB**:

$$3 \times 6 + 2 \times 0 + 1 \times 1 = 18 + 0 + 1 = 19$$
$$3 \times 0 + 2 \times 2 + 1 \times 5 = 0 + 4 + 5 = 9$$
$$3 \times 1 + 2 \times 3 + 1 \times 1 = 3 + 6 + 1 = 10$$

$$\begin{bmatrix} 3 & 2 & 1 \\ 0 & 2 & 4 \end{bmatrix} \begin{bmatrix} 6 & 0 & 1 \\ 0 & 2 & 3 \\ 1 & 5 & 1 \end{bmatrix} = \begin{bmatrix} 19 & 9 & 10 \\ * & * & * \end{bmatrix}.$$

The second row of **A** is then combined with each column of **B** in turn to give the second row of **AB**, so that

$$\begin{bmatrix} 3 & 2 & 1 \\ 0 & 2 & 4 \end{bmatrix} \begin{bmatrix} 6 & 0 & 1 \\ 0 & 2 & 3 \\ 1 & 5 & 1 \end{bmatrix} = \begin{bmatrix} 19 & 9 & 10 \\ 4 & 24 & 10 \end{bmatrix}.$$

Exercise B

*1   The answer to the following matrix product has two rows.

$$\begin{bmatrix} 2 & 8 & 3 \\ 1 & 5 & 0 \end{bmatrix} \begin{bmatrix} 1 & 5 & 4 & 6 \\ 2 & 2 & 1 & 6 \\ 3 & 10 & 0 & 1 \end{bmatrix}$$

(a) How many columns has it?
(b) Show that the number in the first row and the first column of the product is 27.
(c) Complete the calculation.

2   Find **DE** if $\mathbf{D} = \begin{bmatrix} 5 & 1 \\ 2 & 3 \\ 4 & 10 \end{bmatrix}$ and $\mathbf{E} = \begin{bmatrix} 1 & 6 & 3 & 8 \\ 2 & 6 & 4 & 2 \end{bmatrix}$.

3 How many rows and columns have the following matrix products?

(a) $\begin{bmatrix} 2 & 0 & 3 \\ 1 & 4 & 1 \end{bmatrix}\begin{bmatrix} 6 \\ -2 \\ 3 \end{bmatrix}$;   (b) $\begin{bmatrix} 4 & 3 \\ 0 & -1 \end{bmatrix}\begin{bmatrix} 1 & 2 & 0 \\ 0 & 3 & 4 \end{bmatrix}$;

(c) $\begin{bmatrix} 1 & 3 & 4 \end{bmatrix}\begin{bmatrix} 2 & 5 \\ 0 & 3 \\ 1 & 2 \end{bmatrix}$;   (d) $\begin{bmatrix} 3 & 0 & 1 \\ 5 & 7 & 0 \\ -1 & 0 & 2 \end{bmatrix}\begin{bmatrix} 5 \\ 1 \\ 2 \end{bmatrix}$;

(e) $\begin{bmatrix} 3 & 1 & 0 & 1 \\ 2 & 0 & 5 & -2 \end{bmatrix}\begin{bmatrix} 3 \\ 2 \\ 2 \\ 5 \end{bmatrix}$; (f) $\begin{bmatrix} 5 & -1 & 3 \\ 0 & 2 & 1 \end{bmatrix}\begin{bmatrix} 7 & 2 & 0 \\ 0 & 3 & 1 \\ 1 & 4 & 1 \end{bmatrix}$;

(g) $\begin{bmatrix} 3 & 1 \\ 2 & -1 \\ 0 & 2 \end{bmatrix}\begin{bmatrix} 0 & 2 \\ 4 & 1 \end{bmatrix}$;   (h) $\begin{bmatrix} 1 & 6 & 3 \end{bmatrix}\begin{bmatrix} 4 \\ 5 \\ 2 \end{bmatrix}$.

*4 Carry out the combinations of question 3.

5 Find the following matrix products.

(a) $\begin{bmatrix} 2 & 6 \\ 1 & 5 \end{bmatrix}\begin{bmatrix} 4 & 2 \\ 3 & 4 \end{bmatrix}$;   (b) $\begin{bmatrix} 5 & 3 \\ 2 & 10 \end{bmatrix}\begin{bmatrix} 8 & 4 \\ 1 & 6 \end{bmatrix}$;   (c) $\begin{bmatrix} 3 & 0 \\ 4 & 1 \end{bmatrix}\begin{bmatrix} 7 & 5 \\ 2 & 8 \end{bmatrix}$;

(d) $\begin{bmatrix} 9 & -2 \\ -3 & 1 \end{bmatrix}\begin{bmatrix} 5 & 3 \\ 4 & 5 \end{bmatrix}$;   (e) $\begin{bmatrix} -1 & 2 \\ 3 & -6 \end{bmatrix}\begin{bmatrix} 10 & 8 \\ 5 & 4 \end{bmatrix}$;   (f) $\begin{bmatrix} 2 & -3 \\ 4 & -5 \end{bmatrix}\begin{bmatrix} 3 & -6 \\ -1 & -5 \end{bmatrix}$.

*6 If $F = \begin{bmatrix} 2 & 4 \\ 1 & 3 \end{bmatrix}$, $G = \begin{bmatrix} 1 & 7 \\ 5 & 6 \end{bmatrix}$, and $H = \begin{bmatrix} 2 & 3 \\ 10 & 1 \end{bmatrix}$, find the products:

(a) **FG**; (b) **GH**; (c) **FH**; (d) **GF**; (e) **HG**; (f) **HF**.

7 If $A = \begin{bmatrix} 5 & 2 \\ 3 & 1 \end{bmatrix}$, $B = \begin{bmatrix} 0 & -4 \\ 9 & 8 \end{bmatrix}$, and $C = \begin{bmatrix} 7 & 4 \\ 6 & -1 \end{bmatrix}$, find the products:

(a) **AB**; (b) **BA**; (c) **AC**; (d) **CA**; (e) **BC**; (f) **CB**.

*8 Find x if $\begin{bmatrix} 2 & 0 \\ x & 3 \end{bmatrix}\begin{bmatrix} 0 & 4 \\ 2 & 1 \end{bmatrix} = \begin{bmatrix} 0 & 8 \\ 6 & 9 \end{bmatrix}$.

9 Find y if $\begin{bmatrix} 3 & 2 \\ 4 & -5 \end{bmatrix}\begin{bmatrix} y & 1 \\ 3 & -1 \end{bmatrix} = \begin{bmatrix} 5y & 1 \\ -y & 9 \end{bmatrix}$.

10 If $L = \begin{bmatrix} 1 & 2 \\ 4 & 3 \end{bmatrix}$, $M = \begin{bmatrix} 5 & 0 \\ 2 & 6 \end{bmatrix}$ and $N = \begin{bmatrix} 3 & 2 \\ -1 & 1 \end{bmatrix}$, find:

(a) **LM**; (b) **(LM)N**; (c) **MN**; (d) **L(MN)**.
(e) Is it true that **(LM)N = L(MN)**?

11 If $L = \begin{bmatrix} 2 & 9 \\ 8 & 5 \end{bmatrix}$, $M = \begin{bmatrix} 1 & 0 \\ 0 & 1 \end{bmatrix}$ and $N = \begin{bmatrix} 0 & 0 \\ 0 & 0 \end{bmatrix}$, find:

(a) **LM**; (b) **ML**; (c) **LN**; (d) **NL**.

12 If **A** is a (3 row, 2 column) matrix, **B** is (2 row, 4 column) and **C** is (2 row, 3 column), give the number of rows and columns of each of the following products when it exists. If a product cannot be formed, say so.

(*a*) **AB**;   (*d*) **BC**;   (*c*) **AC**;   (*d*) **BA**;   (*e*) **CA**.

3. COMBINING DATA STORAGE MATRICES

In Exercise C we return to data storage matrices like the ones we considered at the beginning of the chapter. It is important to assemble the data in the right way and to set out the matrices in the right order.

Exercise C

*1   A shop selling fireworks charged 5 p each for Bangers, 10 p each for Catherine wheels, 8p each for Fountains and 15p each for Rockets. The following matrix shows the number of each bought by John, Kate and Linda.

	Bangers	Catherine wheels	Fountains	Rockets
John	10	2	3	6
Kate	0	4	6	5
Linda	5	0	5	8

   (*a*) How much did John's fireworks cost?
   (*b*) Write down the (Firework\Price) matrix and combine it with the (Buyer\Firework) matrix above.
   (*c*) State in words what each number in your product matrix tells you.

2   The way in which Sampton rugby fifteen scored in the first four matches of the season is shown in this table:

	Tries	Conversions	Penalties
Match 1	5	1	3
Match 2	3	2	1
Match 3	2	0	3
Match 4	1	1	2

Four points are awarded for a try, two for a conversion and three for a penalty.
   (*a*) Write down the points scheme as a (3 row, 1 column) matrix.
   (*b*) Combine the (Match\Scores) matrix obtained from the table of results with the (Scores\Points) matrix obtained in (*a*).
   (*c*) The scores of the team's opponents were as follows:

	Tries	Conversions	Penalties
Match 1	4	3	2
Match 2	2	0	4
Match 3	3	1	1
Match 4	2	1	1

Which matches did the Sampton team win?

*3 A factory produces three types of portable radio sets called Audiox 1, 2 and 3. Audiox 1 contains 5 transistors, 10 resistors and 8 capacitors, while Audiox 2 contains 7 transistors, 18 resistors and 9 capacitors, and Audiox 3 contains 10 transistors, 24 resistors and 10 capacitors. Arrange this information in matrix form and find the factory's weekly consumption of transistors, resistors and capacitors if its weekly output of sets is 100 of Audiox 1, 250 of Audiox 2 and 80 of Audiox 3.

4 'Bildit' is a constructional toy with standard parts called Flats, Pillars, Blocks, Rods and Caps. It is boxed in sets, numbered 1 to 4. Set 1 has a flat, 4 pillars, 8 blocks, 14 rods and 2 caps. Set 2 has 2 flats, 10 pillars, 12 blocks, 30 rods and 4 caps. Set 3 has 4 flats, 24 pillars, 30 blocks, 60 rods and 10 caps. Set 4 has 10 flats, 40 pillars, 52 blocks, 100 rods and 24 caps.

(a) Tabulate this information in a (4 row, 5 column) matrix.

(b) The manufacturers receive an order for 20 of set 1, 25 of set 2, 10 of set 3 and 6 of set 4. Write this as a matrix with one row and combine your matrices to find the numbers of each part that will be needed.

5 The flats in Bildit (see question 4) cost 6p each, pillars 4p, blocks 1p, rods 2p, and caps 3p.

(a) Combine the (Set\Parts) matrix of question 4 with the (Parts\Cost) matrix obtained from the above information. What information does this give you?

(b) Combine your answer to (a) with the (Order\Sets) matrix from question 4(b). What information does this give you?

(c) Combine the (Order\Parts) matrix which you had as an answer to question 4(b) with the (Parts\Cost) matrix. Comment on your result.

*6 In a triangular athletics match between Leaply, Throfar and Runfast schools, points were awarded as follows: 1st, 6; 2nd, 4; 3rd, 3; 4th, 2; 5th, 1. The individual results are shown by the table

	1st	2nd	3rd	4th	5th
Leaply	4	2	3	2	6
Throfar	2	5	4	4	3
Runfast	4	3	3	4	1

(a) Write the points scheme as a matrix with one column and calculate the scores of each team. Which team won?

(b) Which team would have won if the points scheme had been: 1st, 8; 2nd 5; 3rd, 3; 4th, 2; 5th, 1?

7 A new university hall of residence is to contain 20 flats, 50 double rooms and 30 single rooms. Some of the furniture is to be bought from Oakhearts Ltd: for each flat, 5 chests of drawers, 4 desks, 8 chairs and 1 table; for each double room, 2 chests, 2 desks, 3 chairs and 1 table; for each single room, 2 chests, 1 desk and 2 chairs.

Oakhearts Ltd will charge £20 for a chest of drawers, £30 for a desk, £10 for a chair and £15 for a table.

(a) Use a suitable matrix product to find the total number of each items of furniture to be ordered from Oakhearts Ltd.

(b) Use another matrix product to find the total cost of the furniture for each type of accommodation.

(c) Use your answer to (a) to calculate the total cost of the order. Check by using your answer to (b).

4. ROUTE MATRICES

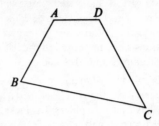

Figure 2

Suppose you draw a quadrilateral *ABCD* and wish to give enough information over the telephone to a friend so that he may draw a congruent quadrilateral (i.e. one of exactly the same size and shape). What information would you give him? You might measure all four sides and all the angles and tell him these. Could he draw a correct diagram with less information?

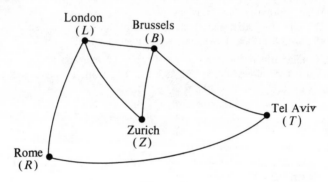

Figure 3

Figure 3 shows part of a map of the routes taken by the aircraft of one particular airline. On this, lengths and directions are unimportant; all that matters is which airports are connected directly. How would you convey this information? One method is to use a *route matrix* in which a 1 means that there is a direct route between the two points (or nodes) and an entry of 0 means that there is no such route.

$$
\begin{array}{c}
\\
\\
\text{From}
\end{array}
\begin{array}{c}
 \\
L \\
B \\
Z \\
R \\
T
\end{array}
\overset{\displaystyle \text{To}}{
\begin{array}{ccccc}
L & B & Z & R & T \\
\end{array}}
\left[
\begin{array}{ccccc}
0 & 1 & 1 & 1 & 0 \\
1 & 0 & 1 & 0 & 1 \\
1 & 1 & 0 & 0 & 0 \\
1 & 0 & 0 & 0 & 1 \\
0 & 1 & 0 & 1 & 0
\end{array}
\right]
$$

Example 2

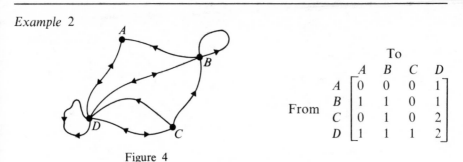

Figure 4

$$\begin{array}{cc} & \text{To} \\ & \begin{array}{cccc} A & B & C & D \end{array} \\ \text{From} \begin{array}{c} A \\ B \\ C \\ D \end{array} & \begin{bmatrix} 0 & 0 & 0 & 1 \\ 1 & 1 & 0 & 1 \\ 0 & 1 & 0 & 2 \\ 1 & 1 & 1 & 2 \end{bmatrix} \end{array}$$

Figure 4 is a road map with some one-way roads and some two-way roads. Notice how this affects the route matrix. Notice also how the loops from B and D (scenic routes round the local beauty spots, perhaps?) are shown in the matrix.

Squaring a route matrix

$$\mathbf{S} = \begin{array}{c} \\ A \\ B \\ C \end{array} \begin{array}{c} \begin{array}{ccc} A & B & C \end{array} \\ \begin{bmatrix} 0 & 1 & 0 \\ 1 & 0 & 1 \\ 1 & 1 & 1 \end{bmatrix} \end{array}$$

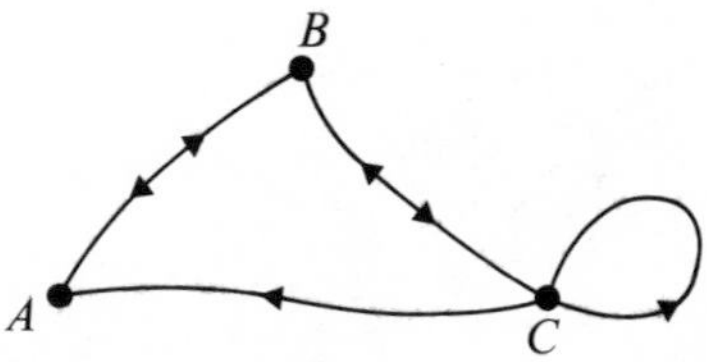

Figure 5

$$\mathbf{S}^2 = \mathbf{SS} = \begin{bmatrix} 0 & 1 & 0 \\ 1 & 0 & 1 \\ 1 & 1 & 1 \end{bmatrix} \begin{bmatrix} 0 & 1 & 0 \\ 1 & 0 & 1 \\ 1 & 1 & 1 \end{bmatrix} = \begin{bmatrix} 1 & 0 & 1 \\ 1 & 2 & 1 \\ 2 & 2 & 2 \end{bmatrix}$$

If we multiply the route matrix for Figure 5 by itself, the result (which we write $\mathbf{S}^2$) shows the number of two-stage routes connecting the various pairs of points. For example, the 2 in the second row and second column indicates that there are 2 such journeys starting and ending at B, namely

$$B \xrightarrow{\text{first stage}} A \xrightarrow{\text{second stage}} B$$

$$B \longrightarrow C \longrightarrow B$$

Check that there are 2 two-stage journeys starting from C and ending at A but none from A to B.

Can you explain why $\mathbf{S}^2$ is the matrix which gives the two-stage journeys? Will this happen whenever we multiply a route matrix by itself?

Exercise D

(Questions 5 and 9 introduce ideas needed in the subsequent questions.)

***1** Compile a route matrix for Figure 6. By multiplying the matrix by itself, find the matrix which describes the two-stage journeys. List all these as, for example, $A \longrightarrow C \longrightarrow B$.

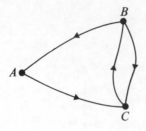

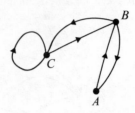

Figure 6   Figure 7

2   Repeat question 1 for Figure 7.

*3   Write down the route matrix S for Figure 8. Find S^2 and explain why the first columns of S and S^2 contain only zeros.

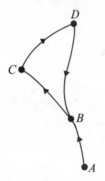

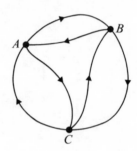

Figure 8   Figure 9

4   Compile a route matrix for Figure 9. Find S^2 and S^4. How many four-stage routes are there:

(a) starting and finishing at the same point;

(b) starting and finishing at different points?

*5   The ideas of route matrices can be applied to the results of games. In Figure 10 the nodes represent four boys Alan, Brian, Charles and David, and the arrow from A to B indicates that Alan has beaten Brian at table-tennis.

When Charles plays David we might expect Charles to win because of the two-stage route $C \longrightarrow A \longrightarrow D$ in the network, showing that Charles beat Alan and Alan beat David. This is called a 'two-stage' dominance.

(a) If in fact David beat Charles, complete the network and write down the matrix **T** for your network.

(b) Find the matrix T^2 giving all the two-stage dominances. Who do you think is the best player?

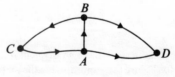

Figure 10

6 Andrew, John, Mark and Simon played each other at squash. Andrew beat John and Mark but lost to Simon. John beat Mark and Simon. Mark beat Simon.
   (a) Draw a network to represent these results.
   (b) Compile a matrix for the network and multiply it by itself. Find the total of one-stage and two-stage dominances for each boy.

7 Figure 11 shows the results of ten matches played by five girls.
   (a) Compile a matrix for the network and multiply it by itself.
   (b) Find the total of one-stage and two-stage dominances for each girl and hence place the girls in order.

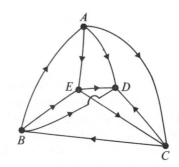

Figure 11

8 A tennis tournament between six girls, in which each girl was to play every other girl, was rained off after each had played four matches.

   Alison beat Catherine; Bridget beat Alison, Catherine and Helen; Catherine beat Helen and Elizabeth; Elizabeth beat Alison and Frances; Frances beat Alison, Bridget and Helen; Helen beat Elizabeth.

   Compile matrices showing one-stage and two-stage dominances and use them to place the girls in order.

*9 Networks and their matrices can be used to describe relations. In Figure 12 the nodes represent people and the arrows show the relation 'is a parent of'. Thus b is a parent of c.

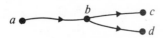

Figure 12

   (a) Write down the route matrix **R** for this network and find **R**². What relation does it represent?
   (b) Form another matrix **R'** by interchanging the rows and columns of **R**. (The first column of **R** becomes the first row of **R'** and so on.) What relation does this represent?
   (c) The matrix **R'** formed in this way is called the *transpose* of **R**. When will a matrix and its transpose be the same? Give an example of a relation for which the matrix and its transpose are the same.

10 Figure 13 (a) shows the relation 'is the daughter of' on a set of five people, and Figure 13(b) shows the relation 'is the sister of' on the same set.
   (a) What can you say about the sex of the members of the set?
   (b) Compile matrices **D** and **S** to represent these relations.
   (c) What relations would be represented by **D'** and **S'**?
   (d) Form the matrix product **DS**. What relation does it represent?
   (e) What matrix product would give a matrix representing the relation 'is an aunt of'?

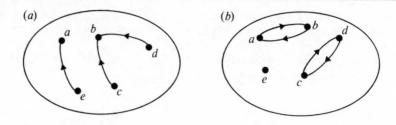

Figure 13

11 Make up an example of your own in which the relation 'is the brother-in-law of' appears as the combination of two other relations.

12 If a matrix R represents the following relations on a set of numbers, what relation is represented by (i) R^2, (ii) R' in each case:
    (a) 'is twice';   (b) 'is a factor of';   (c) 'is the square of'?

5. ADDITION OF MATRICES

The orders for Sharpers' woodwork tools for the week ending 11 February were given in Table 1 at the beginning of the chapter and are repeated here in Table 3. The following week orders were again received from the same three warehouses: these orders are shown in Table 4. Table 5 shows the total orders for the two weeks.

| | *Week ending 11 February* | | | |
	Hammers	Chisels	Screwdrivers	Saws
Whites Ltd	20	30	40	10
Wilsons Ltd	30	50	0	20
Walkers Ltd	20	40	30	30

Table 3

| | *Week ending 18 February* | | | |
	Hammers	Chisels	Screwdrivers	Saws
Whites Ltd	30	0	10	20
Wilsons Ltd	0	0	40	20
Walkers Ltd	20	10	20	10

Table 4

| | *Fortnight ending 18 February* | | | |
	Hammers	Chisels	Screwdrivers	Saws
Whites Ltd	50	30	50	30
Wilsons Ltd	30	50	40	40
Walkers Ltd	40	50	50	40

Table 5

The corresponding matrices are:

$$A = \begin{bmatrix} 20 & 30 & 40 & 10 \\ 30 & 50 & 0 & 20 \\ 20 & 40 & 30 & 30 \end{bmatrix}, B = \begin{bmatrix} 30 & 0 & 10 & 20 \\ 0 & 0 & 40 & 20 \\ 20 & 10 & 20 & 10 \end{bmatrix} \text{ and } C = \begin{bmatrix} 50 & 30 & 50 & 30 \\ 30 & 50 & 40 & 40 \\ 40 & 50 & 50 & 40 \end{bmatrix}.$$

C is obtained from **A** and **B** by adding the corresponding entries, and so is called the sum of **A** and **B**; we write $C = A + B$. Clearly, only matrices of the same shape can be added in this way.

Exercise E

*1   If $A = \begin{bmatrix} 1 & 2 & ^-3 \\ 4 & 0 & 1 \end{bmatrix}$ and $B = \begin{bmatrix} 2 & ^-3 & ^-4 \\ 0 & 5 & 2 \end{bmatrix}$, calculate $A + B$ and $B + A$.

2   If $C = \begin{bmatrix} 1 & 3 \\ 4 & 5 \\ 2 & 6 \end{bmatrix}$ and $D = \begin{bmatrix} 4 & 0 \\ 3 & 3 \\ 1 & 2 \end{bmatrix}$, calculate $C + D$ and $D + C$.

*3   If $A = \begin{bmatrix} 2 & 3 \\ ^-4 & 5 \end{bmatrix}$ and $Z = \begin{bmatrix} 0 & 0 \\ 0 & 0 \end{bmatrix}$,

    (a) calculate $A + Z$;
    (b) find a matrix X such that $A + X = Z$;
    (c) suggest what the matrix ^-A ought to be.

4   If $A = \begin{bmatrix} 3 & 4 & 7 \\ ^-5 & 2 & 3 \end{bmatrix}$ and $B = \begin{bmatrix} 5 & 6 & 9 \\ 0 & 0 & 3 \end{bmatrix}$,

    (a) find a matrix X such that $A + X = B$;
    (b) suggest what the matrix $B - A$ ought to be.

5   If $M = \begin{bmatrix} 4 & ^-7 & 3 \\ 0 & 2 & 5 \end{bmatrix}$,

    (a) calculate $M + M$;
    (b) suggest what the matrix $3M$ ought to be.

SUMMARY

Matrices are used for many purposes including data storage and description of networks.   (Sections 1, 4)

Matrices are multiplied by combining rows of the left-hand matrix with columns of the right-hand matrix. The shape of the product is given by:

(m row, n column) (n row, p column) = (m row, p column).

Only if the number of columns of the left matrix is equal to the number of rows of the right matrix are two matrices compatible for multiplication.

The matrix products **LM** and **ML** are not equal, even if they both exist, except in certain special cases.

$L(MN) = (LM)N$ whenever **L** and **M** are compatible and **M** and **N** are compatible.

If $L = \begin{bmatrix} a & b \\ c & d \end{bmatrix}$, $I = \begin{bmatrix} 1 & 0 \\ 0 & 1 \end{bmatrix}$ and $0 = \begin{bmatrix} 0 & 0 \\ 0 & 0 \end{bmatrix}$ then

$LI = IL = L$ and $L0 = 0L = 0$. (Section 2)

M^2 is used as a shorthand for MM, M^3 for $M(MM)$ or $(MM)M$, and so on.

If $M = \begin{bmatrix} 2 & 5 & 9 \\ 1 & 10 & 6 \end{bmatrix}$, $M' = \begin{bmatrix} 2 & 1 \\ 5 & 10 \\ 9 & 6 \end{bmatrix}$. The matrix M' is called the transpose of M.

Multiplying the route matrix of a network by itself gives the matrix of two-stage routes. (Section 4)

Two matrices of the same shape can be added by adding the corresponding entries in the two matrices. (Section 5)

Summary exercise

1 If $A = \begin{bmatrix} 1 & 2 \\ 3 & 5 \end{bmatrix}$, $B = \begin{bmatrix} 2 & 1 \\ 1 & 0 \end{bmatrix}$ and $C = \begin{bmatrix} 4 \\ 7 \end{bmatrix}$ find:

   (a) AB;   (b) BA;   (c) AC;   (d) BC;   (e) $(AB)C$;   (f) $A + B$.

2 If $P = \begin{bmatrix} 1 & 0 & 2 & 5 \\ 3 & 1 & 4 & 1 \\ 2 & {}^-6 & 0 & 3 \end{bmatrix}$, $Q = \begin{bmatrix} {}^-5 & {}^-1 \\ 0 & 7 \\ 2 & 4 \\ 1 & 1 \end{bmatrix}$ and $R = \begin{bmatrix} 3 & 2 & 0 \\ {}^-4 & 2 & {}^-1 \end{bmatrix}$ find:

   (a) $(PQ)R$;   (b) $P(QR)$;   (c) QRP;   (d) RPQ.

3 For the network in Figure 14, write down the route matrix and multiply it by itself.

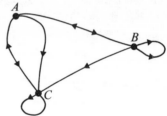

Figure 14

4 Ruritanian Transport has 15 minibuses, 12 coaches and 10 double-deckers. Transylvanian Coachways has 5 minibuses, 20 coaches and 3 double-deckers.

   (a) Write this information as a (2 row, 3 column) matrix.

   (b) The minibuses carry 12 passengers, the coaches 30 passengers and the double-deckers 50 passengers. Write down a suitable product of matrices to give the total number of passengers that each company can carry. Find this product.

Miscellaneous exercise

1 If $A = \begin{bmatrix} 1 & 0 & 0 \\ 0 & 1 & 0 \\ 0 & 0 & 1 \end{bmatrix}$, $B = \begin{bmatrix} 2 & 11 \\ 14 & 8 \\ 6 & 23 \end{bmatrix}$ and $C = \begin{bmatrix} 1 & 0 \\ 0 & 1 \end{bmatrix}$ find

   (a) AB;   (b) BC;   (c) $A(BC)$.

2 If $X = \begin{bmatrix} 1 & 8 & 2 \\ 3 & 4 & 3 \end{bmatrix}$ and $Y = \begin{bmatrix} 5 & 0 \\ 1 & 6 \\ 2 & 7 \end{bmatrix}$, find

   (a) XY;   (b) X';   (c) Y';   (d) $X'Y'$;   (e) $Y'X'$.

Which matrix is the transpose of XY? Can you explain why, using a data storage example?

3 If $D = \begin{bmatrix} 6 & ^-2 \\ -7 & 1 \end{bmatrix}$ find:

   (a) DD;   (b) D^2D;   (c) DD^2;   (d) D^4.

4 If $S = \begin{bmatrix} 0 & 1 \\ 1 & 1 \end{bmatrix}$ find:

   (a) S^2;   (b) S^3;   (c) S^4.

Do you recognise the sequence of numbers occurring in these matrices? Can you guess what S^5, S^6 and S^7 are?

5 (a) If $L = \begin{bmatrix} a & b \\ c & d \end{bmatrix}$ and $M = \begin{bmatrix} p & q \\ r & s \end{bmatrix}$ find LM and ML.

Show that if $LM = ML$ then $br = cq$.

   (b) If $L = \begin{bmatrix} 5 & 2 \\ 3 & 1 \end{bmatrix}$, $M = \begin{bmatrix} p & 4 \\ 6 & s \end{bmatrix}$ and $LM = ML$, find some pairs of possible values

   of p and s.

6 If $N = \begin{bmatrix} e & f \\ g & h \end{bmatrix}$, where none of e, f, g, h is zero, and $NN = \begin{bmatrix} 1 & 0 \\ 0 & 1 \end{bmatrix}$ show that $e = {}^-h$.

Find some suitable pairs of values for f and g if $e = 3$ and $h = {}^-3$.

7 If $U = \begin{bmatrix} a & b \\ c & d \end{bmatrix}$, $V = \begin{bmatrix} e & f \\ g & h \end{bmatrix}$ and $W = \begin{bmatrix} i & j \\ k & l \end{bmatrix}$ find $U(VW)$ and $(UV)W$

8 One difficulty in Exercise D, questions 5–8, has been that we have no means of including draws in the calculations. This can be overcome in the following manner.

   If A beats B, this can be shown by a double arrow (see Figure 15 (a)) and an entry 2 in the matrix in row A and column B.

   If A draws with C, this can be shown by arrows in each direction (see Figure 15(b)) and entries of 1 in the matrix in (i) row A, column C and (ii) row C, and column A.

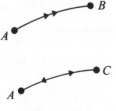

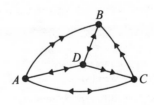

Figure 15   Figure 16

   Alan, Bill, Catherine and Debbie all played each other in a chess tournament and the results are indicated in Figure 16. Compile a matrix for this and multiply it by itself. Who should be awarded the prize?

15

Statistics

1. REPRESENTATION OF DATA

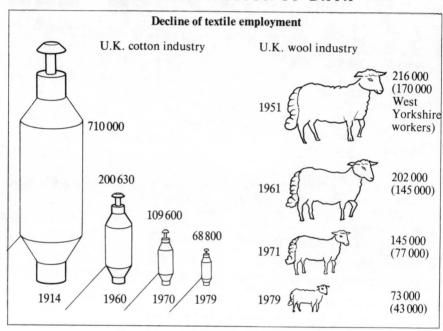

Decline of textile employment

U.K. cotton industry

U.K. wool industry

710 000

200 630

109 600

68 800

1914   1960   1970   1979

1951   216 000 (170 000 West Yorkshire workers)

1961   202 000 (145 000)

1971   145 000 (77 000)

1979   73 000 (43 000)

Figure 1. This diagram has been based on
one that appeared in *The Guardian*, 16 June 1980, p. 15.

Figure 1 is a pictorial way of presenting some statistical facts. Three of the common ways of presenting statistical information are bar charts, pictograms and pie charts. Exercise A shows some examples, some of which are misleading.

Exercise A

1 What are the misleading features of Figure 2?

2 Figure 3 shows the vitamin/mineral content of 1 kg of Doggo compared with 1 kg of shin of beef. What are the misleading features?

3 Figure 4 illustrates the company chairman's statement: 'Profit this year is double that of last year.' Is it a fair representation? What is the ratio of:
   (*a*) the heights of the money bags;
   (*b*) their areas?

84

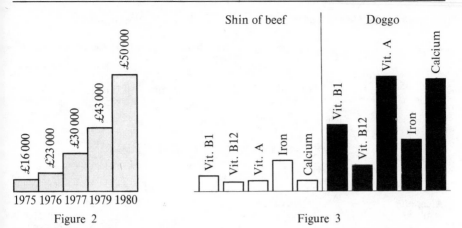

Figure 2

Figure 3

Figure 4

4   Figure 1 illustrates some changes in employment in the textile industry in Britain.
    (a) For the cotton industry write the following ratios in the form 1: n
        (i) number employed in 1960: number employed in 1979;
        (ii) the ratio of the heights of the bobbins illustrating these figures;
        (iii) the ratio of the areas of the pictures of these bobbins;
        (iv) the ratio of the volumes of these bobbins.
    (b) For the wool industry, write the following ratios in the form 1 : n
        (i) number employed in 1951: number employed in 1979;
        (ii) the ratio of the distances from nose to tail of the sheep illustrating these figures;
        (iii) the ratio of the volumes of these sheep.
    (c) Comment on the visual impression given by the diagrams.
5   Figure 5 shows the average household weekly expenditure per person on commodities and services in 1966 and 1976.
    (a) Find the ratio of the radii of the pie charts in the form 1 : n.
    (b) Find the ratio of the areas of the pie charts in the form 1 : n.
    (c) Find the ratio of the expenditures in the two years in the form 1 : n.
    (d) What are the main changes between 1966 and 1976?

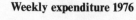

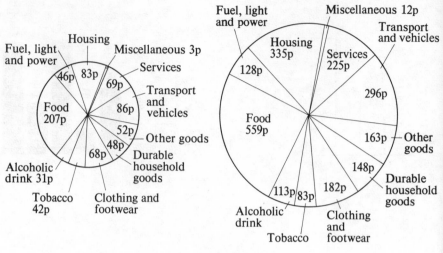

Figure 5

2. FREQUENCIES

Farmer Fairacre weighs 30 potatoes and records their masses (to the nearest 10 g) as follows:

170	220	170	200	190	210	200	190	180	190
220	190	180	210	200	190	180	200	200	190
210	200	210	180	190	180	190	200	170	190

Table 1

How many of the potatoes had a mass of 190 g? How many had a mass of at least 205 g? Answering questions like these is easier if the information is re-organised and the number of potatoes of each mass recorded. From Table 1 we find that 3 potatoes had a mass of 170 g, or, in other words, the *frequency* of 170 is 3. Table 2 is a *frequency table* for the data of Table 1.

Mass in grams (to the nearest 10 g)	Frequency (number of potatoes)
170	3
180	5
190	9
200	7
210	4
220	2

Table 2

Notice that the total frequency (3 + 5 + 9 + 7 + 4 + 2) is 30, the total number of potatoes weighed.

The information about the frequencies can be presented in bar-chart form, called a *frequency diagram* (Figure 6). Since the masses were measured to the nearest 10 g, the 9 potatoes recorded as having a mass of 190 g must have a mass of at least 185 g and less than 195 g. The bar for that mass, therefore, spans the interval 185 to 195.

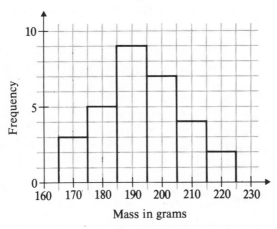

Figure 6

Example 1

A postman makes a note of the number of letters he delivers to each house in Eastmead Street one morning, as follows:

House number	1	3	5	7	9	11	13	15	17	19	21	23	25	27
Number of letters	1	2	1	0	5	1	0	1	1	3	2	1	0	1

House number	29	31	33	35	37	39	40	38	36	34	32	30	28
Number of letters	4	1	1	0	1	1	2	3	1	0	7	1	5

House number	26	24	22	20	18	16	14	12	10	8	6	4	2
Number of letters	2	2	4	2	3	3	0	1	0	2	0	4	1

Construct a frequency table and draw the frequency diagram.

The frequency table is shown in Table 3 and the frequency diagram in Figure 7. Notice that the total frequency is 40, the total number of houses. In the frequency diagram each number on the scale for the number of letters is at the centre of a column, so that the column for 3, for example, spans the interval 2.5 to 3.5. Similarly, the column for 0 spans the interval ⁻0.5 to 0.5.

Number of letters delivered per house	Frequency (number of houses)
0	8
1	15
2	7
3	4
4	3
5	2
6	0
7	1

Table 3

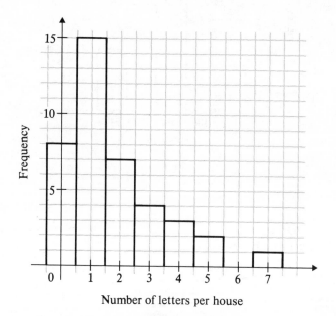

Number of letters per house

Figure 7

Sometimes frequency tables are constructed using groups of events. Table 4 is a record of the number of words in 100 sentences of *Animal Farm* by George Orwell.

23	52	22	33	24	45	30	67	16	25	29	33	21	19	36	12	12	44	10	13
33	40	23	25	25	41	20	20	8	22	25	6	18	21	12	14	40	29	20	31
21	25	16	7	23	10	10	4	10	18	40	24	20	28	25	10	24	32	12	21
25	10	18	20	21	16	28	37	11	38	27	18	23	22	31	25	10	30	22	33
8	25	9	22	9	18	14	8	34	18	27	20	11	21	25	14	51	39	22	4

Table 4

This information might be presented in a frequency table such as Table 5.

Number of words per sentence	1–5	6–10	11–15	16–20	21–25	26–30	31–35	36–40
Frequency	2	14	10	16	29	8	8	7

Number of words per sentence	41–45	46–50	51–55	56–60	61–65	66–70
Frequency	3	0	2	0	0	1

Table 5

Although some of the detail is lost by this grouping, a better general picture is obtained than by using frequencies for each individual number of words between 4 and 67. The frequency diagram drawn from Table 5 is shown in Figure 8. Since the column for 6 would span the interval 5.5 to 6.5, and the column for 10 would span 9.5 to 10.5, the column for the group 6–10 spans the interval 5.5 to 10.5.

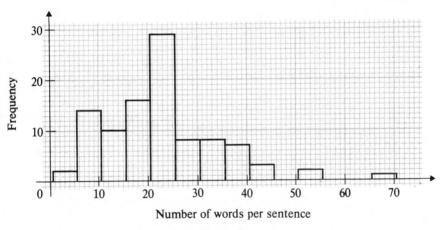

Figure 8

Span of intervals

When drawing frequency diagrams, care must be taken over the span of the columns. Here are some examples:

(1) Measurements are given to the nearest suitable unit. 'The letter weighs 40 g to the nearest 10 g' means that its weight is between 35 g and 45 g. In a frequency diagram the column corresponding to this measurement would span the interval 35 to 45. 'The length of this road is 2.1 m' means that its length is between 2.05 m and 2.15 m, and the corresponding column would span 2.05 to 2.15.

(2) When using groups of measurements, it is common to specify the beginning and end of each group and the span of the corresponding column is the same.

For example, letters might be classified by mass as less than 50 g, at least 50 g but less than 100 g, or at least 100 g but less than 150 g. The columns for these groups would span 0–50, 50–100 and 100–150.

(3) If the population consists of whole numbers (like the number of letters delivered per house), columns are centred on the whole number points.

(4) If a frequency table for groups of whole numbers is being used, a similar principle to (3) is involved and groups such as 6–10, 11–15 are represented by columns spanning 5.5–10.5 and 10.5–15.5.

(5) Ages are measurements given in a different way from (1): 'age 13' means at least 13 years old, but less than 14 years old, and the corresponding column in a frequency diagram would span 13–14.

Exercise B

*1 The heights of 30 tomato seedlings were measured to the nearest centimetre and recorded as follows:

11	10	13	9	8	13	11	11	11	13
11	8	8	14	9	11	10	13	8	12
13	6	8	10	10	9	5	10	9	8

Construct a frequency table and draw the frequency diagram.

2 The times taken for 50 vehicles to cross a toll-bridge were recorded in seconds as follows:

32	28	29	34	28	35	31	29	29	29
31	27	33	30	27	32	30	29	36	37
28	35	25	28	31	29	34	29	26	28
30	29	34	32	32	29	29	31	30	29
34	29	27	30	26	26	27	29	31	26

(*a*) Construct a frequency table and draw the frequency diagram.

(*b*) The bridge is 370 m long and there is a speed limit of 45 km/h. How many of the vehicles were breaking the speed limit? (45 km/h = 12.5 m/s)

*3 The number of goals scored in first-class football matches one Saturday were as follows:

(*a*) Cup

0	4	2	1	3	6	0	2	1	1	2	8	4	4
2	4	0	4	0	3	2	2	3	1	3	4	3	8

(*b*) League

5	2	0	5	2	2	0	4	0	0	1	2	3	4	5	1
5	1	1	4	4	1	3	4	4	3	2	4	1	4	0	1
1	2	4	1	2	4	3	2	3	3	1	4				

(*c*) Scottish league   1 3 3 1 0 3 2 2 3 3 3 3 3 3 2 2 4 2

Construct frequency tables and draw frequency diagrams. Do there appear to be any great differences between the three groups?

4 The number of children in each house in two roads is shown in this table:

(*a*) Westfield Road

1	0	3	3	2	1	0	1	0	2	1	1	1	0	2
1	0	0	3	0	2	1	1	2	2	2	2	1	1	2

(*b*) Eastfield Road

2	4	0	2	3	2	2	3	3	2	2	3
1	4	3	2	1	0	5	3	2	4	3	0

Construct frequency tables and draw frequency diagrams. Comment on the different shapes of the diagrams.

*5 Fifty apples were weighed, with the following results (masses in grams):

90.2	103.1	87.6	91.3	96.5	99.0	94.7	95.8	86.1	93.0
88.3	81.9	89.1	75.4	84.1	85.2	93.9	83.5	90.3	85.8
89.7	74.6	82.0	78.5	92.6	80.8	88.5	98.2	97.0	96.1
91.8	94.3	88.9	96.4	92.7	76.0	101.2	102.4	77.5	80.9
84.8	74.8	79.2	106.5	83.8	104.0	89.3	92.6	88.2	103.9

Construct a frequency table using groups of 'at least 70 g but less than 75 g', and so on, in intervals of 5 g up to 110 g. Draw the frequency diagram. What percentage of the apples had a mass of at least 95 g?

6 The time-tabled times for the 26 weekday trains from Oxford to London in 1980 were, in minutes:

82 109 90 76 67 95 60 112 76 60 65 62 62
106   62 62 62 65 72 69   68 76 66 71 70 87

Construct a frequency table using classes of 60–64 minutes, 65–69 minutes and so on, in intervals of 5 minutes up to 114 minutes. Draw the frequency diagram. How many of the trains would you class as 'slow'?

*7 Sixty 15-year-old girls were tested to find their resting pulse-rates. The following figures were obtained for the number of beats per minute:

72 70 66 74 81 70 74 53 57 62 58 92 74 67 62
91 73 68 65 80 78 67 75 80 84 61 72 72 69 70
76 74 65 84 79 80 76 72 68 65 82 79 71 86 77
69 72 56 70 62 76 56 86 63 73 70 75 73 89 64

Construct a frequency table using groups of 50–54, 55–59, etc., and draw the frequency diagram.
Construct another frequency table using groups of 50–59, 60–69, etc. and draw the corresponding frequency diagram.
Which diagram gives a better representation of the data?

8 The number of runs scored by 78 batsmen who completed their innings in one-day matches one Sunday were as follows:

38 64   7 58 70   6 29 27 24   6   3   5 45
13 12 13 12 21   0   0 23   2   2 34 16   0
 0 15 46   3 14 32 17   5 12 57 35 31   0
 6   2   2   3   8 18 13   1   1 13 15 15   1
 2   7 17   1 21   3 27 30 10   4 47 14 11
26   4 26   1 14 12   5 14   2   6   2 25 22

Construct a frequency table using groups of 0–4, 5–9, etc., and draw the frequency diagram.
Construct another frequency table using groups of 0–9, 10–19, etc., and draw the corresponding frequency diagram.
Which diagram gives a better representation of the data?

9 The following table gives the frequencies of the numbers of words in two samples of 100 sentences from books by each of two authors, Enid Blyton and P.G. Wodehouse. The samples were taken from descriptive passages only and are not necessarily in the correct order.

Number of words	1–5	6–10	11–15	16–20	21–25	26–30	31–45	36–40	41–45	46–50
Sample 1	18	24	30	14	8	3	1	0	2	0
Sample 2	15	22	17	11	12	9	8	2	2	2
Sample 3	22	18	10	14	7	9	6	5	5	4
Sample 4	15	27	32	15	7	3	1	0	0	0

Draw a frequency diagram for each sample. By examining the shapes of the graphs find which samples are taken from the same author.

10 The following table gives the frequencies of the numbers of letters in the words of leading articles from four newspapers.

	1	2	3	4	5	6	7	8	9	10	11	12	13	14	15	16
Newspaper 1	6	53	73	38	25	25	17	14	11	9	5	1	1	1	0	0
Newspaper 2	5	36	35	32	33	20	17	24	8	9	4	2	2	0	0	1
Newspaper 3	8	30	56	57	13	19	13	7	2	6	0	3	0	0	0	0
Newspaper 4	3	34	64	27	35	25	34	7	5	8	7	6	0	1	0	0

Draw frequency diagrams for each set of data. One of the newspapers was *The Times*. Which one do you think it was?

11 Collect your own data similar to that in questions 9 and 10, and display it on suitable frequency diagrams.

3. THE MEAN

Farmer Fairacre sells potatoes in 50-kilogram sacks. He decides to fill his sacks with a certain number of potatoes, weigh the sack, and then add or take away a few potatoes to get the total mass correct. How many should he put in a sack?

The masses of 30 potatoes from his farm were given in Table 2. Assuming that this is a typical sample of potatoes, we could find the approximate number of potatoes in a 50-kilogram sack by finding the average mass of these 30 potatoes and calculating how many potatoes with this mean mass would have a total mass of 50 kg. In order to find the mean mass, we have to find the total mass and divide by 30. We look again at Table 2.

Mass in grams (to the nearest 10 g)	Frequency (number of potatoes)
170	3
180	5
190	9
200	7
210	4
220	2

Table 2

The 3 potatoes with mass 170 g have a total mass of $170 \times 3 = 510$ g, the 5 potatoes with mass 180 g have a total mass of $180 \times 5 = 900$ g, and so on. The complete calculation can be set out as in Table 6.

Mass in grams (x)	Frequency (f)	xf
170	3	170 × 3 = 510
180	5	180 × 5 = 900
190	9	190 × 9 = 1710
200	7	200 × 7 = 1400
210	4	210 × 4 = 840
220	2	220 × 2 = 440
	30	5800

Table 6

(If you are using a calculator with a memory, you can add each entry in the final column into the memory as you find it.)

The total mass of the 30 potatoes is therefore 5800 g, and the mean mass is $\frac{5800}{30}$ g = 193.33 ... g ≈ 193 g. We should expect a 50-kilogram sack to contain about $\frac{50\,000}{193.33}$ potatoes ≈ 259 potatoes.

There is a convention that a mean is given to an accuracy of one more significant figure than the original data; in this case the masses were given to the nearest 10 g, so the mean is given the nearest gram.

Exercise C

*1 Calculate the mean height of the tomato seedlings whose heights are given in the following table:

Height in cm	5	6	7	8	9	10	11	12	13	14
Frequency	1	1	0	6	4	5	6	1	5	1

2 Calculate the mean time to cross the toll-bridge for the 50 vehicles of Exercise B, question 2. What is the speed of a vehicle which takes the mean time?

*3 'Cup football is more exciting than the leagues because more goals are scored, on average.' Use the information from Exercise B, question 3 to investigate whether this is a reasonable statement.

4 What are the mean numbers of children per house in (a) Westfield Road; (b) Eastfield Road? (See Exercise B, question 4.) On the housing estate there are 200 houses similar to those in Westfield Road and 100 houses similar to those in Eastfield Road. How many children would you expect there to be on the whole estate?

*5 The numbers of eggs in 100 tree-sparrow nests were counted, and the results recorded in the following frequency table:

Number of eggs	2	3	4	5	6	7
Frequency	2	7	25	53	12	1

What was the total number of eggs in the 100 nests? What was the mean number of eggs per nest?

6 In a census of 145 randomly selected houses in Umbridge, the following information about the number of children was obtained:

Number of children (under 12 years of age) per house	0	1	2	3	4	5	6
Frequency (number of houses)	81	25	20	10	5	3	1

(a) How many children under 12 are there in the 145 houses? What is the mean number of children per house?

(b) If there are 521 houses in the village, how many children under 12 would you expect there to be in the village?

(c) Can you tell how many children there are, approximately, in the village school, which takes children from 5 to 11 years old?

*7 In a novel there were 128 pages with no misprints, 86 pages with one misprint each, 29 pages with two misprints each, 6 pages with three misprints each, and 1 page with four misprints. Find the mean number of misprints per page.

8 The number of rooms per dwelling at the 1951 and 1971 censuses is given in the following table:

Number of rooms	1	2	3	4	5	6	7	8	9	10 or more
Frequency, 1951	95	457	1346	3399	4220	1548	487	246	110	121
Frequency, 1971 (thousands of dwellings)	294	731	1722	4186	5362	4163	928	420	169	197

(a) Draw frequency diagrams to illustrate the data.

(b) Find the mean number of rooms for each of the two years, stating clearly how you have dealt with the top group.

*9 What was the mean length of the words used in the leading article of newspaper 3 (see Exercise B, question 10)?

10 What was the mean time for the rail journeys given in Exercise B, question 6? Is the mean a useful figure in this case?

4. CALCULATING THE MEAN FROM A GROUPED FREQUENCY TABLE

Look again at the data about the number of words in 100 sentences of *Animal Farm* (Tables 4 and 5).

23	52	22	33	24	45	30	67	16	25	29	33	21	19	36	12	12	44	10	13
33	40	23	25	25	41	20	20	8	22	25	6	18	21	12	14	40	29	20	31
21	25	16	7	23	10	10	4	10	18	40	24	20	28	25	10	24	32	12	21
25	10	18	20	21	16	28	37	11	38	27	18	23	22	31	25	10	30	22	33
8	25	9	22	9	18	14	8	34	18	27	20	11	21	25	14	51	39	22	4

Table 4

Number of words per sentence	1–5	6–10	11–15	16–20	21–25	26–30	31–35
Frequency	2	14	10	16	29	8	8

Number of words per sentence	36–40	41–45	46–50	51–55	56–60	61–65	66–70
Frequency	7	3	0	2	0	0	1

Table 5

If we needed to calculate the mean, we could add up all 100 numbers in Table 4 and divide by 100. Alternatively we could try to use the frequencies of Table 5. The difficulty here is that although we know that, for example, there were 29 sentences with between 21 and 25 words each, we don't know (without referring back to Table 4) the precise lengths of those 29 sentences. However, it might be reasonable to assume that their average length is about midway between 21 and 25 words, and that their total length is about $23 \times 29 = 667$ words. 23 is the *mid-interval value* for the 21–25 group.

The complete calculation for the mean can be set out as in Table 7.

Number of words in a sentence	Mid-interval value (x)	Frequency (f)	xf
1–5	3	2	6
6–10	8	14	112
11–15	13	10	130
16–20	18	16	288
21–25	23	29	667
26–30	28	8	224
31–35	33	8	264
36–40	38	7	266
41–45	43	3	129
46–50	48	0	0
51–55	53	2	106
66–70	68	1	68
		100	2260

Table 7

The mean length of the sentences is therefore approximately
$$\frac{2260}{100} \approx 23 \text{ words}.$$

(Because of the approximation involved in using mid-interval values, it would not be reasonable to give a greater degree of accuracy than these two significant figures.)

Exercise D

*1   The masses of a sample of 50 apples from a fruit farm are recorded in the following table:

Mass in grams	Frequency
At least 70 but less than 75	2
At least 75 but less than 80	5
At least 80 but less than 85	8
At least 85 but less than 90	11
At least 90 but less than 95	11
At least 95 but less than 100	7
At least 100 but less than 105	5
At least 105 but less than 110	1

(*a*) Calculate the mean mass of the apples.

(*b*) If the apples are packed in boxes of 120 apples, what would you expect the total mass of the apples in a box to be?

2   The time-tabled times for the trains from Oxford to London are tabulated as follows:

Time in minutes	60–69	70–79	80–89	90–99	100–114
Number of trains	13	6	2	2	3

Use this table to calculate the mean time. Compare this with the mean calculated directly from the data given in Exercise B, question 6. (See Exercise C, question 10.)

*3   The masses of a group of children at 6 months were as follows:

Mass in kilograms	Freqency
At least 6 but less than 7	5
At least 7 but less than 8	11
At least 8 but less than 9	18
At least 9 but less than 10	8
At least 10 but less than 11	3

Find their mean mass.

4   The ages in years and months of a form of 30 are as follows:

Age	Frequency
At least 13.0 but less than 13.2	4
At least 13.2 but less than 13.4	7
At least 13.4 but less than 13.6	5
At least 13.6 but less than 13.8	5
At least 13.8 but less than 13.10	3
At least 13.10 but less than 14.0	6

Find the mean age of the form.

*5   The resting pulse-rates of 60 girls were recorded in the following table (compare Exercise B, question 7):

Number of beats per minute	Frequency (number of girls)
50–54	1
55–59	4
60–64	6
65–69	10
70–74	18
75–79	9
80–84	7
85–89	3
90–94	2

Find their mean pulse-rate.

6   The heights of 100 saplings are shown in the following table:

Height in centimetres	Frequency
At least 100 but less than 110	3
At least 110 but less than 120	9
At least 120 but less than 130	13
At least 130 but less than 140	28
At least 140 but less than 150	37
At least 150 but less than 160	7
At least 160 but less than 170	3

Find the mean height of the saplings.

SUMMARY

Statistical data can often be given in frequency tables which give the number of times each particular observation, or group of observations, occurs.

(Section 2)

The mean can be calculated from a frequency table by multiplying each number by its frequency and dividing the total by the total frequency.

(Section 3)

When calculating the mean from a frequency table for groups, the mid-interval value for each group should be used.

(Section 4)

Summary exercise

1 The total rainfall (to the nearest cm) in each month in 5 years is given in the following table:

13	2	2	3	7	5	7	12	11	5	3	12
7	9	6	1	4	4	8	8	10	7	6	9
9	7	4	2	9	8	7	7	12	7	7	9
14	1	12	8	4	6	5	5	0	6	8	20
11	6	4	4	4	9	9	9	9	21	12	12

(a) Construct a frequency table and draw a frequency diagram. (Do not group the data.)

(b) Calculate the mean rainfall per month.

2 The heights of 30 boys are given in the following table:

Height in cm	Frequency
At least 150 but less than 156	3
At least 156 but less than 162	9
At least 162 but less than 168	13
At least 168 but less than 174	4
At least 174 but less than 180	1

(a) Show this information on a frequency diagram.

(b) Calculate the mean height of the boys.

Miscellaneous exercise

1   The age distribution of the UK population at the 1911 and 1971 censuses is shown
    in the table below:

Age	Number in age-group in thousands (1911)	(1971)
0–4	4516	4505
5–9	4339	4669
10–14	4114	4213
15–19	3919	3832
20–24	3702	4227
25–29	3559	3610
30–34	3320	3269
35–39	3022	3169
40–44	2584	3330
45–49	2226	3544
50–54	1864	3273
55–59	1487	3362
60–64	1187	3206
65–69	948	2707
70–74	676	2005
75–79	372	1331
80–84	174	791
85 or over	77	472

(*a*) Draw frequency diagrams to illustrate the two sets of data.
(*b*) Calculate the mean age of the populations in 1911 and 1971.
(*c*) What percentage of those aged under 5 in 1911 lived for at least a further 60 years?
(*d*) Comment on the main differences between the two age-distributions.

2   In 1972 it was reported that class sizes in secondary schools in England and Wales were
    as follows:

Number of pupils	Number of classes
1 – 30	111 087
31 – 40	28 175
41 – 50	637
51 or more	1 550

Calculate the mean number of pupils per class. Do you think it is a useful statistic?

3 Before the final game of the season two cricketers A and B had both taken 16 wickets at 9 runs per wicket. In the final game A took 1 wicket for 26 runs and B took 4 wickets for 56 runs. Who had the better average for the whole season?

   Show the points $O(0, 0)$, $P(16, 144)$, $A(17, 170)$ and $B(20, 200)$ on a graph. Calculate the gradients of OP, PA, PB, OA and AB, and explain the connection with the first part of this question.

4 Chlorine has two isotopes, Cl^{35} (atomic mass 35) and Cl^{37} (atomic mass 37). In a particular sample of chlorine, 75% of the molecules present are Cl^{35} and 25% are Cl^{37}. Calculate the average atomic mass of the sample.

5 (a) Draw a frequency diagram on card for the following data:

x	1	2	3	4	5
Frequency	15	17	9	7	2

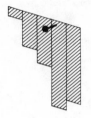

Figure 9

   (b) Calculate the mean and mark it on your diagram.
   (c) Cut out the frequency diagram and find a balance point for it (see Figure 9). Where does it appear to be? Why?

6 The number of clumps of lichen on each of 20 rows of bricks on a 5-metre length of wall were counted, with the following results:

Row	1	2	3	4	5	6	7	8	9	10
Number of clumps	0	10	10	10	8	5	4	5	7	12

Row	11	12	13	14	15	16	17	18	19	20
Number of clumps	5	6	3	1	1	2	0	0	0	0

   (a) Represent these results on a bar chart showing row number $\longrightarrow$ number of clumps.
   (b) Find the mean number of clumps per row, and mark this on your diagram, using a dotted line.
   (c) Assuming that row N is N units from the bottom of the wall, calculate the mean distance of the lichen clumps from the bottom of the wall and mark this on your diagram with a dotted line.
   (d) Which of the means you have calculated do you think is most helpful in thinking about the lichen growth?

REVISION EXERCISE 13

Calculate the following without using your calculator:

1 $14.07 + 3.683 + 971 + 1.087 + 10.15$

2 $596.347 - 472.891$

3 1234.5679×0.0009

4 $0.133 \div 19$

5 $1^3 + 2^3 + 3^3 + 4^3 - (1 + 2 + 3 + 4)^2$

6 $(\frac{1}{2} + \frac{2}{3} + \frac{3}{4} + \frac{4}{5} + \frac{5}{6}) - \frac{11}{20}$

7 $(4\frac{1}{8} - 3\frac{3}{4}) \times 5\frac{1}{3}$

8 $7\frac{7}{8} \div 2\frac{1}{4} - 2\frac{1}{2}$

9 $\frac{1}{6}$ as a percentage.

10 12% of £4625.

11 $(2 + 6 - 3 - 8 + 9 - 2 + 1 - 12)^3$

12 $1 + 2 + 3 + 4 + \ldots + 97 + 98 + 99$

REVISION EXERCISE 14

1 Multiply 0.0003 by 0.014, giving your answer in standard form.

2 A cone has a base radius of 4.4 cm and a height of 11.7 cm. Use Pythagoras' theorem to calculate its slant height, and hence calculate its total surface area. (Area of curved surface $= \pi r s$, where $r =$ base radius and $s =$ slant height.)

3 A clock has an hour hand of length 3.2 cm. At 2.30 p.m. :
   (*a*) what is the angle between the hour hand and the minute hand;
   (*b*) how far is the tip of the hour hand below its position at noon?

4 Copy Figure 1 onto squared paper, and find the coordinates of the centre of the rotation which maps one flag onto the other.

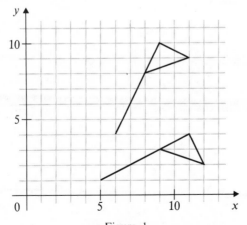

Figure 1

5 A shop makes a profit of 35% if it sells a cassette recorder for £49.95. What was the cost of the recorder to the shop?

6 Calculate the gradient of the line joining $(^-2.1, 3.7)$ to $(1.7, \,^-5.8)$.

7 Solve the equation $\frac{1}{3}(2p - 7) + \frac{1}{2}(3p - 5) = 6$.

8 If 4.7 litres of petrol cost 143 ruples, how many litres of petrol can be bought for 600 ruples?

REVISION EXERCISE 15

1 Divide 5.7×10^4 by 1.9×10^{-5} giving your answer in standard form.

2 What does a price of £5.85 become when reduced by a 15% discount?

3 Calculate the following matrix products:

$(a)\ \begin{bmatrix} 2 & 1 \\ 5 & 3 \end{bmatrix}\begin{bmatrix} 3 & ^-1 \\ ^-5 & 2 \end{bmatrix};\quad (b)\ \begin{bmatrix} 7 & ^-3 \\ ^-4 & 2 \end{bmatrix}\begin{bmatrix} 2 & 3 \\ 4 & 7 \end{bmatrix}.$

4 In triangle ABC, $AC = 108$ cm, $CB = 50$ cm, and angle $ABC = 90°$. Calculate:
(a) the length of AB;   (b) the angle CAB.

5 A positive quarter-turn about the point with coordinates $(0, 3)$ maps the point with coordinates $(2, 2)$ to the point P. Find the coordinates of P.

6 What length of wire would be needed to put a three-strand wire fence all round a circular enclosure of diameter 100 m at a horse show, allowing two gaps of 10 m each for entrances?

7 A new car cost £3500. Each year its value decreased by 20% of its value at the beginning of that year. What was its value after three years?

8 In a quadrilateral $ABCD$ the angle at B is 15° more than the angle at A, the angle at C is twice the angle at B, and the angle at D is the three times the angle at A. Find the four angles.

16

Can you convince me ?

1. CONJECTURES

Exercise A

1 Here are some statements about whole numbers. Do you think that they are always, sometimes, or never, true?
   (*a*) The sum of any two odd numbers is even.
   (*b*) The sum of any two consecutive odd numbers (17 and 19, for example) is divisible by 4.
   (*c*) The sum of any two consecutive even numbers is divisible by 4.
   (*d*) Every even number greater than 2 is the sum of two prime numbers.
   (*e*) The sum of the first n odd numbers is equal to n^2.

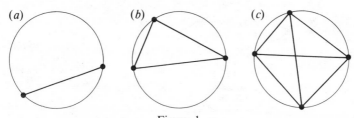

Figure 1

2 Points are drawn on a circle and straight lines are drawn joining the points as shown in Figure 1. With two points, as in Figure 1(*a*), the inside of the circle is divided into two regions. With three points there are four regions.
   (*a*) How many regions are there when four points are used?
   (*b*) How many regions are there when five points are used? Does it matter where you choose to mark the points?
   (*c*) How many regions do you think there would be if (i) six, (ii) seven, points were used? Check your answer by drawing diagrams and counting carefully.

3 (*a*) Copy and complete the following multiplications:
   $$12 \times 9 = 108$$
   $$123 \times 9 =$$
   $$1234 \times 9 =$$
   $$12\,345 \times 9 =$$
   (*b*) Can you spot a pattern? Predict the answers to $1\,234\,567 \times 9$ and $123\,456\,789 \times 9$ and check your answers by calculation.
   (*c*) What is the next multiplication in this pattern?

4 Draw a quadrilateral *ABCD* and mark the middle points *P*, *Q*, *R*, *S* of the four sides *AB*, *BC*, *CD* and *DA*. Is there anything special about the quadrilateral *PQRS*? Try again with a differently shaped quadrilateral *ABCD*.

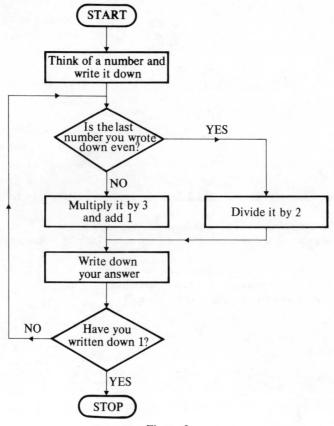

Figure 2

5   (a) Work through the flow chart in Figure 2. For example, if you start with 7, you should
       write down:
       7, 22, 11, 34, 17, 52, 26, 13, 40, 20, 10, 5, 16, 8, 4, 2, 1.
    (b) Did you reach 1 and stop? Do you think this always happens? Are you sure?
6   (a) Find the value of the expression $n^2 + n + 41$ when
       (i) $n = 1$;   (ii) $n = 2$;   (iii) $n = 3$.
    (b) Are all the answers to (a) prime numbers?
    (c) Try another value of n. Do you get a prime number? Will you always get a prime
       number? Are you sure?

2. COUNTER-EXAMPLES

Our experience often leads us to make general statements. For example, in
question 6 of Exercise A we looked at the expression $n^2 + n + 41$. Here is a
table of values of this expression:

n	4	5	6	7	8	9	10	11	12
$n^2 + n + 41$	61	71	83	97	113	131	151	173	197

All the values of $n^2 + n + 41$ in this table are prime numbers. The evidence seems to be accumulating that $n^2 + n + 41$ is always prime. We are now faced with two possibilities: either to prove that this is true, or to find a value of n for which it is not true.

If $n = 40$ then $n^2 + n + 41 = 1681 = 41 \times 41$. So here is a case in which $n^2 + n + 41$ is not prime. This is quite a common situation, where a promising conjecture can be overthrown by a single counter-example. Did this happen to you when answering Exercise A, question 2?

There are, in fact, many values of n for which $n^2 + n + 41$ is not prime; there are at least two more between 40 and 50. But to disprove the conjecture that $n^2 + n + 41$ is always prime all we need is one counter-example.

Exercise B

Find counter-examples to show that each of the statements in questions 1–10 is not true.

1 All numbers ending in 3 are prime.

2 $(n + 1)^2 = n^2 + 1$ for all numbers n.

3 $(n - 1)^2 = n^2 - 1$ for all numbers n.

4 $(a + b)^2 = a^2 + b^2$ for all numbers a and b.

5 $\dfrac{1}{x + y} = \dfrac{1}{x} + \dfrac{1}{y}$ for all numbers x, y.

6 $\dfrac{1}{x - y} = \dfrac{1}{x} - \dfrac{1}{y}$ for all numbers x, y.

7 x^2 is always greater than x.

8 $\dfrac{1}{x}$ is always less than x.

9 Every number is the sum at most three perfect squares. (For example, $5 = 2^2 + 1^2$, $11 = 3^2 + 1^2 + 1^2$.)

10 The sum of the squares of the first n odd numbers is always divisible by the next odd number. (For example, $1^2 + 3^2 + 5^2 + 7^2 + 9^2 = 165$, which is divisible by 11.)

3. IMPLICATION SIGNS

The statement
> 'today is Midsummer's Day $\Rightarrow$ the month is June'

can be read as:
> '*if* today is Midsummer's Day *then* the month is June',

or
> 'today is Midsummer's Day *implies* that the month is June'.

Notice that we are not making any assertions about whether or not today is Midsummer's Day, only about what must happen if it is. (Sometimes it is useful to start with a supposition with turns out to be false.) The complete statement is true, in the northern hemisphere.

Sometimes it is useful to use $\Leftarrow$. The statement above could be rewritten as:
> 'the month is June $\Leftarrow$ today is Midsummer's Day'

which could be read as:

'the month is June if today is Midsummer's Day'

or

'the month is June is implied by today being Midsummer's Day'

The statement

'the month is June $\Rightarrow$ today is Midsummer's Day'

or equivalently,

'today is Midsummer's Day $\Leftarrow$ the month is June'

is the *converse* of the original statement. It is false, since today might be 2 June, which is not Midsummer's Day.

If a statement and its converse are both true, we may use $\Leftrightarrow$. For example: $2x = 6 \Leftrightarrow x = 3$ is a true statement, since it is true both that if $2x = 6$ then $x = 3$ and that if $x = 3$ then $2x = 6$. The $\Leftrightarrow$ sign may be read as 'if and only if'. Here are some further examples:

Statement: If n is odd then n^2 is odd.   (True)
Converse: If n^2 is odd then n is odd.   (True)
                n is odd $\Leftrightarrow n^2$ is odd.   (True)

Statement: $x = 3 \Rightarrow x^2 = 9$.   (True)
Converse: $x^2 = 9 \Rightarrow x = 3$.   (False: x is not necessarily
                                          equal to 3; it might be $^-3$.)
                $x = 3 \Leftrightarrow x^2 = 9$ is therefore false, but
        $x = 3$ or $x = {}^-3 \Leftrightarrow x^2 = 9$ is true.

Statement: The sides of a quadrilateral $ABCD$ are of equal length $\Rightarrow ABCD$
                is a square. (False; why?)
Converse: $ABCD$ is a square $\Rightarrow$ the sides of $ABCD$ are of equal length. (True)

Exercise C

1 Write the following as English sentences.
    (a) Tomorrow is Thursday $\Rightarrow$ yesterday was Tuesday.
    (b) Today is 1 January 1900 $\Rightarrow$ Queen Victoria is alive.
    (c) Triangle ABC is equilateral $\Leftarrow AB = AC$.
    (d) The angles of $PQRS$ are right angles $\Rightarrow PQRS$ is a square.

*2 State whether the statements given in question 1 are true or false. Give your reasons.

*3 Write down the converses of the statements given in question 1. Are they true or false? Give your reasons.

4 State with reasons whether the following statements are true or false.
    (a) N is an even whole number $\Rightarrow 3N$ is an even whole number.
    (b) $x^2 = x \Rightarrow x = 1$.
    (c) $2x + 3 = 17 \Rightarrow x = 7$.
    (d) $a^2 = b^2 \Leftarrow a = b$.

5 Write down the converses of the statements given in question 4. Are they true or false? Give your reasons.

*6   State with reasons whether the following statements are true or false.
   (a) $n(A) = 5$ and $n(B) = 3 \Rightarrow n(A \cup B) = 8$.
   (b) $A \subset B \Rightarrow A \cap B = A$.
   (c) $A \cap B = \varnothing \Rightarrow A = \varnothing$.
   (d) $A' = \varnothing \Leftarrow A = \mathcal{E}$.

7   Write down the converses of the statements given in question 6. Are they true or false? Give your reasons.

8   (a) State whether the following statements are true or false.
      (i) $3x + 4 = 19 \Leftrightarrow x = 5$.
      (ii) N is an even whole number $\Leftrightarrow N^2$ is divisible by 4.
      (iii) $x = 5 \Leftrightarrow x > 4$.
      (iv) In the quadrilateral $ABCD$, $AC = BD \Leftrightarrow ABCD$ is a rectangle.
   (b) For the statements which are false, replace $\Leftrightarrow$ by $\Rightarrow$ or $\Leftarrow$ to make the statements true.

9   (a) Insert $\Rightarrow$ or $\Leftarrow$ to make the following into true statements about numbers (p and q are assumed to be whole numbers).
      (i) p is even pq is even.
      (ii) $p + q$ is odd pq is even.
      (iii) $x = 0$ $xy = 0$.
      (iv) $ab = ac$ $b = c$.
   (b) For each of the statements (i)–(iv), explain why $\Leftrightarrow$ cannot be used.

4. PROOF

If we have a conjecture which we suspect to be true and for which we cannot find a counter-example, then we try to construct a chain of reasoning which will enable us to deduce the result from some fairly simple assumptions.

Example 1
   Prove that the sum of two odd numbers is even.

M is an odd number $\Leftrightarrow M$ is not exactly divisible by 2
$\qquad\qquad\qquad\qquad \Leftrightarrow M$ has a remainder 1 when divided by 2
$\qquad\qquad\qquad\qquad \Leftrightarrow M = 2p + 1$ for some number p.
M and N are odd numbers $\Leftrightarrow M = 2p + 1$ and $N = 2q + 1$ for some
$\qquad\qquad\qquad\qquad\qquad\qquad\qquad\qquad\qquad$ numbers p, q
$$\Rightarrow M + N = 2p + 1 + 2q + 1$$
$$= 2p + 2q + 2$$
$$= 2(p + q + 1)$$
$$\Rightarrow M + N \text{ is divisible by 2}$$
$$\Rightarrow M + N \text{ is even.}$$

Exercise D

*1   (a) What is the next even number after $2n$?
   (b) What is the sum of $2n$ and the next even number? Show that this is never a multiple of 4.

2 (a) What is the difference between two consecutive odd numbers?
   (b) What is the next odd number after $2n + 1$?
   (c) What is the sum of $2n + 1$ and the next odd number? Show that this is a multiple of 4.

*3 Prove that the difference between two even numbers is even.

4 Prove that the difference between two odd numbers is even.

*5 Prove that the square of an even number is divisible by 4.

6 Prove that the product of two even numbers is divisible by 4.

5. USE OF DIAGRAMS

Diagrams can be used in several ways to illustrate many results, and perhaps convince us of their truth. For example, Pythagoras' theorem may be illustrated by the diagrams of Figure 3. In Figure 3(a) the four right-angled triangles (with sides of lengths a, b and c) and the square of side c fit together to make a square of side $a + b$. In Figure 3(b) the square of side c has been replaced by squares of sides a and b and the pieces rearranged to form, again, a square of side $a + b$. It follows that the area of the square of side c must be equal to the sum of the areas of the squares of sides a and b, and so $c^2 = a^2 + b^2$.

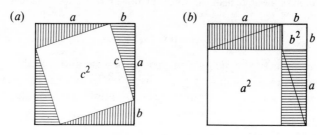

Figure 3. $c^2 = a^2 + b^2$.

Areas of rectangles can often be used to illustrate the distributive rule. Figures 4, 5 and 6 show some examples. The diagrams imply that a, b, c, d, x and y are all positive, but the algebraic statements are true whether the quantities are positive or negative. Figure 6 gives us a useful way of setting out a table to help with problems involving removal of brackets.

	x	3
2	$2x$	6

Figure 4. $2(x + 3) = 2x + 6$.

	x	y
a	ax	ay

Figure 5. $a(x + y) = ax + ay$.

	c	d
a	ac	ad
b	bc	bd

Figure 6. $(a + b)(c + d) = ac + ad + bc + bd$.

Example 2

Multiply out and simplify:

(a) $(p + 5)(3p - 2)$;

(b) $(q - 4)(q - 3)$.

(a) $(p + 5)(3p - 2) = p(3p - 2) + 5(3p - 2)$
$$= 3p^2 - 2p + 15p - 10$$
$$= 3p^2 + 13p - 10$$

or, using a table like Figure 6:

Collecting together the terms in the loop, we see that
$(p + 5)(3p - 2) = 3p^2 + 13p - 10$.

(b) $(q - 4)(q - 3) = q(q - 3) - 4(q - 3)$
$$= q^2 - 3q - 4q + 12$$
$$= q^2 - 7q + 12$$

or, from a table:

$$(q - 4)(q - 3) = q^2 - 7q + 12$$

Difference of two squares

$(a + b)(a - b) = a(a - b) + b(a - b)$
$$= a^2 - ab + ba - b^2$$
$$= a^2 - b^2$$

Compare the table:

	a	^-b
a	a^2	^-ab
b	ab	$^-b^2$

This result can be useful for calculating $a^2 - b^2$ to a greater degree of accuracy than can be obtained directly on a calculator.

Example 3

Multiply out $(3p + 4q)(3p - 4q)$.

Since this is of the form $(a + b)(a - b)$, we can write down directly:
$$(3p + 4q)(3p - 4q) = (3p)^2 - (4q)^2$$
$$= 9p^2 - 16q^2.$$

Example 4

Calculate $0.234\,56^2 - 0.234\,55^2$.

Direct calculation gives $0.000\,004\,69$.

If we require greater accuracy we could use

$$0.234\,56^2 - 0.234\,55^2 = (0.234\,56 + 0.234\,55)(0.234\,56 - 0.234\,55)$$
$$= 0.469\,11 \times 0.000\,01$$
$$= 0.000\,004\,691\,1 \quad \text{which is the exact answer.}$$

Squares

We saw in Exercise B, question 4 that $(a + b)^2$ is not always equal to $a^2 + b^2$. In fact,

$$(a + b)^2 = (a + b)(a + b)$$
$$= a(a + b) + b(a + b)$$
$$= a^2 + ab + ba + b^2$$
$$= a^2 + 2ab + b^2$$

and this is true for all values of a and b, positive or negative. The result can also be demonstrated by the area diagram shown in Figure 7.

Figure 7

There is a similar result for $(a - b)^2$, which can be obtained by replacing b by ^-b in the previous working, or from the following table:

$$(a - b)^2 = a^2 - 2ab + b^2$$

Example 5

Multiply out:

(*a*) $(5p + 4q)^2$;   (*b*) $(5p - 4q)^2$.

(*a*) Using $(a + b)^2 = a^2 + 2ab + b^2$,
$$(5p + 4q)^2 = (5p)^2 + 2 \times 5p \times 4q + (4q)^2$$
$$= 25p^2 + 40pq + 16q^2.$$

(*b*) Using $(a - b)^2 = a^2 - 2ab + b^2$,
$$(5p - 4q)^2 = (5p)^2 - 2 \times 5p \times 4q + (4q)^2$$
$$= 25p^2 + 40pq + 16q^2.$$

Exercise E

*1 Multiply out:
  (a) $2(x - 4)$;   (b) $a(b + 3)$;   (c) $2a(x - 4)$;
  (d) $2p(3q + 5)$;   (e) $3x(4y - 5z)$;   (f) $2x(x + 7)$.

2 Multiply out:
  (a) $3(2x + 7)$;   (b) $p(3q - 7)$;   (c) $3m(n + 5)$;
  (d) $3a(2b - 5c)$;   (e) $4a(5 - 2a)$;   (f) $2x(3x - 4y)$.

*3 Multiply out and simplify:
  (a) $(a + 1)(2a + 1)$;   (b) $(p + q)(2p + q)$;
  (c) $(2p - 3)(3p + 2)$;   (d) $(2x - 3y)(3x + 2y)$;
  (e) $(a + 7)(2a - 5)$;   (f) $(a + 7b)(2a - 5b)$.

4 Multiply out and simplify:
  (a) $(q + 4)(2q - 3)$;   (b) $(t - 9)(t + 6)$;
  (c) $(3t - 4)(5t + 9)$;   (d) $(2r - 3)(3r - 4)$;
  (e) $(2r + 3s)(4r - 5s)$;   (f) $(R - r)(2R + r)$.

*5 Multiply out:
  (a) $(a + 3)(a - 3)$;   (b) $(b + 5)(b - 5)$;
  (c) $(2b + 5)(2b - 5)$;   (d) $(9p + 4q)(9p - 4q)$;
  (e) $(r - 7t)(r + 7t)$;   (f) $(4 + 3a)(4 - 3a)$.

6 Multiply out:
  (a) $(x + 7)(x - 7)$;   (b) $(y - 2)(y + 2)$;
  (c) $(2p - 3)(2p + 3)$;   (d) $(5p + 3q)(5p - 3q)$;
  (e) $(4p - 7t)(4p + 7t)$;   (f) $(5 - 3t)(5 + 3t)$.

*7 Multiply out:
  (a) $(x + 3)^2$;   (b) $(2x + 1)^2$;   (c) $(a - 5)^2$;
  (d) $(2p + 3)^2$;   (e) $(3a + 2b)^2$;   (f) $(3a - 2b)^2$.

8 Multiply out:
  (a) $(x - y)^2$;   (b) $(3p + 2)^2$;   (c) $(a - \frac{1}{2})^2$;
  (d) $(r - 3s)^2$;   (e) $(3 - p)^2$;   (f) $(4x - 3y)^2$.

*9 Calculate exactly:
  (a) $50\,563^2 - 49\,437^2$;   (b) $90^2 - 89.99^2$;   (c) $123\,456\,789^2 - 123\,456\,788^2$.

10 Calculate exactly:
  (a) $400\,003^2$;   (b) $399\,997^2$;   (c) $5.000\,01^2$.

*11 In Figure 8 the square $PQRS$ has been drawn with its vertices on the sides of the square $EFGH$. Write down expressions involving a and b for:
  (a) the area of the square $EFGH$;
  (b) the area of the triangle EPQ;
  (c) the area of the square $PQRS$.
  Simplify your answer to (c) as much as possible.
  How does this prove Pythagoras' theorem?

12 In Figure 9, triangles ASD, DRC and CQB are the images of triangle BAP under successive quarter-turns about the centre of the square $ABCD$; $BP = a$ and $AP = b$. Write down expressions involving a and b for;
  (a) PQ;
  (b) the area of $PQRS$;
  (c) the area of triangle BAP;
  (d) the area of $ABCD$.

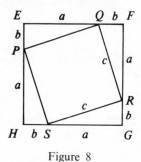

Figure 8

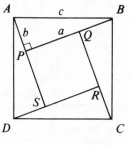

Figure 9

Simplify your answer to (*d*) as much as possible.

How does this prove Pythagoras' theorem?

(This diagram was published by the Indian mathematician Bhāskara (1114–1158); he could not use the algebraic explanation: the signs + and − did not appear in manuscripts until 1481, the = sign was introduced by Robert Recorde in the first English book on arithmetic in 1557, and the notation a^2 was not in common use until the seventeenth century.)

6. TESTS OF DIVISIBILITY

In this section we look at some quick ways of deciding whether one number is divisible by another. The first proofs are set out for four-figure numbers, but can be extended to deal with larger numbers. The *digits* of the number 4372 are 4, 3, 7 and 2, and $4372 = 4 \times 1000 + 3 \times 100 + 7 \times 10 + 2$. In general if the digits of a four-figure number are a, b, c and d (in that order) then the number is $1000a + 100b + 10c + d$.

Divisibility by 2

A number N is divisible by 2 ⟺ its last digit is even.

Proof: $N = 1000a + 100b + 10c + d$
$ = 2(500a + 50b + 5c) + d$
So N is divisible by 2 ⟺ d is divisible by 2
$ ⟺$ the last digit is even.

Divisibility by 3

A number N is divisible by 3 ⟺ the sum of its digits is divisible by 3.

Proof: $N = 1000a + 100b + 10c + d$
$ = 999a + 99b + 9c + a + b + c + d$
$ = 3(333a + 33b + 3c) + (a + b + c + d)$
So N is divisible by 3 ⟺ $a + b + c + d$ is divisible by 3, which is the result we require.

Divisibility by 11

Add and subtract the digits of any number N alternately; if the result is divisible by 11, then so is the original number. For example, 54 879 is divisible by 11 because $5 - 4 + 8 - 7 + 9 = 11$.

Proof for a five-figure number:
$$N = 10\,000a + 1000b + 100c + 10d + e$$
$$= (9999a + a) + (1001b - b) + (99c + c) + (11d - d) + e$$
$$= 9999a + 1001b + 99c + 11d + (a - b + c - d + e)$$
$$= 11(909a + 91b + 9c + d) + (a - b + c - d + e)$$
So N is divisible by 11 $\Leftrightarrow a - b + c - d + e$ is divisible by 11, which is the result we require.

Exercise F

*1 Use the above divisibility tests to write the following numbers as products of prime factors:
   (*a*) 1452;   (*b*) 3159;   (*c*) 1782;   (*d*) 5324.

2 Adapt the proof about divisibility by 2 to prove rules for divisibility by (*a*) 5;   (*b*) 10.

3 (*a*) Writing a number N as $100n + 10c + d$, where c and d are the last two digits of N, adapt the proof about divisibility by 2 to prove a rule for divisibility by 4.

   (*b*) Make a further adaptation to prove a rule for divisibility by 8.

4 Adapt the proof about divisibility by 3 to prove a rule for divisibility by 9.

5 How can you test whether a number is divisible by 6?

*6 Here is an illustration of a rule for testing divisibility by 7, applied to the number 18 347.

   183|47 $183 \times 2 = 366 +$
                                  47
                                  ———
                                413
   4|13 $4 \times 2 = $ $8 +$
                                    13
                                  ———
                                  21

21 is divisible by 7.
Therefore so is 413.   Therefore so is 18 347.
   Write a number N as $100n + 10c + d$. Use the fact that 98 is a multiple of 7 to explain why the rule works.

7 (*a*) Use the fact that 95 is a multiple of 19 to adapt the method given in question 6 to produce a method of testing for divisibility by 19.

   (*b*) Adapt further to obtain methods for testing for divisibility by 13 and 17. (Hint: $91 = 7 \times 13$; $102 = 6 \times 17$.)

*8 Write the following numbers as products of prime factors:
   (*a*) 315;   (*b*) 2574;   (*c*) 3465;   (*d*) 17 303.

9 Write the following numbers as products of prime factors:
   (*a*) 432;   (*b*) 9801;   (*c*) 9295;   (*d*) 1 127 357.

*10 (a) What are the factors of 111?

(b) Write down the prime factors of (i) 222;   (ii) 777;   (iii) 1221.

11 (a) What are the factors of 1001?

(b) Use your answer to explain why the following method for testing for divisibility by 7 works.

18 ¦ 347   347 −   329 is divisible by 7.
                18   Therefore 18 347 is divisible by 7.

                ___

                329

                ___

(c) Explain why the same procedure could be used for testing for divisibility by 13.

SUMMARY

A conjecture can be disproved by a single counter-example, but cannot be proved by a number of examples.   (Sections 1 and 2)

'$3n + 1 = 7 \Rightarrow n = 2$' can be read as 'if $3n + 1$ is equal to 7 then n is equal to 2'.

'$n = 2 \Rightarrow 3n + 1 = 7$'   is the converse of this statement. It can also be written as '$3n + 1 = 7 \Leftarrow n = 2$'   which can be read as '$3n + 1 = 7$ if $n = 2$'.

'$3n + 1 = 7 \Leftrightarrow n = 2$' can be read as '$3n + 1 = 7$ if and only if $n = 2$'.

(Section 3)

$$a(x + y) = ax + ay$$
$$(a + b)(c + d) = ac + ad + bc + bd$$
$$(a + b)(a - b) = a^2 - b^2$$
$$(a + b)^2 \quad = a^2 + 2ab + b^2$$
$$(a - b)^2 \quad = a^2 - 2ab + b^2$$

(Section 5)

Summary exercise

1 (a) Calculate the matrix product $\begin{bmatrix} 1 & 2 \\ 0 & 1 \end{bmatrix} \begin{bmatrix} 1 & 2 \\ 0 & 1 \end{bmatrix}$.

(b) Is it always true that $\begin{bmatrix} 1 & k \\ 0 & 1 \end{bmatrix} \begin{bmatrix} 1 & k \\ 0 & 1 \end{bmatrix} = \begin{bmatrix} 1 & k^2 \\ 0 & 1 \end{bmatrix}$?

2 Prove that the product of two odd numbers is odd.

3 (a) State whether the following statements are true or false:

(i) N is divisible by $3 \Rightarrow N^2$ is divisible by 9.

(ii) $x^2 > 4 \Leftarrow x < {}^-2$.

(iii) Three hours ago it was 8 a.m. $\Rightarrow$ It is now 11 a.m.

(iv) Three hours ago it was N o'clock $\Rightarrow$ It is now $N + 3$ o'clock.

(b) Write down the converses of the four statements above.

(c) State whether the converses are true or false.

4 Multiply out and simplify:

(a) $4p(5q - 3r)$;   (b) $(p - 3)(p - 2)$;

(c) $(p - 6)(p + 1)$;   (d) $(2p + 5q)(3p - 7q)$.

5 Multiply out:
   (a) $(x + 9)(x - 9)$;   (b) $(2 - 3t)(2 + 3t)$;
   (c) $(3t + 1)^2$;   (d) $(2 - 3r)^2$.

6 Write the following numbers as products of prime factors:
   (a) 324;   (b) 343;   (c) 4389;   (d) 12 144.

Miscellaneous exercise

1 (a) Explain why the product of two consecutive numbers is even.
   (b) Explain why the product of three consecutive numbers is divisible by 6.
   (c) Explain why if the first of three consecutive numbers is even their product is divisible by 24.

2 Drawing one straight line divides a plane into two regions. With two straight lines there are four regions. (See Figure 10.)
   (a) How many regions are there when three straight lines are drawn? Does it matter where the straight lines are drawn?
   (b) Find how many regions there are when   (i) four,   (ii) five,   lines are drawn.
   (c) Can you make a general statement about the number of regions when n lines are drawn?

(a)   (b)   (c)

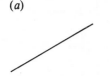 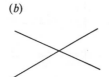 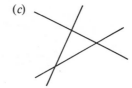

Figure 10

3 $5\frac{1}{2}$ is between 5 and 6. $5 \times 6 = 30$. $(5\frac{1}{2})^2 = (\frac{11}{2})^2 = \frac{121}{4} = 30\frac{1}{4}$.
   Similarly $(7\frac{1}{2})^2 = 7 \times 8 + \frac{1}{4} = 56\frac{1}{4}$.
   (a) Investigate whether this method works for $(1\frac{1}{2})^2$ and $(3\frac{1}{2})^2$.
   (b) Multiply out: (i) $(n + \frac{1}{2})^2$;   (ii) $n(n + 1)$ and use your answers to explain the method.

4 A right-angled triangle has hypotenuse of length x. The other two sides are of lengths 8   and $x - 2$. Use Pythagoras' theorem to find x.

5 A piston of radius 2.347 cm is designed to fit inside a cylinder of radius 2.355 cm (see Figure 11). Find the cross-sectional area of the gap between the piston and cylinder. What are the upper and lower bounds for your answer?

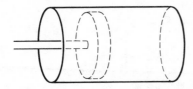

Figure 11

6 The process of 'top-ending' a number is defined as placing the first digit (from the left) at the end. For example, top-ending 563 gives 635 and top-ending 4720 gives 7204.

(a) If x is a number between 0 and 99, what number is obtained when $200 + x$ is top-ended?

(b) Find a number N between 200 and 300 such that top-ending N gives $\frac{3}{4}N$.

(c) Find a five-figure number N such that top-ending N gives $\frac{9}{5}N$.

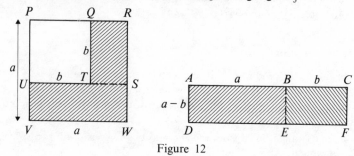

Figure 12

7   Explain how Figure 12 illustrates that $a^2 - b^2 = (a + b)(a - b)$.

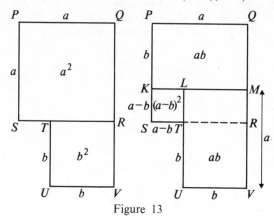

Figure 13

8   Explain how Figure 13 illustrates that $(a - b)^2 = a^2 - 2ab + b^2$.

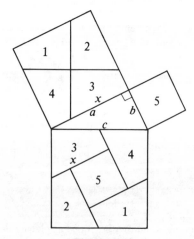

Figure 14

9 Explain how Figure 14 (Perigal's dissection) demonstrates Pythagoras' theorem. Can you write x in terms of a and b?

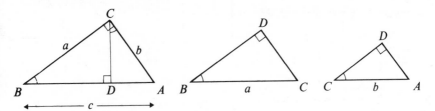

Figure 15

10 In Figure 15 the three triangles are similar.
  (a) What is the ratio of the lengths of the sides of the three triangles?
  (b) What is the ratio of their areas?
  (c) Explain how you can deduce Pythagoras' theorem from (b).

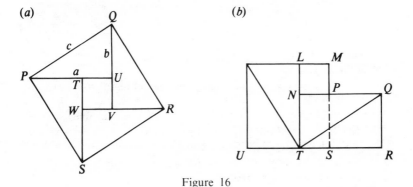

Figure 16

11 Explain how Figure 16 demonstrates Pythagoras' theorem.

Generalising

12 The sum of two consecutive odd numbers is divisible by 4. Can you make similar statements about
  (a) the sum of three consecutive odd numbers;
  (b) the sum of four consecutive odd numbers?
  Prove your assertions.

13 (a) Prove that the sum of the squares of five consecutive integers is divisible by 5. (Hint: take the middle integer as n, so that the five integers are $n-2, n-1, n, n+1, n+2$.)
  (b) Can you make similar statements about the sum of the squares of (i) three consecutive integers; (ii) seven consecutive integers; (iii) nine consecutive integers?
  (c) Can you make a general statement about the values of k for which the sum of the squares of k consecutive integers is divisible by k?
  (d) Can you prove any of your statements in (b) and (c)?

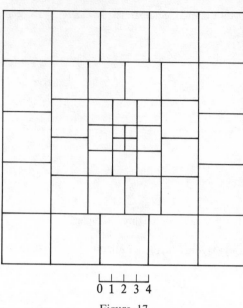

A   P   B

S   Q

D   R   C

Figure 18

0 1 2 3 4

Figure 17

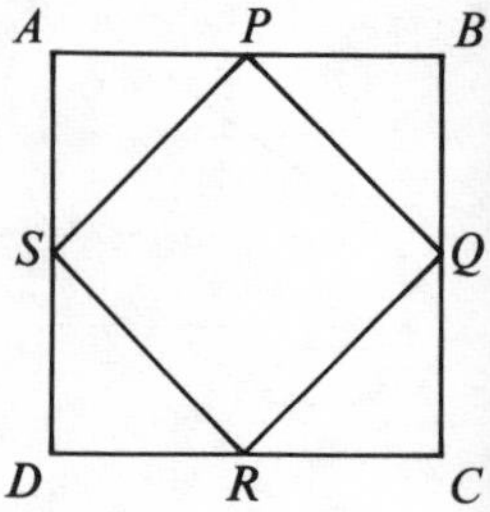

14 Look at Figure 17.

    (a) How many squares have been drawn of side (i) 1 unit;   (ii) 2 units; (iii) 3 units?

    (b) Explain why the total area is $4(1^3 + 2^3 + 3^3 + 4^3)$ square units.

    (c) Explain why the area can also be written as $4(1 + 2 + 3 + 4)^2$ square units.

What general statement can be made about $1^3 + 2^3 + 3^3 + 4^3 + \ldots + n^3$?

15 (a) P, Q, R, S are the midpoints of the sides of a square $ABCD$ (see Figure 18). What kind of quadrilateral is PQRS?

    (b) What kind of quadrilateral is $PQRS$ if $ABCD$ is

        (i) a rectangle;   (ii) a parallelogram;   (iii) any quadrilateral?

    (c) (i) What is the image of PS under enlargement, centre A and scale factor 2?

        (ii) What is the image of QR under enlargement, centre C and scale factor 2?

        (iii) What do your answers to (i) and (ii) tell you about PS and QR? How does this justify your answer to (b) (iii)?

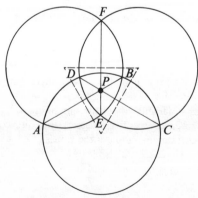

Figure 19

16 Three circles with equal radii are drawn with their centres at the vertices of an equilateral triangle (see Figure 19). From considerations of symmetry it is clear that the three chords joining the points of intersection of each pair of circles
(i) all pass through a point P (the centre of rotational symmetry of the diagram);
(ii) cut at angles of 120°.
Investigate whether (i) and (ii) appear to be still true if:
  (*a*) the centres of the circles are not at the vertices of an equilateral triangle;
  (*b*) the circles do not have equal radii but their centres are at the vertices of an equilateral triangle;
  (*c*) the circles do not have equal radii nor are their centres at the vertices of an equilateral triangle.

17 Figure 20 shows part of a tessellation of equilateral triangles. Explain why
  (i) $AX = BY = CZ$;
  (ii) AX, BY and CZ are concurrent (i.e. they all pass through a point P);
  (iii) AX, BY and CZ cut at angles of 120°;
  (iv) $AP + BP + CP = AX$.
(Hint for (iv): notice that triangle BPX is 'half' of an equilateral triangle; what is the relationship between the lengths of BP and PX?) Investigate whether (i)–(iv) appear to be true if:
  (*a*) the tessellation is of non-equilateral triangles (see Figure 21);
  (*b*) ABC is not equilateral, but ABZ, ACY and BCX are equilateral (see Figure 22).

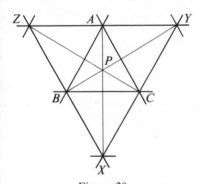

Figure 20

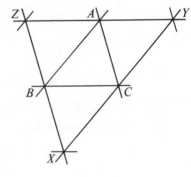

Figure 21

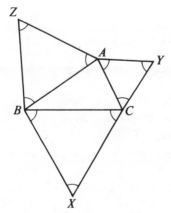

Figure 22

Fallacies

18   The area of the square in Figure 23 is 64 square units.

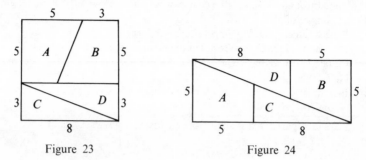

Figure 23   Figure 24

The area of the rectangle in Figure 24 is 65 square units.

But both diagrams are constructed from the trapeziums *A* and *B* and the two triangles *C* and *D*. It follows that

$$64 = 65.$$

Try drawing the diagram. Can you explain what has happened?

19 $1 = 2$.

'Proof': $a = b \Rightarrow ab = b^2$
$\Rightarrow ab - a^2 = b^2 - a^2$
$\Rightarrow a(b - a) = (b + a)(b - a)$
$\Rightarrow a = b + a$
$\Rightarrow a = a + a = 2a$
$\Rightarrow 1 = 2$.

Only one of the steps is incorrect. Which one is it?

20   All numbers are equal to 1.

'Proof': For any number *a*,
$(a - 1)^2 = a^2 - 2a + 1$ and $(1 - a)^2 = 1 - 2a + a^2 = a^2 - 2a + 1$
Hence $a - 1 = 1 - a$
$2a = 2$
$a = 1$
What is incorrect about this argument?

21   Every triangle is isosceles.

'Proof': In any triangle ABC, draw the bisector of the angle BAC and the mediator of BC. Call their point of intersection P (see Figure 25).

Since P is on the mediator of BC, $PB = PC$.

Since AP bisects the angle BAC, reflection in the line AP maps the line AB to the line AC. So the image of B under this reflection, B', is on AC, and $PB' = PB = PC$.

That is, B' is on AC and B' is the same distance from P as C is from P.
So B' must be at C.

This reflection maps AB to AC. Therefore $AB = AC$.

Triangle ABC is isosceles.

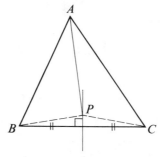

Figure 25

Draw an accurate diagram and discover what is wrong with this 'proof'.

17

Transformations and matrices

1. RULES FOR TRANSFORMATIONS

Figure 1 shows a quadrilateral $ABCD$ and its image $A'B'C'D'$ under enlargement, centre the origin and scale factor 2. From the diagram we can see that the point A with coordinates $(3, 1)$ is mapped to the point A' with coordinates $(6, 2)$.

Also: $B(^-1, 3)$ is mapped to $B'(^-2, 6)$,

$C(^-2, ^-3)$ is mapped to $C'(^-4, ^-6)$

and $D(1, ^-2)$ is mapped to $D'(2, ^-4)$.

In each case the coordinates are doubled, since $\underset{\sim}{O}A' = 2\underset{\sim}{O}A$ and so on. If we write (x', y') for the coordinates of the image of the point with coordinates (x, y) we can write

$$x' = 2x$$
$$y' = 2y.$$

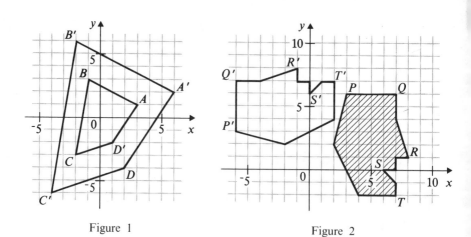

Figure 1 Figure 2

Figure 2 shows an object (shaded) and its image under the quarter-turn about the origin. In this case the point P with coordinates $(3, 6)$ is mapped to the point P' with coordinates $(^-6, 3)$.

Also: $Q\,(7, 6)$ is mapped to $Q'\,(^-6, 7)$,

$R\,(8, 1)$ is mapped to $R'\,(^-1, 8)$,

$S\,(6, 0)$ is mapped to $S'\,(0, 6)$

and $T\,(7, ^-2)$ is mapped to $T'\,(2, 7)$.

In general, if (x, y) are the coordinates of any point of the object, then the coordinates of its image are $(^-y, x)$. Using (x', y') for these new coordinates, the transformation can be given by the rule

$$x' = {}^-y$$
$$y' = x.$$

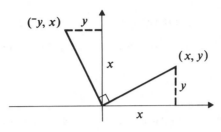

Figure 3

Exercise A

(All questions should be attempted; the answers will be needed in Exercise B.)
For each of the transformations in questions 1–8:
(a) draw the image of the quadrilateral $ABCD$ shown in Figure 4;
(b) write down the coordinates of the images of A, B, C and D;
(c) write down a rule for the transformation in the form $x' = ...$
$$y' = ...$$

*1 Reflection in the x-axis.

2 Reflection in the y-axis.

*3 The half-turn about the origin.

4 The three-quarter turn about the origin.

*5 Reflection in the line $y = x$.

6 The identity transformation.

*7 Reflection in the line $x + y = 0$.

8 Enlargement, centre the origin and scale factor 3.

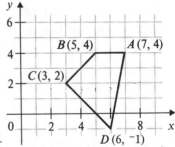

Figure 4

2. MATRICES FOR TRANSFORMATIONS

The rules we have met so far in this chapter have included

$$x' = 3x \qquad x' = {}^-y \qquad x' = x$$
$$y' = 3y, \qquad y' = x, \qquad y' = {}^-y.$$

In each case we have a number of xs and ys on the right-hand side, and we could use a (2 row, 2 column) matrix to store the information about how many of each we have. For example, the rule for the quarter-turn about the origin is:

$$x' = {}^-y$$
$$y' = x$$

which can be written as:

$$x' = 0x + {}^-1y$$
$$y' = 1x + 0y$$

and therefore represented by the matrix

$$\begin{bmatrix} 0 & {}^-1 \\ 1 & 0 \end{bmatrix}.$$

Similarly, the rule for enlargement, centre the origin and scale factor 2, is $\begin{aligned} x' &= 2x = 2x + 0y \\ y' &= 2y = 0x + 2y \end{aligned}$ and it is therefore represented by the matrix $\begin{bmatrix} 2 & 0 \\ 0 & 2 \end{bmatrix}.$

Exercise B

Write down the (2 row, 2 column) matrices for each of the transformations of Exercise *A*, questions 1–8.

3. INTERPRETING A MATRIX

Any (2 row, 2 column) matrix can be interpreted as a rule for a transformation. For example, the matrix $\begin{bmatrix} 3 & {}^-2 \\ 2 & 3 \end{bmatrix}$ represents the transformation given by the rule

$$x' = 3x - 2y$$
$$y' = 2x + 3y.$$

If the transformation **S** given by this rule maps the point *A* with coordinates (5, 4) to the point **S**(*A*), then the coordinates of **S**(*A*) are

$$x' = 3 \times 5 - 2 \times 4 = 7$$
$$y' = 2 \times 5 + 3 \times 4 = 22.$$

Notice that this result is also obtained by using the matrix product

$$\begin{bmatrix} 3 & {}^-2 \\ 2 & 3 \end{bmatrix}\begin{bmatrix} 5 \\ 4 \end{bmatrix} = \begin{bmatrix} 7 \\ 22 \end{bmatrix}$$

where the coordinates of *A* and **S**(*A*) appear in the column matrices $\begin{bmatrix} 5 \\ 4 \end{bmatrix}$ and $\begin{bmatrix} 7 \\ 22 \end{bmatrix}.$ Similarly from the matrix products

$$\begin{bmatrix} 3 & {}^-2 \\ 2 & 3 \end{bmatrix}\begin{bmatrix} 4 \\ 6 \end{bmatrix} = \begin{bmatrix} 0 \\ 26 \end{bmatrix} \text{ and } \begin{bmatrix} 3 & {}^-2 \\ 2 & 3 \end{bmatrix}\begin{bmatrix} 3 \\ 8 \end{bmatrix} = \begin{bmatrix} {}^-7 \\ 30 \end{bmatrix}$$

we can deduce that **S** maps *B* (4, 6) to **S**(*B*) (0, 26) and *C* (3, 8) to **S**(*C*) (⁻7, 30). (See Figure 5.)

All three results can be combined in the single matrix product

$$\begin{array}{ccc} A & B & C \end{array} \qquad \begin{array}{ccc} S(A) & S(B) & S(C) \end{array}$$
$$\begin{bmatrix} 3 & {}^-2 \\ 2 & 3 \end{bmatrix}\begin{bmatrix} 5 & 4 & 3 \\ 4 & 6 & 8 \end{bmatrix} = \begin{bmatrix} 7 & 0 & {}^-7 \\ 22 & 26 & 30 \end{bmatrix}.$$

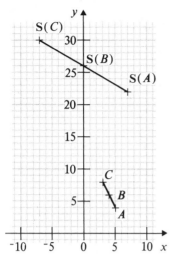

Figure 5

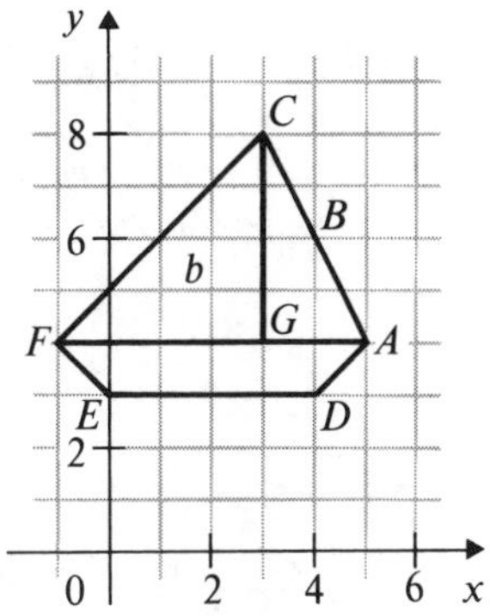

Figure 6

Exercise C

Questions 1–5 refer to the transformation **S** given by the matrix $\begin{bmatrix} 3 & {}^-2 \\ 2 & 3 \end{bmatrix}$.

*1 Find the coordinates of the images of the points $D(4, 3)$, $E(0, 3)$, $F({}^-1, 4)$ and $G(3, 4)$ under the transformation **S**.

2 (a) Use the answers in the section above and your answers to question 1 to draw **S**(b) where b is the 'boat' in Figure 6. (You will need values of x between about ${}^-12$ and 10 and values of y between 0 and 30.)
   (b) What does the transformation **S** do?

*3 (a) Calculate the matrix product $\begin{bmatrix} 3 & {}^-2 \\ 2 & 3 \end{bmatrix} \begin{bmatrix} 0 & 1 & 2 & 3 & 4 \\ 3 & 3 & 3 & 3 & 3 \end{bmatrix}$.
   (b) The points with coordinates $(0, 3)$, $(1, 3)$, $(2, 3)$, $(3, 3)$ and $(4, 3)$ are evenly spaced along the 'keel' of the boat b, the line $y = 3$.
     (i) Show these points and their images under **S** on a diagram.
     (ii) Are the images on a straight line? Are they evenly spaced?
     (iii) What is the image of the line $y = 3$?

4 (a) Calculate the matrix product $\begin{bmatrix} 3 & {}^-2 \\ 2 & 3 \end{bmatrix} \begin{bmatrix} 3 & 3 & 3 & 3 & 3 \\ 4 & 5 & 6 & 7 & 8 \end{bmatrix}$.
   (b) The points with coordinates $(3, 4)$, $(3, 5)$, $(3, 6)$, $(3, 7)$ and $(3, 8)$ are evenly spaced along the 'mast' of the boat b, the line $x = 3$.
     (i) Show these points and their images under **S** on a diagram.
     (ii) Are the images on a straight line? Are they evenly spaced?
     (iii) What is the image of the line $x = 3$?

*5 What is the image of the point $(0, 0)$ under the transformation **S**?

6 The transformation **M** is represented by the matrix $\begin{bmatrix} 0.6 & 0.8 \\ 0.8 & {}^-0.6 \end{bmatrix}$.

(a) Copy and complete the matrix product

$$\begin{bmatrix} 0.6 & 0.8 \\ 0.8 & ^-0.6 \end{bmatrix} \begin{bmatrix} 1 & 6 & 7 & 5 & 0 & 5 \\ 3 & 3 & 6 & 10 & 5 & 5 \end{bmatrix} = \begin{bmatrix} 3 & * & * & * & * & 7 \\ * & 3 & * & ^-2 & * & * \end{bmatrix}$$

and hence write down the coordinates of the images of the points $A(1, 3)$, $B(6, 3)$, $C(7, 6)$, $D(5, 10)$, $E(0, 5)$ and $F(5, 5)$ under the transformation **M**.

(b) Draw the boat d shown in Figure 7 and its image $\mathbf{M}(d)$.

(c) Describe the transformation **M** as precisely as you can.

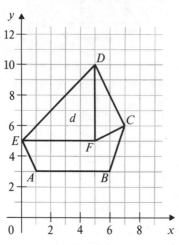

Figure 7

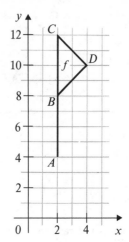

Figure 8

*7   The transformation **N** is represented by the matrix $\begin{bmatrix} 0.8 & ^-0.6 \\ 0.6 & 0.8 \end{bmatrix}$.

(a) Find the coordinates of the images of the points A, B, C, D and E, shown in Figure 7, under the transformation **N**.

(b) Draw the boat d shown in Figure 7 and its image $\mathbf{N}(d)$.

(c) What is the image of the point $(0, 0)$ under **N**?

(d) Describe the transformation **N** as precisely as you can.

8   The transformation **T** is represented by the matrix $\begin{bmatrix} \frac{1}{2} & \frac{1}{2} \\ -\frac{1}{2} & \frac{3}{2} \end{bmatrix}$.

(a) Find the coordinates of the images of the points A, B, C and D, shown in Figure 8, under the transformation **T**.

(b) Draw the flag f shown in Figure 8 and its image $\mathbf{T}(f)$.

(c) Can you describe the effect of **T** on f?

*9   (a) Calculate the matrix product $\begin{bmatrix} 1 & 2 \\ ^-1 & 3 \end{bmatrix} \begin{bmatrix} 6 & 5 & 4 & 3 \\ 0 & 1 & 2 & 3 \end{bmatrix}$.

(b) The points with coordinates $(6, 0)$, $(5, 1)$, $(4, 2)$ and $(3, 3)$ are evenly spaced along the line with equation $x + y = 6$. Show, on a diagram, their images under the transformation represented by the matrix $\begin{bmatrix} 1 & 2 \\ ^-1 & 3 \end{bmatrix}$.

(i) Are these images on a straight line?

(ii) Are the images evenly spaced?

10 What is the image of the point (0, 0) under the transformation represented by the matrix $\begin{bmatrix} a & b \\ c & d \end{bmatrix}$?

4. COMBINING TRANSFORMATIONS

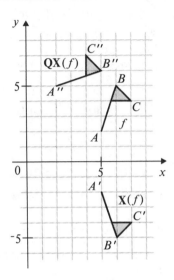

Figure 9

Figure 9 shows a flag f, its image $\mathbf{X}(f)$ under reflection in the x-axis, and $\mathbf{QX}(f)$, the image of $\mathbf{X}(f)$ under the quarter-turn $\mathbf{Q}$ about the origin. Notice that $\mathbf{QX}(f)$ is the image of f under the reflection $\mathbf{X}$ followed by the rotation $\mathbf{Q}$.

The rule for $\mathbf{Q}$ is $\begin{aligned} x' &= {}^-y \\ y' &= x \end{aligned}$ and so the matrix for $\mathbf{Q}$ is $\begin{bmatrix} 0 & {}^-1 \\ 1 & 0 \end{bmatrix}$.

The rule for $\mathbf{X}$ is $\begin{aligned} x' &= x \\ y' &= {}^-y \end{aligned}$ and so the matrix for $\mathbf{X}$ is $\begin{bmatrix} 1 & 0 \\ 0 & {}^-1 \end{bmatrix}$.

We now investigate the relation between these matrices and the matrix for $\mathbf{QX}$. The effect of $\mathbf{X}$ on the flag f can be found from the matrix product

$$\begin{bmatrix} 1 & 0 \\ 0 & {}^-1 \end{bmatrix} \overset{\begin{matrix} A & B & C \end{matrix}}{\begin{bmatrix} 5 & 6 & 7 \\ 2 & 5 & 4 \end{bmatrix}} = \overset{\begin{matrix} A' & B' & C' \end{matrix}}{\begin{bmatrix} 5 & 6 & 7 \\ {}^-2 & {}^-5 & {}^-4 \end{bmatrix}}.$$

The effect of $\mathbf{Q}$ on the flag $\mathbf{X}(f)$ can be found from the matrix product

$$\begin{bmatrix} 0 & {}^-1 \\ 1 & 0 \end{bmatrix} \overset{\begin{matrix} A' & B' & C' \end{matrix}}{\begin{bmatrix} 5 & 6 & 7 \\ {}^-2 & {}^-5 & {}^-4 \end{bmatrix}} = \overset{\begin{matrix} A'' & B'' & C'' \end{matrix}}{\begin{bmatrix} 2 & 5 & 4 \\ 5 & 6 & 7 \end{bmatrix}}.$$

Combining these, we have

$$\begin{array}{ccccccccc} \mathbf{Q} & \mathbf{X} & A & B & C & \mathbf{Q} & A' & B' & C' & A'' & B'' & C'' \end{array}$$

$$\begin{bmatrix} 0 & ^-1 \\ 1 & 0 \end{bmatrix}\begin{bmatrix} 1 & 0 \\ 0 & ^-1 \end{bmatrix}\begin{bmatrix} 5 & 6 & 7 \\ 2 & 5 & 4 \end{bmatrix} = \begin{bmatrix} 0 & ^-1 \\ 1 & 0 \end{bmatrix}\begin{bmatrix} 5 & 6 & 7 \\ ^-2 & ^-5 & ^-4 \end{bmatrix} = \begin{bmatrix} 2 & 5 & 4 \\ 5 & 6 & 7 \end{bmatrix}$$

so that we obtain the effect of **QX** by multiplying by their matrices *in that order*.

$$\begin{bmatrix} \text{matrix} \\ \text{for } \mathbf{QX} \end{bmatrix} = \begin{bmatrix} \text{matrix} \\ \text{for } \mathbf{Q} \end{bmatrix}\begin{bmatrix} \text{matrix} \\ \text{for } \mathbf{X} \end{bmatrix}.$$

In fact the rule for multiplying matrices given in Chapter 14 was chosen so that multiplying matrices would correspond to combining transformations in this way. For any transformations **A** and **B** represented by matrices,

$$\begin{bmatrix} \text{matrix} \\ \text{for } \mathbf{AB} \end{bmatrix} = \begin{bmatrix} \text{matrix} \\ \text{for } \mathbf{A} \end{bmatrix}\begin{bmatrix} \text{matrix} \\ \text{for } \mathbf{B} \end{bmatrix}.$$

Exercise D

*1   If t is the triangle with vertices $P(2, 0)$, $Q(4, 0)$ and $R(4, 3)$,

A is the transformation represented by the matrix $\begin{bmatrix} 0 & 1 \\ 1 & 0 \end{bmatrix}$

and   **B** is the transformation represented by the matrix $\begin{bmatrix} ^-1 & 0 \\ 0 & 1 \end{bmatrix}$,

(a) find the coordinates of the vertices of **A**(t) and of **BA**(t), and draw a diagram showing t, **A**(t) and **BA**(t);

(b) describe precisely the transformations **A**, **B** and **BA**.

The transformation **C** is given by the matrix product $\begin{bmatrix} ^-1 & 0 \\ 0 & 1 \end{bmatrix}\begin{bmatrix} 0 & 1 \\ 1 & 0 \end{bmatrix}$.

(c) Calculate this product.

(d) Find the coordinates of the vertices of **C**(t), and show **C**(t) on your diagram. What can you deduce about **C**?

2   If v is the triangle with vertices $K(2, 1)$, $L(4, ^-1)$ and $M(4, 4)$,

C is the transformation represented by the matrix $\begin{bmatrix} 0 & ^-1 \\ ^-1 & 0 \end{bmatrix}$

and   **D** is the transformation represented by the matrix $\begin{bmatrix} 0 & 1 \\ ^-1 & 0 \end{bmatrix}$,

(a) find the coordinates of the vertices of **C**(v) and of **DC**(v), and draw a diagram showing v, **C**(v) and **DC**(v);

(b) describe precisely the transformations **C**, **D** and **DC**.

The transformation **E** is given by the matrix product $\begin{bmatrix} 0 & 1 \\ ^-1 & 0 \end{bmatrix}\begin{bmatrix} 0 & ^-1 \\ ^-1 & 0 \end{bmatrix}$.

(c) Calculate this product.

(d) Find the coordinates of the vertices of **E**(v), and show **E**(v) on your diagram. What can you deduce about **E**?

*3   If the transformation **M** is represented by the matrix $\begin{bmatrix} 0 & 1 \\ 1 & 0 \end{bmatrix}$ and the transformation **N** is given by the matrix $\begin{bmatrix} 0 & 1 \\ ^-1 & 0 \end{bmatrix}$,

(a) calculate the products (i) $\begin{bmatrix} \text{matrix} \\ \text{for M} \end{bmatrix}\begin{bmatrix} \text{matrix} \\ \text{for N} \end{bmatrix}$ and (ii) $\begin{bmatrix} \text{matrix} \\ \text{for N} \end{bmatrix}\begin{bmatrix} \text{matrix} \\ \text{for M} \end{bmatrix}$.

(b) If t is the triangle with vertices at $A(2, 1)$, $B(5, 2)$ and $C(5, 4)$,
    (i) find the coordinates of the vertices of $\mathbf{M}(t)$, $\mathbf{N}(t)$, $\mathbf{MN}(t)$ and $\mathbf{NM}(t)$;
    (ii) show t, $\mathbf{M}(t)$, $\mathbf{N}(t)$, $\mathbf{MN}(t)$ and $\mathbf{NM}(t)$ on a single diagram.

(c) Describe precisely the transformations $\mathbf{M}$, $\mathbf{N}$, $\mathbf{MN}$ and $\mathbf{NM}$.

4 If the transformation $\mathbf{P}$ is represented by the matrix $\begin{bmatrix} 2 & ^-1 \\ 1 & 2 \end{bmatrix}$ and the transformation $\mathbf{Q}$ is represented by the matrix $\begin{bmatrix} 0.2 & ^-0.4 \\ 0.4 & 0.2 \end{bmatrix}$,

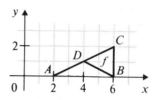

Figure 10

(a) find the coordinates of the images of the points A, B, C and D on the flag f shown in Figure 10 under the transformations (i) $\mathbf{P}$; (ii) $\mathbf{QP}$;

(b) show f, $\mathbf{P}(f)$ and $\mathbf{QP}(f)$ on a diagram;

(c) describe precisely the transformation $\mathbf{QP}$;

(d) calculate the product $\begin{bmatrix} \text{matrix} \\ \text{for Q} \end{bmatrix}\begin{bmatrix} \text{matrix} \\ \text{for P} \end{bmatrix}$.

*5 If $\mathbf{I} = \begin{bmatrix} 1 & 0 \\ 0 & 1 \end{bmatrix}$, $\mathbf{X} = \begin{bmatrix} 1 & 0 \\ 0 & ^-1 \end{bmatrix}$, $\mathbf{Y} = \begin{bmatrix} ^-1 & 0 \\ 0 & 1 \end{bmatrix}$ and $\mathbf{H} = \begin{bmatrix} ^-1 & 0 \\ 0 & ^-1 \end{bmatrix}$, copy and complete the combination table below. (For example the entry given shows that $\mathbf{XY} = \mathbf{H}$.) What transformations are represented by the matrices $\mathbf{I}$, $\mathbf{X}$, $\mathbf{Y}$ and $\mathbf{H}$?

		Right matrix		
		I	X	Y	H
	I				
Left	**X**			**H**	
matrix	**Y**				
	H				

6 If $\mathbf{I} = \begin{bmatrix} 1 & 0 \\ 0 & 1 \end{bmatrix}$, $\mathbf{Q} = \begin{bmatrix} 0 & ^-1 \\ 1 & 0 \end{bmatrix}$, $\mathbf{H} = \begin{bmatrix} ^-1 & 0 \\ 0 & ^-1 \end{bmatrix}$ and $\mathbf{T} = \begin{bmatrix} 0 & 1 \\ ^-1 & 0 \end{bmatrix}$, copy and complete the combination table below. What transformations are represented by the matrices $\mathbf{I}$, $\mathbf{Q}$, $\mathbf{H}$ and $\mathbf{T}$?

		Right matrix		
		I	Q	H	T
	I				
Left	**Q**				
matrix	**H**				
	T				

7 If $\begin{matrix} x' = ax + by \\ y' = cx + dy \end{matrix}$ and $\begin{matrix} x'' = px' + qy' \\ x'' = rx' + sy' \end{matrix}$, show that $\begin{matrix} x'' = (pa + qc)x + (pb + qd)y \\ y'' = (ra + sc)x + (rb + sd)y \end{matrix}$.

Compare this with the matrix product $\begin{bmatrix} p & q \\ r & s \end{bmatrix}\begin{bmatrix} a & b \\ c & d \end{bmatrix}$.

5. TRANSFORMATIONS AND VECTORS

Exercise E

1   Figure 11 shows a flotilla of boats. Find their images under the transformation represented by the matrix $\begin{bmatrix} 1 & ^-2 \\ 2 & 1 \end{bmatrix}$. Show the images on a diagram (with values of x and y between $^-15$ and 15). Use your diagram to answer questions 2–5.

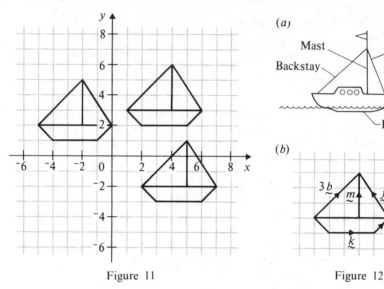

Figure 11   Figure 12

*2   The keel of each boat in Figure 11 is given by the vector $\underset{\sim}{k} = \begin{bmatrix} 3 \\ 0 \end{bmatrix}$.
What vector(s) correspond to the keels of the images?

3   The mast of each boat in Figure 11 is given by the vector $\underset{\sim}{m} = \begin{bmatrix} 0 \\ 3 \end{bmatrix}$.
What vector(s) correspond to the masts of the images?

*4   The forestay of each boat in Figure 11 is given by the vector $\underset{\sim}{f} = \begin{bmatrix} ^-2 \\ 3 \end{bmatrix}$.
What vector(s) correspond to the forestays of the images?

5   (a) The bow of each boat in Figure 11 is given by the vector $\underset{\sim}{b} = \begin{bmatrix} 1 \\ 1 \end{bmatrix}$.
What vector(s) correspond to the bows of the images?
(b) The backstay of each boat in Figure 11 is given by the vector $3b$. What vector corresponds to the backstays of the images? What is its relation to the vector of the images of the bows?

6   Find the images of the points with coordinates (3, 0), (0, 3), ($^-2$, 3), (1, 1) and (3, 3). Compare your answers with your answers to questions 2–5.

7–12   Repeat questions 1–6 with the same flotilla, but using the matrix $\begin{bmatrix} 3 & 1 \\ 1 & 2 \end{bmatrix}$. (You will need to allow for values of x and y between about $^-15$ and 20 in your diagram.)

Vectors and position vectors

You will have noticed in Exercise E, question 4, that the images of all the forestays were equal and parallel. The transformation appears to map the vector $\begin{bmatrix} -2 \\ 3 \end{bmatrix}$ to the vector $\begin{bmatrix} -8 \\ -1 \end{bmatrix}$.

Figure 13 shows another boat and its image under the transformation represented by the matrix $\begin{bmatrix} 1 & -2 \\ 2 & 1 \end{bmatrix}$. Notice that again the image of $\underset{\sim}{f} = \begin{bmatrix} -2 \\ 3 \end{bmatrix}$ is $\begin{bmatrix} -8 \\ -1 \end{bmatrix}$.

But F has coordinates $(^-2, 3)$ and F' has coordinates $(^-8, ^-1)$: components of vectors are transformed in the same way as the coordinates of points. A method of proof of this result is suggested in the Miscellaneous exercise, questions 4, 5 and 6.

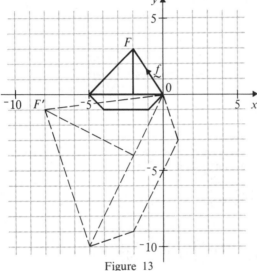

Figure 13

The vector $\underset{\sim}{OF} = \begin{bmatrix} -2 \\ 3 \end{bmatrix}$ is called the position vector of F relative to O.

Throughout this chapter we have really been considering transformations of position vectors, but general vectors are transformed in the same way. This result can often be used to find the image of a complicated figure under a transformation.

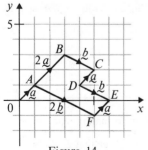

Figure 14

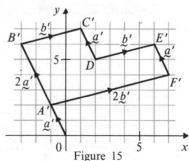

Figure 15

Figure 14 shows a figure drawn using the vectors $\underset{\sim}{a} = \begin{bmatrix} 1 \\ 1 \end{bmatrix}$ and $\underset{\sim}{b} = \begin{bmatrix} 2 \\ -1 \end{bmatrix}$. Its image under the transformation represented by the matrix $\begin{bmatrix} 1 & -2 \\ 1 & 1 \end{bmatrix}$ can quickly be drawn using

$$\underset{\sim}{a}' = \begin{bmatrix} 1 & -2 \\ 1 & 1 \end{bmatrix}\begin{bmatrix} 1 \\ 1 \end{bmatrix} = \begin{bmatrix} -1 \\ 2 \end{bmatrix}$$

$$\text{and } \underset{\sim}{b}' = \begin{bmatrix} 1 & -2 \\ 1 & 1 \end{bmatrix}\begin{bmatrix} 2 \\ -1 \end{bmatrix} = \begin{bmatrix} 4 \\ 1 \end{bmatrix}.$$

The image is shown in Figure 15.

Exercise F

*1 (a) Calculate $\begin{bmatrix} 1 & -2 \\ 0 & 1 \end{bmatrix}\begin{bmatrix} 1 \\ 2 \end{bmatrix}$ and $\begin{bmatrix} 1 & -2 \\ 0 & 1 \end{bmatrix}\begin{bmatrix} 2 \\ 0 \end{bmatrix}.$

(b) Use your answers to (a) to draw the image of the flag in Figure 16 under the transformation represented by the matrix $\begin{bmatrix} 1 & -2 \\ 0 & 1 \end{bmatrix}.$

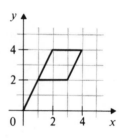

Figure 16

2 (a) Calculate $\begin{bmatrix} 1 & 0 \\ -1 & 3 \end{bmatrix}\begin{bmatrix} 1 \\ 2 \end{bmatrix}$ and $\begin{bmatrix} 1 & 0 \\ -1 & 3 \end{bmatrix}\begin{bmatrix} 2 \\ 0 \end{bmatrix}.$

(b) Use your answers to (a) to draw the image of the flag in Figure 16 under the transformation represented by the matrix $\begin{bmatrix} 1 & 0 \\ -1 & 3 \end{bmatrix}.$

*3 If $\underset{\sim}{p} = \begin{bmatrix} 2 \\ 1 \end{bmatrix}$ and $\underset{\sim}{q} = \begin{bmatrix} -3 \\ 1 \end{bmatrix},$

(a) calculate $\underset{\sim}{r} = \underset{\sim}{p} + 2\underset{\sim}{q}$;

(b) show $\underset{\sim}{p}, \underset{\sim}{q}$ and $\underset{\sim}{r}$ on a diagram;

(c) find the images $\underset{\sim}{p}', \underset{\sim}{q}'$ and $\underset{\sim}{r}'$ of $\underset{\sim}{p}, \underset{\sim}{q}$ and $\underset{\sim}{r}$ under the transformation represented by the matrix $\begin{bmatrix} 1 & -3 \\ 0 & 2 \end{bmatrix}$ and show them on a diagram. Is it true that $\underset{\sim}{p}' + 2\underset{\sim}{q}' = \underset{\sim}{r}'$?

4 If $\underset{\sim}{a} = \begin{bmatrix} 3 \\ -3 \end{bmatrix}$ and $\underset{\sim}{b} = \begin{bmatrix} 1 \\ -4 \end{bmatrix},$

(a) calculate $\underset{\sim}{c} = 2\underset{\sim}{a} - 3\underset{\sim}{b}$;

(b) show $\underset{\sim}{a}, \underset{\sim}{b}$ and $\underset{\sim}{c}$ on a diagram;

(c) find the images $\underset{\sim}{a}', \underset{\sim}{b}'$ and $\underset{\sim}{c}'$ of $\underset{\sim}{a}, \underset{\sim}{b}$ and $\underset{\sim}{c}$ under the transformation represented by the matrix $\begin{bmatrix} 3 & -1 \\ 1 & 2 \end{bmatrix}$ and show them on a diagram. Is it true that $2\underset{\sim}{a}' - 3\underset{\sim}{b}' = \underset{\sim}{c}'$?

SUMMARY

Many geometrical transformations can be given by a rule of the form
$$x' = ax + by$$
$$y' = cx + dy$$
where (x', y') are the coordinates of the image of the point with coordinates (x, y).   (Section 1)

Such a transformation can then be represented by the matrix
$$\begin{bmatrix} a & b \\ c & d \end{bmatrix}.$$ (Section 2)

x' and y' are then given by a matrix product:
$$\begin{bmatrix} x' \\ y' \end{bmatrix} = \begin{bmatrix} a & b \\ c & d \end{bmatrix}\begin{bmatrix} x \\ y \end{bmatrix}.$$

The images of a set of points such as $(2, 3), (4, 5)$ and $(6, 7)$ can be found by calculating the matrix product
$$\begin{bmatrix} a & b \\ c & d \end{bmatrix}\begin{bmatrix} 2 & 4 & 6 \\ 3 & 5 & 7 \end{bmatrix}$$

and interpreting the columns of the product matrix as the coordinates of the images.   (Section 3)

If **A** and **B** are two transformations which can be represented by matrices,
$$\begin{bmatrix} \text{matrix} \\ \text{for } \mathbf{AB} \end{bmatrix} = \begin{bmatrix} \text{matrix} \\ \text{for } \mathbf{A} \end{bmatrix}\begin{bmatrix} \text{matrix} \\ \text{for } \mathbf{B} \end{bmatrix}.$$

(**AB** is the transformation equivalent to the transformation **B** followed by **A**.)
                                                                                (Section 4)

The vector $\underset{\sim}{O}P = \begin{bmatrix} x \\ y \end{bmatrix}$ is called the *position vector* of the point P with coordinates (x, y).

For all transformations which can be represented by a (2 row, 2 column) matrix:

(a) The origin is fixed.

(b) Points evenly spaced along a straight line are mapped to points evenly spaced along a straight line.

(c) Parallel lines are mapped to parallel lines.

(d) Vectors are mapped by the same rule as position vectors:
$$\begin{bmatrix} p' \\ q' \end{bmatrix} = \begin{bmatrix} a & b \\ c & d \end{bmatrix}\begin{bmatrix} p \\ q \end{bmatrix}.$$ (Section 5)

Summary exercise

1   (a) Write down the images under reflection in the line $y = {}^-x$ of the points with coordinates:
(i) $(4, {}^-1)$;   (ii) $(3, 1)$;   (iii) $({}^-2, 3)$;   (iv) (x, y).

(b) Write down the matrix representing the reflection.

2 (a) Find the coordinates of the images of the points A, B, C, D and E on the flag f shown in Figure 17 under the transformation $\mathbf{R}$ represented by the matrix $\begin{bmatrix} \frac{3}{5} & \frac{-4}{5} \\ \frac{4}{5} & \frac{3}{5} \end{bmatrix}$.

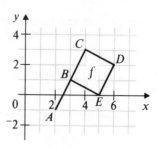

Figure 17

(b) Show $\mathbf{R}(f)$ on a diagram.

(c) What is the image of the vector $\underset{\sim}{BC} = \begin{bmatrix} 1 \\ 2 \end{bmatrix}$ under $\mathbf{R}$?

(d) Describe the transformation $\mathbf{R}$ precisely.

3 (a) Find the coordinates of the images of the points A, B, C, D and E on the flag f shown in Figure 17 under the transformation $\mathbf{M}$ represented by the matrix $\begin{bmatrix} \frac{-3}{5} & \frac{4}{5} \\ \frac{4}{5} & \frac{3}{5} \end{bmatrix}$.

(b) Show $\mathbf{M}(f)$ on a diagram.

(c) What is the image of the vector $\underset{\sim}{CD} = \begin{bmatrix} 2 \\ -1 \end{bmatrix}$ under $\mathbf{M}$?

(d) Describe $\mathbf{M}$ as precisely as you can.

4 (a) Find the matrix representing the transformation $\mathbf{RM}$ where $\mathbf{R}$ and $\mathbf{M}$ are the transformations given in questions 2 and 3 respectively.

(b) Find the image of the flag f in Figure 17 under $\mathbf{RM}$ and show $\mathbf{RM}(f)$ on a diagram.

(c) Describe $\mathbf{RM}$ precisely.

Miscellaneous exercise

1 The transformation $\mathbf{S}$ is represented by the matrix $\begin{bmatrix} 1 & -1 \\ 1 & 1 \end{bmatrix}$.

The square $ABCD$ has vertices $A(0, 2)$, $B(^-2, 0)$, $C(0, ^-2)$ and $D(2, 0)$.

(a) Find the coordinates of $\mathbf{S}(A)$, $\mathbf{S}(B)$, $\mathbf{S}(C)$ and $\mathbf{S}(D)$. Show $ABCD$ and its image under $\mathbf{S}$ on a diagram.

(b) Find the coordinates of $\mathbf{S}^2(A)$, $\mathbf{S}^2(B)$, $\mathbf{S}^2(C)$ and $\mathbf{S}^2(D)$ and show these points on your diagram. (Remember that $\mathbf{S}^2(A)$ means $\mathbf{SS}(A)$.)

(c) Describe the transformations $\mathbf{S}$ and $\mathbf{S}^2$.

(d) What is the matrix representing $\mathbf{S}^2$?

2 (a) Find the image of the rectangle shown in Figure 18 under the transformation represented by the matrix $\begin{bmatrix} -2 & 0 \\ 0 & -2 \end{bmatrix}$.

(b) Calculate the fraction $\dfrac{\text{area of image}}{\text{area of object}}$.

(c) Describe the transformation.

3 The 'face' in Figure 19 is to be given a quarter-turn $\mathbf{Q}$ about the point $A(1, 2)$.

(a) Calculate the coordinates of $\mathbf{Q}(B)$ by the following method:

(i) Write down the column matrix representing the vector $\underset{\sim}{AB}$.

(ii) Multiply this by the matrix representing a quarter-turn: $\begin{bmatrix} 0 & -1 \\ 1 & 0 \end{bmatrix}$.

(iii) Deduce the coordinates of **Q**(*B*).

(*b*) Repeat the procedure in (*a*) for each of the points *C*, *D*, *E*, *F* and *G*. Draw the image of the face under **Q**.

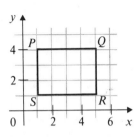

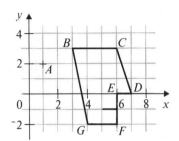

Figure 18   Figure 19

4   The transformation **Z** is represented by the matrix $\begin{bmatrix} 1 & 2 \\ 3 & 4 \end{bmatrix}$ and the points *A* and *B* have coordinates (p, q) and $(p + 3, q + 2)$ respectively.

(*a*) Find the coordinates of $A' = Z(A)$ and $B' = Z(B)$.

(*b*) Write down the vectors $\underset{\sim}{AB}$ and $\underset{\sim}{A'B'}$ as column matrices.

(*c*) Find the coordinates of the image of the point (3, 2) under **Z**. Compare your answer with your answers to (*b*).

5   Repeat question 4, using the same matrix, but with the points $A(p, q)$ and $C(p + r, q + s)$. In part (*c*), find the image of the point (r, s).

6   Repeat question 5, using the same points *A* and *C*, but using the matrix $\begin{bmatrix} a & b \\ c & d \end{bmatrix}$.

REVISION EXERCISE 16

1 If $p = 5$, $q = {}^-2$ and $r = 3$, find the values of:
   (a) $3p^2$;   (b) $q^2 + r^2$;   (c) $p - q - r$;   (d) $pq + qr + pr$.

2 Calculate the angles of a right-angled triangle if its shortest side is of length 8.2 cm and its area is 49.6 cm^2.

3 The scores of twenty pupils in a test were 8, 9, 15, 11, 12, 8, 10, 18, 9, 11, 13, 10, 17, 14, 15, 11, 10, 9, 11, 9.
   (a) Construct a frequency table and find the mean mark.
   (b) Another five pupils took the test and gained a mean mark of 14. What is the mean of all 25 marks?

4 Draw the graph of $y = 2x - 3$ for values of x between $^-1$ and 5. What is its gradient?

5 If $A = \begin{bmatrix} 4 & 1 \\ 2 & 0 \end{bmatrix}$ and $B = \begin{bmatrix} ^-3 & 2 \\ 6 & ^-4 \end{bmatrix}$ calculate:
   (a) **AB**;   (b) **A** + **B**.

6 A television set, normally priced at £269.95, is offered in a sale at £199.99. What is the percentage saving on the normal price?

7 An alloy cylinder of radius 2.1 cm and height 9.7 cm has a mass of 1.196 kg. Calculate the density of the alloy in kg/m^3.

8 The distance from the centre of Pittsfield to the centre of Springfield is 66 km in a straight line. From Springfield to Greenfield is 53 km, and from Greenfield to Pittsfield is 56 km. A television transmitter is to be erected to serve all three towns, and the search for a suitable site will start at Worthington. The distances from Worthington to Pittsfield, Greenfield and Springfield are all equal. Make an accurate scale drawing to find this distance.

REVISION EXERCISE 17

1 Write $\dfrac{1}{1250}$ in standard form.

2 If $\mathscr{E} = \{$letters of the alphabet$\}$, $A = \{f, i, s, h\}$ and $B = \{c, h, i, p, s\}$:
   (a) list the members of $A \cup B$;
   (b) list the members of $A \cap B$;
   (c) find $n(A' \cap B')$.

3 If $A = \begin{bmatrix} 4 & 2 & ^-6 \\ ^-2 & ^-1 & 4 \end{bmatrix}$ and $B = \begin{bmatrix} 2 & 1 \\ 1 & ^-3 \\ 3 & 1 \end{bmatrix}$ calculate **AB** and **BA**.

4 Write without brackets and simplify:
   (a) $2(x - 3) + 3(x - 2) - 4(3 - x)$;
   (b) $3(c - 1) + 2c(1 - c) - c(3 - c)$;
   (c) $a(2a - b) - ab + b(b + 2a)$;
   (d) $x(y - z) + y(z - x) + z(x - y)$.

5 Find the perimeter (P) and area (A) of the polygon in Figure 1 in terms of x and y in as simple a form as possible. Use your answer to write x in terms of P and y.

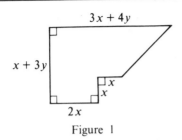

Figure 1

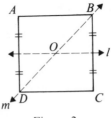

Figure 2

6   The square $ABCD$ is reflected in the line l and then in the line m (see Figure 2). What single transformation would have the same effect? What would be the effect of performing the two reflections in the reverse order?

7   Calculate the areas of the sector OAB and the triangle OAB shown in Figure 3.

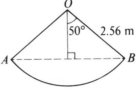

Figure 3

18

Graphs and inequalities

1. STRAIGHT-LINE GRAPHS

We saw in Chapter 12 that if y is proportional to x then the graph of $x \longrightarrow y$ is a straight line through the origin with gradient equal to the constant of proportionality. For example, if an aircraft is flying at a steady speed of 15 km/min and d is the number of kilometres travelled in t minutes, then $d = 15t$ and the graph of $t \longrightarrow d$ is as shown in Figure 1. The gradient of the line is 15.

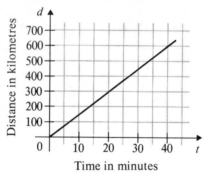

Figure 1

We also saw that the equation of a straight line that does not go through the origin can be written down from its gradient and the y-coordinate of the point where it crosses the y-axis.

Example 1

A company sells cassette tapes at prices shown in Table 1.

Playing-time in minutes (t)	60	90	120
Price in pence (C)	59	79	99

Table 1

(a) What would you expect a 30-minute cassette to cost?
(b) Write down the equation connecting C and t.

Figure 2 shows the graph of $t \longrightarrow C$.

(a) From the graph we can read off the expected cost of a 30-minute cassette: 39p.

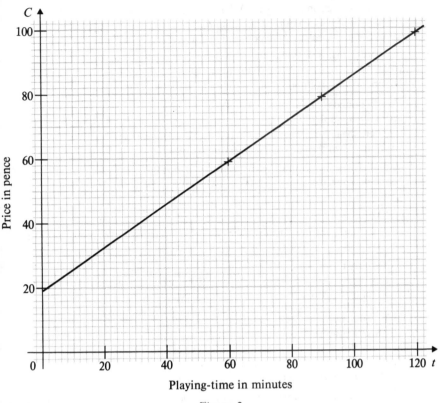

Figure 2

(b) The graph passes through the points (0, 19) and (120, 99) so its gradient is $\dfrac{99-19}{120-0}=\dfrac{80}{120}=\dfrac{2}{3}$. Since the line crosses the C-axis when $C=19$, the equation is $C=\frac{2}{3}t+19$. This could be thought of as 19 p for the empty spool together with $\frac{2}{3}$ p for every minute of playing-time.

Exercise A

*1 A greengrocer is selling potatoes at 60p for 5 kg.

    (a) Copy and complete the following table:

Number of kg of potatoes	(x)	1	3	5	7	9
Cost in pence	(y)			60		

    (b) Draw the graph of $x \longrightarrow y$. What is its gradient?

    (c) Write down an equation connecting x and y.

2 A train is travelling at a steady speed, covering 10.5 km in 4.2 minutes.

    (a) Copy and complete the following table:

Time in minutes	(t)	1.4	4.2	8.4	10	
Distance travelled in km	(d)		10.5			30

(b) Draw the graph of $t \longrightarrow d$. What is its gradient?

(c) What is the speed of the train in km/min?

(d) Write down an equation connecting d and t.

*3 A mail-order firm adds a standard packing charge to the actual cost of all items ordered. Total costs are shown in the table below:

Number of pairs of tights	(t)	2	6	10
Cost in pounds	(C)	2	4	6

(a) Draw a graph of $t \longrightarrow C$.

(b) State the packing charge and actual cost of each pair of tights.

(c) Write down the equation connecting C and t.

4 The total charge for printing headed paper is shown below:

Number of sheets	(x)	300	500	800
Price in pounds	(y)	14	20	29

(a) Draw a graph of $x \longrightarrow y$.

(b) State the charge for setting up the type, also the actual cost of printing per sheet.

(c) Write down the equation connecting x and y.

*5 The quarterly telephone bills for a house are shown for one year:

		Spring	Summer	Autumn	Winter
Number of units used	(n)	720	390	540	680
Cost in pounds	(C)	40.80	27.60	33.60	39.20

(a) Draw a graph of $n \longrightarrow C$.

(b) Write down the rental charge for having a telephone, even if not used.

(c) Give the actual cost per unit used.

(d) Write down the equation connecting C and n.

6 A car driver joined a motorway at 11.37 a.m. and passed signs giving the distance to his destination as follows:

Distance in km to destination	(d)	120	84	57
Time in minutes after noon	(t)	$^-8$	12	27

Draw a suitable graph and hence find:

(a) when he could expect to reach his destination;

(b) the length of his motorway journey;

(c) his average speed;

(d) the equation connecting d and t.

What assumptions have you made?

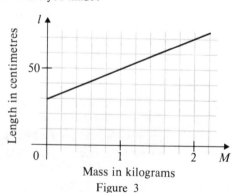

Mass in kilograms

Figure 3

*7   Figure 3 shows how the length of an elastic string varies when different masses are hung from it.
   (a) Calculate the gradient of the line and write down the equation connecting l and M.
   (b) The string breaks when it is stretched to four times its unstretched length. What mass hung on it would cause it to break?

8   A cyclist sets out on a journey at a steady speed. After t hours of cycling, the distance d kilometres that she still has left to travel is given by the formula $d = 14 - 9t$.
   (a) How long is the journey?
   (b) What is the cyclist's speed?
   (c) How many minutes does she take for the whole journey?

2. LINEAR EQUATIONS

Suckers cost 4 pence each and Tastees cost 5 pence each. Peter intends to spend £1 on them. He could do this in various ways; for example, he could buy 20 Suckers and 4 Tastees or just 20 Tastees. These possibilities, and some others, are shown in Table 2.

Number of Suckers (s)	0	25	20	10
Number of Tastees (t)	20	0	4	16

Table 2

Can you complete the two missing entries?

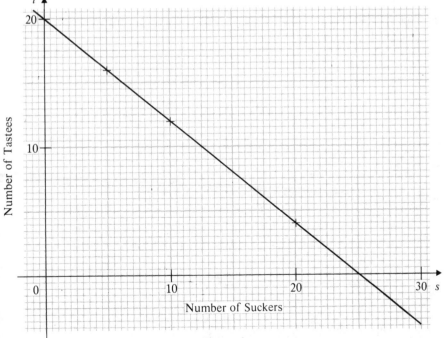

Figure 4

The corresponding points are shown in Figure 4, where they have been joined by a straight line. Notice that in this example it would not matter which axis we used for s and which for t; it is usual to use alphabetical order.

s Suckers at 4 pence each will cost $4s$ pence;
t Tastees at 5 pence each will cost $5t$ pence;
the total cost is 100 pence.

So we have the equation $4s + 5t = 100$.

The graph has gradient $^-0.8$ and crosses the t-axis at $(0, 20)$, so its equation is
$$t = {}^-0.8s + 20$$
which looks very different. But multiplying both sides of this equation by 5 gives
$$5t = {}^-4s + 100$$
$$\Leftrightarrow 4s + 5t = 100.$$

So we have two forms of the same equation. Both have their uses and it is useful to be able to obtain one from the other.

Does every point on the graph give a possible pair of values for s and t? For example, $(15, 8)$ shows that Peter could have bought 15 Suckers and 8 Tastees for £1. However, some points, such as $(18, 5.6)$, or $(30, {}^-4)$ (selling 4 Tastees so as to be able to buy 30 Suckers), may not be acceptable in practice.

Example 2

450 ruples are spent on cement at 27 ruples per kilogram and sand at 20 ruples per kilogram. Write down an equation connecting x, the number of kilograms of cement, and y, the number of kilograms of sand, and draw the corresponding graph.

x kilograms of cement cost $27x$ ruples, and y kilograms of sand cost $20y$ ruples. So we have the equation
$$27x + 20y = 450.$$

To draw the graph, we need to find some pairs of values satisfying this equation. First we find the points where the graph crosses the axes.
$$x = 0 \Leftrightarrow 20y = 450 \Leftrightarrow y = \frac{450}{20} = 22\tfrac{1}{2}$$
$$y = 0 \Leftrightarrow 27x = 450 \Leftrightarrow x = \frac{450}{27} = 16\tfrac{2}{3}$$

So the graph crosses the axes at $(0, 22\tfrac{1}{2})$ and $(16\tfrac{2}{3}, 0)$. Also,
$$x = 10 \Leftrightarrow 270 + 20y = 450 \Leftrightarrow 20y = 180 \Leftrightarrow y = 9$$
and $\qquad x = 6 \;\Leftrightarrow 162 + 20y = 450 \Leftrightarrow 20y = 288 \Leftrightarrow y = 14.4$

so the points $(10, 9)$ and $(6, 14.4)$ are on the graph, which is shown in Figure 5.

Using the points $(10, 9)$ and $(6, 14.4)$ we find that the gradient of the line is
$\dfrac{14.4 - 9}{6 - 10} = \dfrac{5.4}{^-4} = {}^-1.35$. As a check, we can rearrange the equation as follows:
$$27x + 20y = 450$$
$$\Leftrightarrow \qquad 20y = {}^-27x + 450$$
$$\Leftrightarrow \qquad y = {}^-1.35x + 22.5$$
so the gradient is $^-1.35$ and the line crosses the y-axis at $(0, 22.5)$.

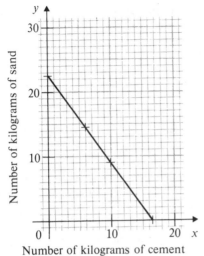

Number of kilograms of cement

Figure 5

Exercise B

*1 An agent sold some tickets for a concert, x of them at £3 each and y of them at £2 each. His total sales were £96.

    (a) Calculate how many £2 tickets were sold if the number of £3 tickets sold was:
      (i) 10;   (ii) 30;   (iii) 0.

    (b) Calculate how many £3 tickets were sold if the number of £2 tickets sold was:
      (i) 15;   (ii) 30;   (iii) 0.

    (c) (i) Use your answers to (a) and (b) to copy and complete the following table of values of x and y:

Number of £3 tickets (x)	10	30	0			
Number of £2 tickets (y)				15	30	0

      (ii) Write down the equation connecting x and y.

    (d) Show the information that you tabulated in (c) on a graph. Write down the equation of the graph. What is its gradient?

2 Strawberries cost 80 ruples for a kilogram and cream costs 120 ruples for a litre. A total of 480 ruples is spent on x kilograms of strawberries and y litres of cream.

    (a) How many litres of cream were bought if the number of kilograms of strawberries bought was: (i) 3;   (ii) 0?

    (b) How many kilograms of strawberries were bought if the number of litres of cream bought was: (i) 0;   (ii) 1?

    (c) (i) Use your answers to (a) and (b) to copy and complete the following table of values of x and y:

Number of kilograms of strawberries (x)	3	0		
Number of litres of cream (y)			0	1

      (ii) Write down an equation connecting x and y.

    (d) Show the information that you tabulated in (c) on a graph. Write down the equation of the graph. What is its gradient?

*3 A farmer spends £96 on fertilisers: £12 per hectare (ha) of wheat and £16 per hectare of kale. He has w hectares of wheat and k hectares of kale.

(a) Make a table showing some possible pairs of values of w and k.

(b) Show this information on a graph.

(c) Write down the equation of your graph.

(d) Use your graph to find:

    (i) how many hectares of kale he has if he has 5 ha of wheat;

    (ii) how many hectares of wheat he has if he has 5 ha of kale.

4 200 soldiers were airlifted using h Hawks and k Kestrels. A Hawk carries 8 people, and a Kestrel carries 10.

(a) Make a table showing some possible pairs of values of h and k.

(b) Show this information on a graph.

(c) Write down the equation of your graph.

(d) With the soldiers went 32 tonnes of equipment, 2 tonnes in each Hawk and 1 tonne in each Kestrel. Write down another equation connecting h and k and show it on your graph.

(e) How many Hawks and Kestrels were used?

*5 With values of x between $^-2$ and 10, draw graphs of the following equations:

(a) $2x + 3y = 20$;   (b) $x + 4y = 6$;

(c) $4x + 3y = 28$;   (d) $5x + 2y = 40$.

*6 Rewrite the equations of question 5 in the form $y = kx + c$.

7 With values of x between $^-3$ and 9, draw graphs of the following equations:

(a) $x + y = 8$;   (b) $3x + 2y = 21$;

(c) $2.3x + 4.5y = 19.2$;   (d) $1.3x + 1.2y = 10.5$.

8 Rewrite the equations of question 7 in the form $y = kx + c$.

*9 Draw the graphs of $3x + y = 12$ and $y = 2x + 2$ on the same diagram, for values of x between 0 and 5. What pair of values of x and y satisfies both equations?

10 Draw the graphs of $3x + 2y = 24$ and $x + y = 11$ on the same diagram. What pair of values of x and y satisfies both equations?

11 Find the gradient of the line $px + qy = r$ and the coordinates of the points where it crosses the x-axis and y-axis.

12 (a) Find the coordinates of the points where the line with equation $\frac{x}{5} + \frac{y}{8} = 1$ crosses the axes. What is the gradient of the line?

(b) Find the coordinates of the points where the line with equation $\frac{x}{a} + \frac{y}{b} = 1$ crosses the axes. What is the gradient of the line?

3. INEQUALITIES

A garden centre supplies compost at 10 pence per kilogram with a £3 delivery charge. The total payment for x kilograms is therefore £y with $y = \frac{1}{10}x + 3$. The graph of this equation is shown in Figure 6. Every point on the line for $x > 0$ represents a possible number of kilograms with the corresponding payment. For example, $(35, 6\frac{1}{2})$ represents 35 kg bought for £6.50.

What does a point above the line represent? $(20, 6)$ represents 20 kg bought with a payment of £6. The payment is more than it should be:

$$x = 20 \text{ and } y = 6 \Rightarrow y > \tfrac{1}{10}x + 3.$$

Similarly every point below the line, such as $(40, 2)$, corresponds to a payment less than that required:

$$x = 40 \text{ and } y = 2 \Rightarrow y < \tfrac{1}{10}x + 3.$$

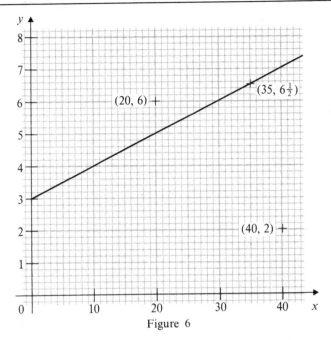

Figure 6

In general,
$$y > kx + c \text{ at all points above the line } y = kx + c$$
$$y < kx + c \text{ at all points below the line } y = kx + c.$$
Similarly, every line is a boundary between two regions, given by replacing the $=$ sign in the equation by $>$ and $<$. The easiest way to check which side is which is to use some specific points.

Example 3

Show on graphs the regions for which:

(a) $x \le 3$;   (b) $3x + 2y < 12$;   (c) $2x - y \ge 5$.

We shall shade out the regions not required so that the regions we want can be clearly labelled.

(a) Figure 7 shows the line $x = 3$. All points to the right of this line have x-coordinates greater than 3, so these points are not in the required region. We shade it out. The line itself is included in the region we want.

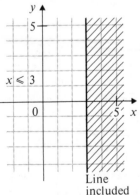

Figure 7

(b) The line $3x + 2y = 12$ passes through the points $(0, 6)$, $(4, 0)$ and $(2, 3)$; it is shown in Figure 8. The point $(3, 4)$ is above the line; for this point, $3x + 2y = 9 + 8 = 17$, which is greater than 12, so this is not a point we want, and we shade out this side of the line. The line itself is also not required, since on the line $3x + 2y$ is equal to 12. As a final check, we choose a point in the unshaded region, such as $(2, 1)$. Here $3x + 2y = 6 + 2 = 8$, which is less than 12, confirming that this point is in the region we require.

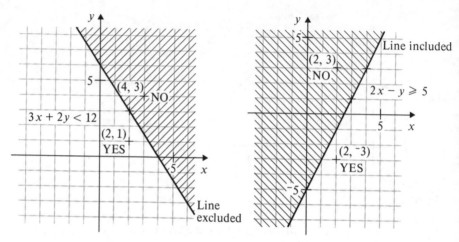

Figure 8   Figure 9

(c) The line $2x - y = 5$ passes through $(0, {}^-5)$, $(3, 1)$ and $(4, 3)$; it is shown in Figure 9. At $(2, 3)$, a point above the line, $2x - y = 4 - 3 = 1$, which is less than 5, so this is not a point we want. We shade out this side of the line. On the line itself, $2x - y$ is equal to 5, so we want the points on the line. At $(2, {}^-3)$, a point below the line, $2x - y = 4 - {}^-3 = 7$, so this is a point we require. The required region is shown unshaded in Figure 9. Notice that the line is included.

Exercise C

In all your answers shade the unwanted regions. Indicate clearly whether a boundary line is included in, or excluded from, a required region.

*1 With values of x and y between ${}^-5$ and 5, draw graphs to show the following regions:

    (a) $y > \frac{1}{2}x + 3$;   (b) $y \leqslant 2x - 3$;   (c) $x > 2$;

    (d) $y < 3$;   (e) $x + y \geqslant 3$;   (f) $2x + 3y < 6$.

2 With values of x and y between ${}^-5$ and 5, draw graphs to show the following regions:

    (a) $x - 2y \leqslant 3$;   (b) $x + 2y \geqslant 0$;   (c) $2x - 3y \leqslant 6$;

    (d) $4y - 5x < 10$;   (e) $y > 2x$;   (f) $x \geqslant 3y$.

3 With values of x and y between ${}^-5$ and 5, draw graphs to show the following regions:

    (a) $\{(x, y) : x > 2\} \cap \{(x, y) : y < 3\}$;

(b) $\{(x, y): y > 2x\} \cap \{(x, y): x + y < 3\}$;

(c) $\{(x, y): y < 2, y > x - 3\}$;

(d) $\{(x, y): 2x + 3y < 6, 2x + 3y > {}^-6\}$.

4 Draw a graph to show the region of points whose coordinates satisfy all five of the following inequalities:
$$x \geqslant 0, \quad y \geqslant 0, \quad 2x + y \geqslant 4, \quad x + 3y \geqslant 9, \quad x + y \leqslant 6.$$
Put a dot on your graph at each point satisfying all five inequalities and having integer coordinates.

*5 A post office has to transport 900 parcels using lorries which can take 150 parcels at a time and vans which can take 60 parcels.

(a) (i) How many parcels can be carried by x lorries?

   (ii) How many parcels can be carried by y vans?

(b) Use your answers to (a) to explain why, if x lorries and y vans are used, $5x + 2y \geqslant 30$.

(c) The costs of each journey are £5 by lorry and £4 by van; the total cost must be less than £44. Write down another inequality which must be satisfied by x and y.

(d) Represent these inequalities on a graph and mark with dots the points corresponding to possible values of x and y.

(e) What are:

   (i) the largest number of vehicles which could be used;

   (ii) the smallest number of vehicles which could be used?

6 A school trip uses 36-seater buses and 12-seater minibuses. The hire cost of a bus is 100 ruples and the hire cost of a minibus is 80 ruples.

(a) Write down expressions for:

   (i) the number of passengers that can be carried by x buses and y minibuses;

   (ii) the hire cost of x buses and y minibuses.

(b) If 240 passengers have to be carried and the total hire cost must not exceed 1000 ruples, write down two inequalities that must be satisfied by x and y.

(c) Represent these inequalities on a graph and mark with dots the points corresponding to possible values of x and y.

(d) What are:

   (i) the largest number of vehicles which could be used;

   (ii) the smallest number of vehicles which could be used?

*7 On a trip round the bay the 'Mudlark' can take up to the equivalent of 24 children, an adult counting as two children.

(a) How many children are equivalent to x adults and y children? Write down an inequality which must be satisfied by x and y.

(b) Adults pay 50 pence and children 20 pence, which must bring in at least £5 to cover the running costs. Show that $5x + 2y \geqslant 50$.

(c) Represent these two inequalities on a graph.

(d) Use your graph to find:

   (i) the greatest profit that can be made on a trip;

   (ii) the largest number of passengers that can be carried without making a loss.

8 The Ruritanian Rhubarb Canning factory employs x unskilled workers and y skilled workers.

(a) Express the following information as inequalities:

   (i) the total number of workers is at least 75;

   (ii) unskilled workers are paid 160 ruples an hour, skilled workers are paid 240 ruples an hour and the total wage bill is less than 14 400 ruples per hour;

(iii) the number of skilled workers is at least one quarter of the number of un-skilled workers.

(b) Represent these inequalities on a graph.

(c) Use your graph to find the greatest numbers of (i) unskilled; (ii) skilled, workers that could be employed.

SUMMARY

$y = kx + c$ gives a straight-line graph with gradient k and crossing the y-axis at $(0, c)$.   (Section 1)

$px + qy = r$ gives a straight-line graph with gradient $\dfrac{^-p}{q}$.   (Section 2)

$y > kx + c$ describes the region above the line $y = kx + c$.
$y < kx + c$ describes the region below the line $y = kx + c$.

Regions such as $3x - 4y < 7$ can be found by drawing the line $3x - 4y = 7$ and testing points on each side to discover whether they belong to the required region.   (Section 3)

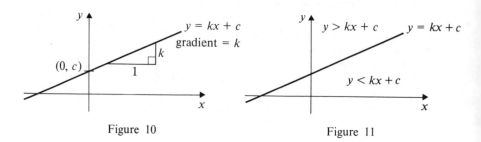

Figure 10   Figure 11

Summary exercise

1 A standard dispenser is sold containing different lengths of adhesive tape, as shown in the following table:

Length of tape in metres	(l)	3	6	10
Cost in pence	(C)	31	43	59

(a) Draw a graph of $l \longrightarrow C$. What is its gradient?

(b) What is the cost: (i) of the dispenser; (ii) per metre of tape?

(c) Write down an equation connecting C and l.

2 The table shows the distance travelled and the number of litres of petrol remaining in the tank on a long car journey.

Distance in kilometres	(d)	75	200	350	500
Number of litres of petrol in tank	(p)	44	34	22	10

(a) Draw a graph of $d \to p$ and find its equation.

(b) How many litres of petrol were there in the tank at the beginning of the journey?

(c) How far will the car have gone when it runs out of petrol, if no more petrol is put in the tank?

(d) What is the rate of petrol consumption, in litres per 100 km?

3 A builder spends a total of £14 on screws at £3 per kg and nails at £2 per kg. Make a table to show possible quantities and show the information on a graph. Give the equation of your graph.

4 (a) With values of x between $^-4$ and 6, draw graphs of the following equations:
  (i) $3x + 5y = 18$; (ii) $3.4x + 1.2y = 15.6$.
  (b) Rewrite these equations in the form $y = kx + c$.

5 Draw graphs to show the regions representing the following inequalities:
  (a) $x < 3$; (b) $y > ^-1$; (c) $y \leqslant \frac{1}{2}x$; (d) $3x - 4y \leqslant 8$.

Miscellaneous exercise

1 A triangle has vertices $A(0, 0)$, $B(1, 7)$ and $C(^-2, 4)$.
  (a) Draw the triangle and find the equations of the lines which form the three sides.
  (b) Write down three inequalities satisfied by the coordinates of all the points inside the triangle.

2 Find the coordinates of the vertices of the triangle whose sides have equations
  $2x + y = 8$, $x + y = 3$ and $y - 2x = 12$.

3 Boadicea's mercenaries were either swordswomen, who were paid 2 denarii a day, or charioteers, who were paid 1 denarius a day. The Iceni fund-raisers could only guarantee her 180 denarii a day. The Amalgamated Union of Swordswomen insisted that the number of swordswomen employed was at least as great as the number of charioteers, but in the interests of mobility the number must not exceed four times the number of charioteers. Boadicea decided to employ at least 50 swordswomen.
  (a) Write down four inequalities corresponding to these conditions and represent them on a graph.
  (b) What was the greatest number of mercenaries employed?
  (c) What was the least number of mercenaries employed?

4 Pineapples cost p cowries each and mangos q cowries each. 4 pineapples and 9 mangos cost 120 cowries.
  (a) Write down an equation connecting p and q and represent it on a suitable graph.
  (b) If 2 pineapples and 3 mangos cost 48 cowries, write down another equation and draw the corresponding line on your graph. What is the price of a pineapple?

19

Configurations

1. PARALLEL LINES

Over the centuries, geometry has formed a large part of mathematics. One of the areas of interest has been to investigate precisely what assumptions about planes, lines and points need to be made in order to deduce particular geometrical results. Much discussion has been concerned with parallel lines and we start this chapter with some simple results about angles and parallel lines. In each case some lines of reasoning are suggested but you should realise that these are based on various assumptions which are not discussed here. Important results which may be referred to later in the chapter are labelled with capital letters.

(A) In Figure 1 (*a*) the angles $x°$ and $y°$ are equal. Some ways of reasoning:
    (1) $x + z = 180$, $y + z = 180$ so $x = y$.
    (2) A rotation about P of $x°$ (or $y°$) maps line l onto line m.
    (3) A half-turn about P maps $x°$ onto $y°$.

(B) In Figure 1(*b*) the angles $x°$ and $y°$ are equal.
    (1) $x°$ and $y°$ are the angles between the direction of l and the direction of the parallel lines m and n.
    (2) A translation $\underset{\sim}{PQ}$ maps x onto y.

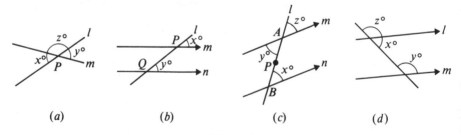

(*a*)   (*b*)   (*c*)   (*d*)

Figure 1

(C) In Figure 1(*c*) the angles $x°$ and $y°$ are equal.
    (1) the same reason as (B) (1).
    (2) $x = z$ (result (B)) and $y = z$ (result (A)) so $x = y$.
    (3) A half-turn about P, the midpoint of AB, maps $x°$ onto $y°$.

(D) In Figure 1(*d*) $x + y = 180$.
    (1) $x + z = 180$ and $y = z$ (result (B)).
    (2) Euclid (*c.* 300 BC) included among his assumptions that if $x + y < 180$ then the lines l and m would meet at some point to the right of the figure. From this he deduced our result. (What happens if $x + y > 180$?)

Exercise A

Find the unknown angles (marked with letters) in the diagrams of Figure 2. State which of the results (A) to (D) you use in each case.

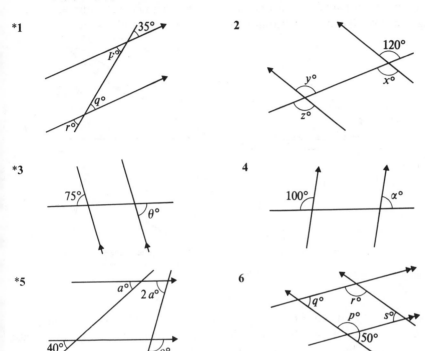

Figure 2

2. THE TRIANGLE

We start by looking at the general triangle with no particular symmetry (a scalene triangle) and then the isosceles and equilateral triangles. As well as re-stating results which may be familiar, we give some indication of *why* the results are true.

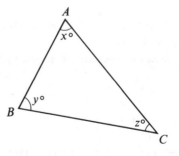

Figure 3

(E)   The sum of the angles of a triangle is 180°.
      In Figure 3 $x + y + z = 180$ or $\angle CAB + \angle ABC + \angle BCA = 180°$.

Justification of result

First method. Place a pencil along one side of a triangle and turn it about each angle in turn as shown in Figure 4. What do you notice about the final position of the pencil compared with its first position? What angle has it turned through altogether? What can you say about the angles of a triangle?

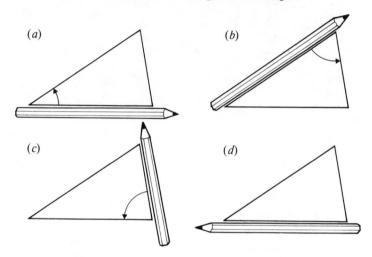

Figure 4

Second method. Cut out a triangle in paper and fold it as shown in Figure 5 so that *B* lies on the side *AC*. Now fold along the dotted lines so that *C* and *A* are at *B*. How does this show that the angles add up to 180°?

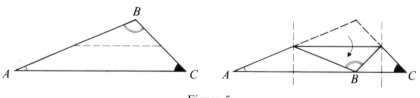

Figure 5

Third method (Euclid). This method uses some of the results mentioned earlier in this chapter.

We extend the side *BC* to *D* and draw a line *CE* parallel to *BA*. (See Figure 6). Give reasons for the following steps:

(1) $\angle ECD = y°$,
(2) $\angle ECA = x°$,
(3) $z° + \angle ECA + \angle ECD = 180°$.

Hence $x + y + z = 180$.

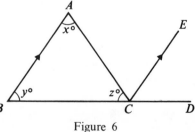

Figure 6

It follows from the above that as $\angle ACD = \angle ACE + \angle ECD$ then $\angle ACD = x° + y°$. We thus have a new result:

(F)   The exterior angle of a triangle (in this case ∠ ACD) is equal to the sum of
      the two interior angles opposite to it (in this case ∠ CAB and ∠ ABC).

Exercise B

Find the angles marked with letters in the diagrams of Figure 7.

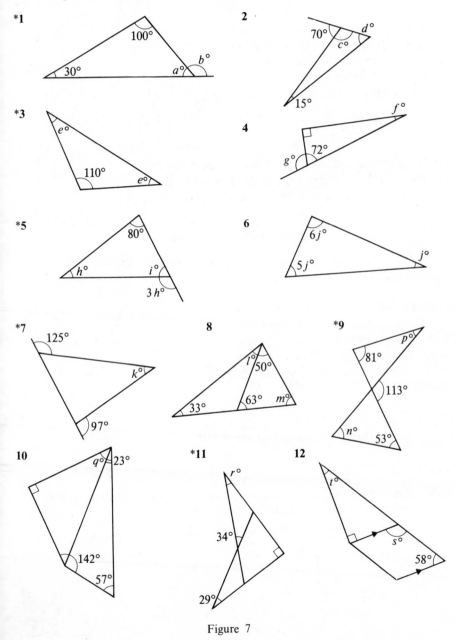

Figure 7

The isosceles triangle

The prefix 'iso' means equal and an isosceles triangle is, by definition, one in which two sides are equal in length.

(G) In an isosceles triangle the angles opposite the equal sides are also equal. In Figure 8, $x = y$.

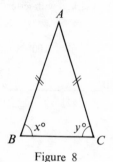

Draw an isosceles triangle on a piece of paper and cut it out. Fold it so that the equal sides AB and AC (see Figure 8) map onto each other. Crease in the fold and then open the triangle out again.

Figure 8

(1) What can be said about the 'base' angles B and C?
(2) What can be said about the angles formed at A by the fold?
(3) What can be said about the way in which the fold meets the line BC?

The equilateral triangle

The word equilateral means 'equal sides' but is stronger than isosceles in that it means that *all* sides of the triangle are equal.

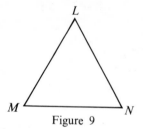

Consider the equilateral triangle LMN in Figure 9. As $LM = LN$ then the triangle can be thought of as being isosceles. What can be said about $\angle LMN$ and $\angle LNM$? Further, what can be said about $\angle LMN$ and $\angle MLN$? Why?

Figure 9

Explain why it follows that:
(H) In an equilateral triangle all angles are 60°.

Exercise C

In questions 1–8, find the angles marked with letters in the diagrams of Figure 10. Similar markings on the sides of triangles indicate equal lengths.

*1

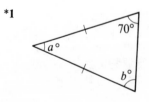

2

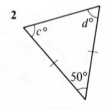

*3

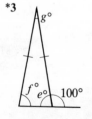

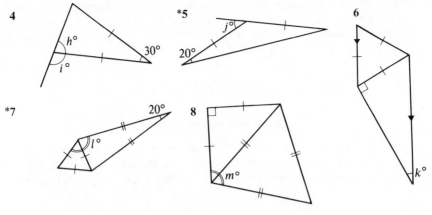

Figure 10

*9 (a) One angle of an isosceles triangle is 40°. Find possible values for the other two angles.

  (b) One angle of an isosceles triangle is 120°. Find possible values for the other two angles. What is the essential difference between this and part (a)?

10 Figure 11 represents a kitchen step stool in the opened position. When the lower steps are closed up the inclined stays rotate about A and B. Through what angle do they rotate as the steps are put away?

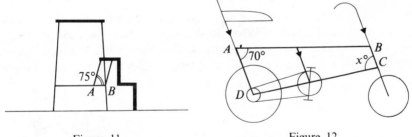

Figure 11   Figure 12

*11 Figure 12 represents the framework of a 'Chopper' bicycle. Given that the lower part of the frame, CD, makes an angle of 20° with the ground, and that AB is parallel to the ground, find angle $x°$.

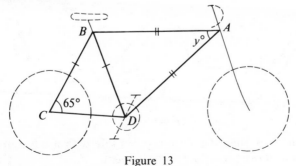

Figure 13

12 Figure 13 represents the framework of a racing cycle. For simplicity assume it is composed of two isosceles triangles. The strut *CD* from the centre of the rear wheel to the pedals makes an angle of 5° with the ground, and *AB* is parallel to the ground. Find angle *y*°.

3. POLYGONS

Angle sum of a polygon

The method of investigating the sum of the angles of a triangle shown in Figure 4 can be adapted for polygons. This time, however we concentrate, initially, on the *exterior* angles. Some exterior angles are marked in the polygon in Figure 14.

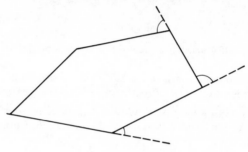

Figure 14

Place a pencil along one side of a polygon and turn it through each *exterior* angle as shown in Figure 15. What do you notice about the final position of the pencil compared with its first position? What angle has it turned through altogether? What can you say about the exterior angles of the polygon in Figure 15?

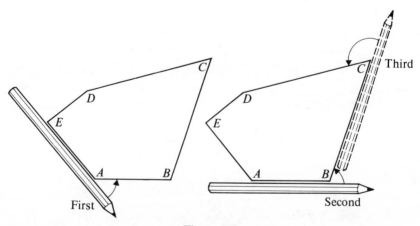

Figure 15

Draw a differently shaped polygon, preferably with a different number of sides. Repeat the above procedure and comment.

Is the same result concerning *exterior* angles also true for triangles? Turn back to Figure 4 and check.

It should be clear that:

(I)   The sum of the exterior angles of any polygon is 360°.

Figure 16 shows part of a polygon with an interior angle and its corresponding exterior angle. Answer the following questions.

(1) What is the sum of each interior angle and its corresponding exterior angle?

(2) If the polygon has 5 sides (a pentagon) what will be the total sum of its exterior and interior angles?

(3) The exterior angles total 360°. What then is the total of the interior angles?

Interior angle / Exterior angle

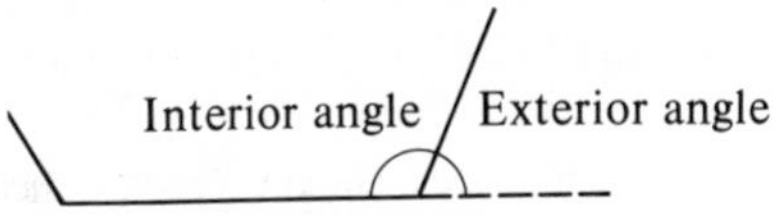

Figure 16

Repeat the steps (1), (2), (3) above for polygons of 4, 6 and 8 sides.
Make a table:

Number of sides	(n)	3	4	5	6	8
Sum of interior angles	$(S°)$	180°		540°		
Sum of interior angles as multiples of 180°		1		3		

Can you find the relation between n and S?

In general the sum of all the interior and exterior angles in $180n°$. Since the total of the exterior angles is 360°, the total of the interior angles is

$$180n° - 360° = 180(n - 2)°.$$

So we have the result:

(J)   The sum of the interior angles of an n-sided polygon is $180(n - 2)°$.

Exercise D

*1   What is the sum of the interior angles of a quadrilateral (4 sides)?

(*a*) A quadrilateral has three interior angles 62°, 134° and 27°. What is the size of the fourth angle?

(*b*) A quadrilateral has three angles each of 65°. What is the size of the fourth angle?

(*c*) A quadrilateral has angles $x°, 2x°, 3x°, 4x°$. Find the value of x.

(*d*) Three of the angles of a quadrilateral are equal. The fourth angle is 120°; find the others.

2   What is the sum of the interior angles of a pentagon (5 sides)?

(*a*) The angles of a pentagon are $x°, 2x°, 54°, 123°$ and 90°. Find x.

(*b*) The angles of a pentagon are $x°, 2x°, (x + 30)°, (x - 10)°$ and $(x + 40)°$. Find x.

(*c*) The angles of a pentagon are in the ratio $1:3:3:4:4$. Find them.

*3   (*a*) Use the result $S = 180(n - 2)$ to find the sum of the interior angles of a decagon (10 sides). If the polygon is regular, what is the size of each interior angle?

(*b*) Use the fact that the sum of the exterior angles of any polygon is 360° to write down the size of the exterior angle of a regular decagon. Hence write down the size of each interior angle.

4   Calculate the size of the exterior and interior angles of the following regular polygons:
    (a) pentagon;   (b) hexagon;   (c) octagon;   (d) dodecagon.

*5 If a regular polygon has exterior angles of 20° how many sides has it?

6   If a regular polygon has interior angles of 170° find its exterior angles and the number
    of sides.

*7 If a regular polygon has interior angles of 150°, calculate the number of sides.

8   (a) If a regular polygon has interior angles of 130°, calculate the number of sides.
    (b) What went wrong in part (a)?
    (c) Which of the following could not be the exterior angles of a regular polygon?
        20°, 25°, 35°, 72°, 60°, 120°, 45°, 80°, 8°, 24°.

9   Consider the n-sided polygon indicated in Figure 17. Lines are drawn from an interior
    point P to each vertex.
    (a) How many triangles are there with a vertex at P?
    (b) What is the total angle-sum of all these triangles?
    (c) What part of the total is given by the angles meeting at P?
    (d) Explain why this shows that the sum of the interior angles is (180n − 360)°.

Figure 17   Figure 18

10 Lines are drawn from one vertex of an n-sided polygon to the other vertices, as indicated
    in Figure 18.
    (a) How many triangles does this procedure produce?
    (b) What is the total angle-sum of all these triangles?
    (c) Explain why this shows that the sum of the interior angles of the polygon
        is 180(n − 2)°.

4. SYMMETRIES OF TRIANGLES AND QUADRILATERALS

Figure 19 reminds you of the two types of symmetry.

Line symmetry

(a)

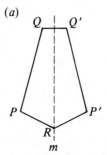

Rotational symmetry

(b)

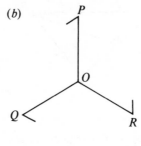

The complete figure is symmetrical about the line *m*. *P'Q'* is the reflection of *PQ* in *m*. *m* is the mediator of *PP'* and of *QQ'*.

A rotation of 120° maps *OP* onto *OQ*, *OQ* onto *OR* and *OR* onto *OP*. The effect of three such rotations is to map the figure onto itself; the figure has rotational symmetry of order 3.

Figure 19

Exercise E

In the diagrams for this exercise a broken line indicates a line of symmetry.

*1   Use the diagram in Figure 20 as a basis for drawing a triangle with one line of symmetry. What sort of triangle is it? Has it any other sort of symmetry?

Figure 20

2   Draw a triangle with *two* lines of symmetry. Perhaps start with your answer to question 1 and change its shape a bit until it has two lines of symmetry. What sort of triangle do you now have? Has it any more symmetries in addition to those you have built in?

*3   Draw a triangle *ABC* as in Figure 21, and let *X* be the midpoint of *AC*. Use tracing-paper to draw the image of *ABC* after a half-turn about *X*. What sort of figure do the original triangle and its image together form?

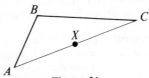

Figure 21

4   The answer to question 3 is 'a parallelogram'. Use the method in question 3 to draw another parallelogram and label it *ABCD* as in Figure 22. Let its diagonals meet at *O* and make a copy of the complete diagram on your tracing-paper. Use this to say what you can about

(a) the lengths AB and CD;

(b) the angles ABC and ADC;

(c) the lengths OB and OD.

Check that opposite sides are parallel.

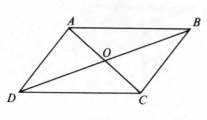 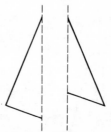 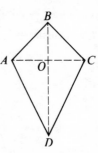

Figure 22   Figure 23   Figure 24

*5   Use the diagram in Figure 23 as a basis for constructing two quadrilaterals each with one line of symmetry. One result is a *kite*, the other is an *arrowhead*.

6   Use tracing-paper, or a geoliner, to construct a kite and label it $ABCD$ as in Figure 24. Let the diagonals meet at O. What can you say about:

(a) the lengths AB and BC;

(b) the lengths OA and OC;

(c) the angles at O;

(d) the angles ADO and ODC;

(e) the triangles ABD and CBD?

7   Repeat question 6 in the case of an arrowhead. How can you describe the difference between a kite and an arrowhead? We say that the arrowhead is a *non-convex* quadrilateral. Try to find out the meaning of this term.

8   In Figure 25 one side of the quadrilateral is shown. Both dotted lines are axes of symmetry. Copy the diagram and com-lete the full picture.

Label the figure $ABCD$ (be careful about the order of the letters); it is a *rhombus*.

What can you say about

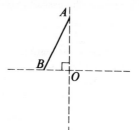

(a) the lengths of the sides of the figure;

(b) the lengths AO and OC;

(c) the angles ABO and CBO?   Figure 25

Has the figure, in addition to the given line symmetry, any other symmetries?

9   (a) How would AB have to be placed in Figure 25 so that the resulting quadrilateral would be a square?

(b) List all the symmetries of a square.

10   Complete Figure 26 so that your figure is a quadrilateral with AB as part of one of its sides and with both the broken lines as lines of symmetry. What kind of quadrilateral do you obtain?

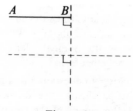

Figure 26

5. RELATIONS BETWEEN QUADRILATERALS

Most quadrilaterals have no special properties, but, as we have seen in Exercise E, quadrilaterals with particular properties have particular names.

(1) Quadrilaterals with point symmetry (rotational symmetry of order 2) are called *parallelograms* (see Figure 27). We shall write
$$P = \{\text{parallelograms}\}.$$

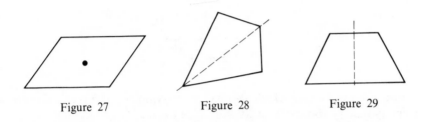

| Figure 27 | Figure 28 | Figure 29 |

(2) Quadrilaterals with line symmetry in a diagonal are called *kites* (see Figure 28). We shall write
$$K = \{\text{kites}\}.$$

(3) Quadrilaterals with line symmetry in a mediator of a side are called *isosceles trapeziums* (see Figure 29). We shall write
$$I = \{\text{isosceles trapeziums}\}.$$

Parallelograms need not have line symmetry so a parallelogram is not necessarily a kite. If we try to draw a parallelogram which is also a kite, we find that we have a *rhombus*. (See Figure 30.) So $P \cap K = \{\text{rhombuses}\} = D$ (for diamonds). Notice that rhombuses have line symmetry in both their diagonals as well as having point symmetry.

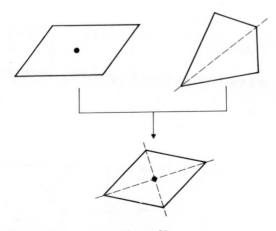

Figure 30

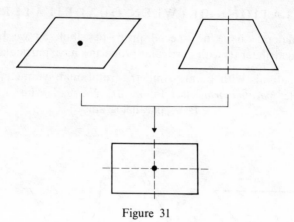

Figure 31

An isosceles trapezium which also has point symmetry is a rectangle, which has line symmetry about both mediators. (See Figure 31).

$$P \cap I = \{\text{rectangles}\} = R.$$

Finally, $D \cap R = \{\text{squares}\} = S$. Notice that S is a subset of all the previous sets.

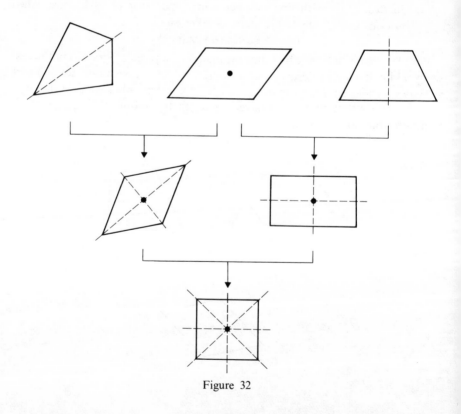

Figure 32

Exercise F

1 Write down as many subset relations such as $S \subset P$ as you can find in the following collections of sets:
  (a) P, K, D, S;   (b) P, I, R, S.

2 Write down any other intersection relations such as $S \cap P = S$ that you can find in the following collections of sets:
  (a) P, K, D, S;   (b) P, I, R, S.

*3 Which quadrilaterals have reflection symmetry in both their diagonals?

4 Which quadrilaterals have rotational symmetry of order 2?

*5 Which quadrilaterals have rotational symmetry of order 2 and no other symmetry?

6 Which quadrilaterals have diagonals which are perpendicular?

*7 Which quadrilaterals have sides which are all equal?

8 Which quadrilaterals have sides any pair of which is either parallel or perpendicular?

*9 (a) Which set is equal to $K \cap I$?
  (b) Copy the Venn diagram shown in Figure 33, indicating clearly the regions representing the sets D, R and S.

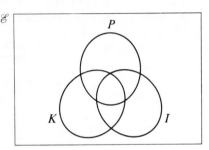

Figure 33

10 Copy and complete the following statements:
  (a) A quadrilateral in which the diagonals bisect each other must be a ...
  (b) A parallelogram in which the diagonals are equal must be a ... ;
  (c) A quadrilateral in which the diagonals bisect each other at right angles must be a ...
  (d) A quadrilateral in which the diagonals bisect each other and are equal must be a ...

SUMMARY

Parallel lines

Angles marked $x°$ are equal.
$x + y = 180.$

(Section 1)

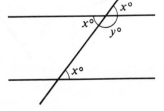

Figure 34

Angle sum of a triangle

The angles of a triangle add up to 180°.
The exterior angle is equal to the sum of
the two opposite interior angles.

(Section 2)

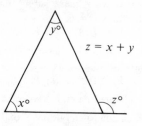

Figure 35

Angle sum of a polygon

The exterior angles of any polygon add up to 360°. The sum of the interior
angles of an n-sided polygon is $180(n - 2)°$.

A regular polygon is one with all sides equal and all angles equal.

(Section 3)

Symmetry of triangles

(lines of symmetry are shown dotted)

   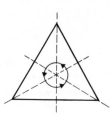

Isosceles triangle
One line of symmetry

Equilateral triangle
Three lines of symmetry, rotational
symmetry of order 3

Figure 36

Symmetries of quadrilaterals

   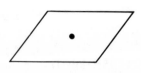   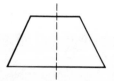

Kite
A diagonal line of
symmetry

Parallelogram
A centre of rotational
symmetry of order 2

Isosceles trapezium
A mediator line of
symmetry

Figure 37

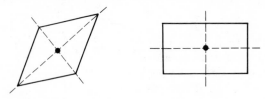

Rhombus   Rectangle

Two lines of symmetry and a centre of rotational symmetry of order 2

Square

Four lines of symmetry and a centre of rotational symmetry of order 4

Figure 37 (continued)

(Sections 4, 5)

Summary exercise

In questions 1–5 calculate the angles marked with letters in Figure 38.

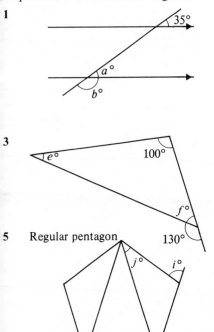

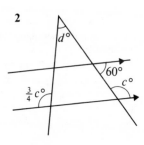

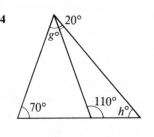

Figure 38

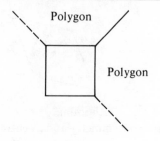

Figure 39

6 A square and two identical regular polygons are fitted together as shown in Figure 39. How many sides do the polygons have?

7 Name quadrilaterals with the following symmetries:
(a) reflection symmetry in both diagonals (only);
(b) half-turn symmetry, and no other;
(c) reflection symmetry in the mediators of both pairs of opposite sides.

8 If $\mathscr{E} = \{\text{quadrilaterals}\}$, $P = \{\text{parallelograms}\}$ and $D = \{\text{rhombuses}\}$, what can be said about:
(a) $P \cap D$;
(b) $P \cup D$;
(c) X if $P \cap X = D$?

9 If a figure has reflection symmetry in two perpendicular axes, what, if any, other symmetry must it possess?

10 A certain style of panelled soccer ball has two regular pentagons and a regular hexagon meeting at a point (see Figure 40). This seems to be impossible. Why? It does in fact happen. Explain.

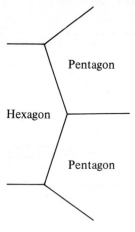

Figure 40

Miscellaneous exercise

1 In Figure 41, O is the centre of the circle through A, B and C.
(a) What can be said about the lengths of AO and OC?
(b) What kind of triangle is AOC?
(c) Calculate angle AOP.
(d) Calculate angle BOP similarly.
(e) Find angles AOB and ACB.

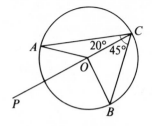

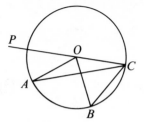

Figure 41   Figure 42

2 In Figure 42, O is the centre of the circle through A, B and C.
   (a) Why is triangle OAC isosceles?
   (b) Name another isosceles triangle in the diagram.
   (c) If angle $OCA = 30°$ find angles OAC and POA.
   (d) If angle $OCB = 74°$ find angles OBC and POB.
   (e) Find angles AOB and ACB.

3 Repeat question 1 with angle $ACO = x°$ and angle $OCB = y°$. What can you deduce about the general relation between the angles AOB and ACB?

4 Figure 43 shows a triangle XOY where the angle at O is a right-angle, and the angle at X is 15°. X is reflected in OY to give the point U and Y is reflected in OX to give V.
   (a) What type of quadrilateral is $XYUV$? Why?
   (b) The image of Y under reflection in UV is T. What kind of triangle is YUT? Why?

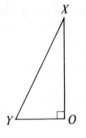

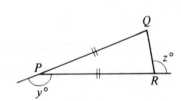

Figure 43   Figure 44

5 If in Figure 44 $PQ = PR$, find an equation connecting y and z.

6 If in a triangle ABC the internal bisectors of the angles at B and C meet at I and angle $BIC = 100°$, find angle BAC.

7 If $S = \{$squares$\}$, $K = \{$kites$\}$, $P = \{$parallelograms$\}$ and $D = \{$rhombuses$\}$, draw sketches to illustrate possible members of the following sets, showing all lines and centres of symmetry:
   (a) $K \cap R'$;   (b) $P \cap R'$;   (c) $D \cap S'$;   (d) $S \cap K'$.

8 $ABCD$ and $PQRS$ are two quadrilaterals. Insert $\Rightarrow$, $\Leftarrow$ or $\Leftrightarrow$ to make the following into true statements.
   (a) $ABCD$ is a rhombus $ABCD$ has at least two lines of symmetry.
   (b) AB is parallel to DC and $AD = BC$ $ABCD$ is a parallelogram.
   (c) The angles at A, B, C, D are equal to $ABCD$ is similar to $PQRS$
       the angles at P, Q, R, S respectively
   (d) $PR = QS$ $PQRS$ is a rectangle.

20

Probability

1. ORDER OUT OF CHAOS

In 1654 a gambler, the Chevalier de Méré, asked a French mathematician, Blaise Pascal, to help him in deciding how to share the stake money in a game of dice. Pascal discussed the problem with Fermat, another eminent mathematician, and in solving the problem they started the theory of probability. Today the theories that were developed from a game of dice are used extensively in economics, industry, science and sociology. To help us develop these theories, consider the following:

(1) The chance of a fourth division team winning the FA cup is nil.
(2) The chance of a die showing a four on the next throw is one in six.
(3) Cambridge are 5 to 2 favourites for the Boat Race.
(4) Tomorrow will almost certainly be sunny.

In each of the above statements an attempt has been made to forecast the result of some future event and to indicate its likelihood using phrases such as 'nil', 'one in six', 'almost certainly'. To develop these ideas we need the results of some very basic experiments.

Experiments

It is suggested that you share the work of performing and recording results. A calculator will be useful.

Experiment 1

Toss a single coin 50 times and note the results scoring 0 for a tail and 1 for a head. Make a table like Table 1. Use a calculator to evaluate the fourth row (to 3 s.f.) for $N = 1, 2, 3, ..., 9, 10, 15, 20, ..., 45, 50$.

Number of throw (N)	1	2	3	4	5	6	...
Score	0	1	1	0	1	1	
Running total (r)	0	1	2	2	3	4	
$\dfrac{r}{N}$	0	0.500	0.667	0.500	0.600	0.667	...

Table 1

Plot a graph of $N \longrightarrow \dfrac{r}{N}$, joining up the points with a dotted line.

Experiment 2
Throw a die 50 times recording 1 every time you throw a six, and 0 otherwise. Make a table of results along the lines followed in Experiment 1 and draw a graph of $N \longrightarrow \dfrac{r}{N}$.

Experiment 3
Toss a drawing-pin onto a table 50 times recording 1 every time it lands with its point up, and 0 otherwise. Record your results and make a table showing running totals as in the two previous experiments. Plot a graph of $N \longrightarrow \dfrac{r}{N}$.

Experiment 4
You need some coloured counters in a box. Shake the box and without looking pick out a counter. Record 1 if it is of a particular colour, say yellow, and record 0 otherwise. Replace the counter, shake the box and repeat, say, 50 times. Record the results as in previous cases.

2. RELATIVE FREQUENCY

You should now look at the graphs you have drawn and discuss them. In particular what would you expect to happen if you had extended the experiments to include many times more results?

We need some technical names. In Experiment 2, for example, the throw of a die is called a *trial* and the occurrence (or otherwise) of a six is an *event*. If, after N trials, the event (of a six) has occurred r times we say that the relative frequency (of a six) is the fraction r/N. The graphs you have plotted have been of relative frequency (r/N) against the number of trials (N). On one occasion when Experiment 4 was done the graph of results was as shown in Figure 1 and we would perhaps expect graphs for all the experiments to be similar. You may well have found that the dotted line 'settles down' to a particular value of r/N. What was

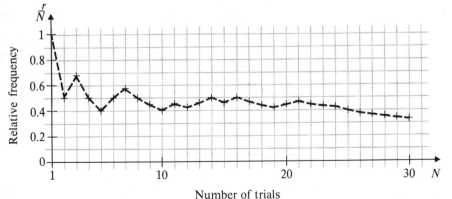

Number of trials

Figure 1

this value in the case of Experiment 1? Can you give a *simple* reason why the graph should settle down to around this value?

Can you give *simple* reasons for the limiting values (i.e. settling down values) of r/N in the other experiments? Try to answer this before reading further.

As a die is symmetrical and has six faces, a score of six is just as likely as any other score. We would expect a six to be thrown on one-sixth of all occasions and the relative frequency, r/N, tends to $\frac{1}{6}$. However, there is no such symmetry argument in the case of a drawing-pin and the limiting value of r/N can only be found by experiment.

Exercise A

These questions could well be answered by discussion with others in the class.

*1 A card is drawn from a standard pack, its suit is recorded and the card is replaced and the pack shuffled. The trial is repeated many times. Roughly what proportion (fraction) of cards drawn would you expect to be Hearts?

 2 Roughly how many threes would you expect to get with 30 throws of a die? How many with 300 throws? Would you be very surprised if you had only 4 threes in your 30 throws? In your 300 throws? Why?

*3 What would be the value of r/N if you never had success with the trial under consideration? What would be its value if you always had success? Why could the value of r/N never be greater than 1?

 4 A match box contains 12 beads of which 3 are red, 4 blue, and 5 green. The box is shaken, a bead pulled out and its colour noted. It is then replaced, the box shaken and the trial repeated many times. If green was drawn 50 times how many times do you think red might have been drawn? How many times do you think the trial might have been repeated?

 5 Bill and Ben were tossing two coins to see how many heads they obtained. Before they started, the conversation went:

Bill:'There are three possibilities, we either get no heads or one head or two heads. So if we toss them 100 times we should get one head about 33 times.'

Ben: 'I disagree. As the coins are different we can get one head in two ways (on either coin) so we should get one head more than 33 times.'

Who do you think was right? Try the experiment and see.

 6 In playing games such as Monopoly it is usual to throw two dice together and total the score indicated on them. What possible scores are there?

  Is the chance of scoring 2 the same as that of scoring 8? Throw a pair of dice 100 times and keep a record of the total scored each time. Plot your results as a frequency diagram. Does it appear that the chances of some scores occurring are better than others? What fraction of your trials gave a score of

  (a) 2;   (b) 4;   (c) 7?

3. PROBABILITY

Consider again Experiment 2. The value of r/N tended to $\frac{1}{6}$ (≈ 0.167) as N became large. We say that the *probability* of throwing a six is $\frac{1}{6}$, and write $P(\text{scoring a six}) = \frac{1}{6}$.

Provided the experiment is done fairly, the relative frequency, r/N, always tends to a limit and it is this value that is known as the probability of the event. In many cases there are simple reasons why probabilities should take particular values. For example, when tossing a coin, P (head) $= \frac{1}{2}$ because there are two equally probable results, heads or tails, and similarly, when drawing a card from a pack, P (Hearts) $= \frac{1}{4}$. But it is important to realise that there are other cases where the probabilities can only be determined by repeated observations: for example, P(drawing-pin lands point up) or P (it will rain in Winchester on St Swithun's Day).

An event which never happens would have relative frequency 0, the smallest possible value for a relative frequency. An event which always happens would have relative frequency 1, the largest possible value. The probability of an event is between 0 and 1 (inclusive).

Use of set notation

The set of the possible outcomes of throwing a die is:
$$\mathscr{E} = \{1, 2, 3, 4, 5, 6\}.$$
Suppose that we are interested in the probability of throwing either a 2 or a 3. The set of outcomes we are interested in is:
$$S = \{2, 3\}.$$
Then, since from the symmetry of the die all scores are equally likely, the probability is equal to:
$$\frac{\text{the number of elements in } S}{\text{the number of elements in } \mathscr{E}}.$$
Thus the probability of throwing either a 2 or a 3 is $\dfrac{2}{6} = \dfrac{1}{3}$. You will remember that this is usually written:
$$P(S) = \frac{n(S)}{n(\mathscr{E})} = \frac{2}{6} = \frac{1}{3},$$
where $P(S)$ denotes the probability of event S, and $n(S)$ and $n(\mathscr{E})$ denote the numbers of elements in S and E respectively.

Example 1
Find the probability of cutting a pack of playing cards and obtaining an ace.

In this case the set of possible outcomes is:
$$\mathscr{E} = \{\text{the 52 cards in a pack of playing cards}\},$$
and the event we are interested in is:
$$S = \{\text{ace of Hearts, ace of Clubs, ace of Diamonds, ace of Spades}\}.$$
The probability of obtaining an ace is:
$$P(S) = \frac{n(S)}{n(\mathscr{E})} = \frac{4}{52} = \frac{1}{13}.$$

Exercise B

*1 A box contains 7 red biros and 3 blue ones. George takes a biro without looking. What is the probability that he takes
(*a*) a red one;   (*b*) a blue one?

2 A bag contains 40 balls of which 5 are green, 15 are black and the rest are yellow. Marion takes a ball from the bag without looking. Find the probability that she takes
(*a*) a black ball;   (*b*) a yellow ball;   (*c*) a ball which is not green.

*3 A box contains 3 red, 2 yellow and 5 blue counters. Frances takes a counter from the box without looking. What is the probability that she takes
(*a*) a blue counter;   (*b*) a red counter?

4 In a raffle for a box of chocolates 258 tickets are sold. What is the probability that you will win the box of chocolates if you have bought 3 tickets?

*5 The names of Arthur, Brenda, Christine, Donald and Edward are put in a hat and one name is drawn out. What is the probability that
(*a*) a girl is chosen;
(*b*) a boy is chosen;
(*c*) Christine is chosen;
(*d*) Edward is not chosen?

6 What is the probability of drawing a picture card from a pack of playing cards (joker excluded)?

*7 If the probability that a person chosen at random will be left-handed is $\frac{1}{20}$, what is the probability that a person chosen at random will be right-handed?

8 What is the connection between $P(A)$, the probability that an event A happens, and $P(A')$, the probability that A does not happen?

4. COMBINED EVENTS

In Exercise A, question 6, you may have been surprised to find that the chance of scoring, say, 7 is considerably more than scoring 12. This is where intuition leads us astray. Suppose, for argument's sake, that you have a red die and a blue die. In how many different ways can they land when thrown together?

The possibilities can be neatly represented on squared paper as in Figure 2. Each cross represents a possible outcome. The circled cross, for example, represents a 5 on the red die and a 4 on the blue die. This can conveniently be

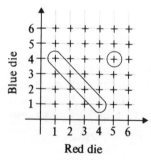

Red die

Figure 2

represented as the ordered pair (5, 4). We say an ordered pair because the order is important. (5, 4) is not the same as (4, 5). What do you think (4, 5) represents?

Example 2
  Calculate the probability of scoring a total of 5 with two dice.

$$\mathscr{E} = \{\text{the different ways in which two dice can land}\},$$
$$S = \{(4, 1), (3, 2), (2, 3), (1, 4)\}.$$

(The points corresponding to S are shown in the loop in Figure 2.) Hence the probability of scoring 5 is:

$$P(S) = \frac{n(S)}{n(\mathscr{E})} = \frac{4}{36} = \frac{1}{9}.$$

Example 3
  Find the probability of a 5 showing when two dice are thrown.

  The points corresponding to a 5 showing are indicated by F in Figure 3. The set has 11 members, so

$$P(\text{a 5 showing}) = \frac{11}{36}.$$

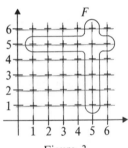

Figure 3

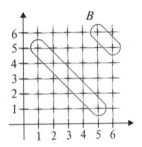

Figure 4

Example 4
  Find the probability of scoring a total of 6 or 11 with two dice.

In Figure 4 sets A and B have been labelled, corresponding to scores of 6 and 11 respectively. $n(A \cup B) = 7$, so

$$P(\text{score of 6 or 11}) = \frac{n(A \cup B)}{n(\mathscr{E})} = \frac{7}{36}.$$

  It is often best to draw a diagram to illustrate all possible outcomes but there are occasions when it is just as quick to list them. For example, if a coin is tossed twice we could either draw a diagram

		First	
Second	T	×	×
	H	×	×
		H	T

or we could list the possibilities (H, H), (H, T), (T, H), (T, T) as a set of ordered pairs; these are, of course, the same as the 'coordinates' of the points shown in the diagram.

Exercise C

*1   A penny and a 5p piece are tossed together. Copy and complete the table below of all possible results.

1p coin   H ...
_____

5p coin   H ...

What are the probabilities that:

   (a) they both show heads; (b) exactly one head shows; (c) they both show tails? Add together your answers to (a), (b) and (c).

2   Draw a diagram such as Figure 2 to show the possible ways in which two dice can fall.

   (a) What is the probability of a total score of 5?

   (b) What is the probability of a total score of 6?

   (c) What is the most probable total score?

   (d) Calculate the probabilities of each of the possible scores. What is the sum of these probabilities?

*3   A married couple intend to have two children. Using G for girl and B for boy, write down the set of ordered pairs which represent the possible families.

Assuming that a boy is as likely as a girl, what is the probability of one of each?

4   Two dice in the form of tetrahedra, with the numbers 1, 2, 3, 4 on their faces, are thrown. The numbers on the two faces which are down are added together.

   (a) Find: (i) the lowest score; (ii) the highest score.

   (b) Represent the set of possible outcomes on a diagram similar to Figure 2.

   (c) What are the probabilities of each possible total score?

*5   The names of Andrew, Betty, Christine and David are put in a hat to select two representatives for an inter-form competition. Make a list of all the possible pairs of names that could be drawn from the hat. What are the probabilities of drawing:

   (a) Andrew and David;   (b) a boy and a girl;

   (c) a pair which includes Betty;   (d) a pair which does not include David?

6   A coin is thrown three times. Using H for 'head', and T for 'tail', write down the set of ordered triples which represent the possible outcomes. What are the probabilities of:

   (a) three 'heads'; (b) two 'heads'; (c) one 'head';

   (d) no 'heads';   (e) all alike?

*7   (a) If you were to write out the set of ordered triples when three dice are thrown, how many elements would there be?

   (b) Could they be represented on a diagram like Figure 2? Suggest a modification.

   (c) What is the probability of a triple 6?

8   A number is selected at random from the set $\{1, 2, 3, 4, 5, 6, 7, 8, 9, 10, 11, 12\}$.

   (a) What is the probability that it is even?

   (b) What is the probability that it is divisible by 3?

   (c) What is the probability that it is the either even or divisible by 3 (or both)?

*9   Draw a diagram to represent the draw of a card from a standard pack with the face values 2, 3, ... J, Q, K, A horizontally and the suit H, C, D, S vertically. A single card is chosen at random from the pack.

(a) Find P(Club).
(b) Find P(Ace).
(c) Find P(Ace and Club).
(d) Find P(Ace or Club).
Write down, and explain, a relation between the probabilities you have found.

10   Refer back to the four statements (1), (2), (3), (4) made at the beginning of this chapter.
   (i) On what basis do you think statement (1) was made?
   (ii) On what basis do you think statement (2) was made?
   (iii) In (3) the phrase '5 to 2 favourites' means that the bookmakers reckon that the

   probability of Cambridge winning is $\dfrac{5}{5+2} = \dfrac{5}{7}$. What do you think is then the

   probability that Oxford will win? What about a dead-heat?
   On what basis do you think such figures are put forward?
   (iv) On what basis do you think statement (4) was made?

5. THE LUCK OF THE DRAW

Have you ever won a large Premium Bond prize or a draw for a Cup Final ticket or a raffle for a fabulous holiday in the Bahamas? These are some examples of occasions when it is necessary to select a winner (or person or object) from among a set of possible winners (or persons or objects). This needs to be done in a fair manner so that no particular person is favoured more than any other. We say that the selection is done *on a random basis*, or, more simply, *at random*. Possible methods are to draw names out of a hat (raffles) or balls out of a bag (FA Cup draw) or to toss a coin (to see who chooses ends at hockey).

   We also use the phrase *at random* in talking about probability; for instance, in question 7 of Exercise B the probability that a person chosen at random was left-handed was 1/20.

   On the first day of every month a list of winning numbers of Premium Bonds is chosen at random by a computer known as ERNIE. (What do the initials E.R.N.I.E. stand for?) This produces combinations of numbers and letters such as 1 JP 297658 or 3 CP 257615. Many millions of bonds are sold and the probability of a particular number coming up is very small, but not zero!

   Some of the questions in Exercise D indicate ways in which you may make up some random numbers for yourself.

Exercise D

1   What is the connection between tables (a) and (b) below?

(a) 3 coins can land	(b) Binary numeral	(c) Natural numbers
T, T, T	000	0
T, T, H	001	1
T, H, T	010	2
T, H, H	011	3
H, T, T	100	4
H, T, H	101	5
H, H, T	110	6
H, H, H	111	7

As any one of the eight possibilities in (a) is as probable as any other, we can obtain a random number between 0 and 7 (inclusive) by tossing three coins and noting the order of heads and tails.

Use this method to generate, say, 80 random digits between 0 and 7. Find how many times each digit occurs and see if the system is working fairly.

2   Adapt question 1 to find random numbers between 0 and 15.

3   How many coins would you need to give random numbers between 0 and 63? Between 0 and 127? What range of random numbers could you generate, in a similar manner, with ten coins? How would you adapt this method to give random numbers between 0 and 100?

4   Icosahedral dice are used in Wargaming. Each digit 0 to 9 is repeated twice on the twenty faces. If possible use some (can you make your own?) to generate some random numbers.

5   Three-figure tables could be used to give a sequence of digits in several ways. One possibility would be to use the last digits in the sines of the angles.
    (a) Do you think this would give a random distribution of the digits 0–9?
    (b) Do you think the same would be true if the first digits were used?

6   Surveys and opinion polls are carried out by making random selections of people to question. Here are some items for discussion.
    (a) You want to select three pupils at random from your school for a survey about travel to school. What is wrong with going to the school entrance a few minutes before school begins and selecting a group of three who are coming in together?
    (b) A firm of porridge oat manufacturers wanted to find out how popular porridge was for breakfast. They opened a London telephone directory at random and contacted everyone on that page. They found that 80% had porridge for breakfast. Can you explain what had gone wrong with their random sample?
    (c) You want to predict the result of the local elections and to do this you go into the main street at 11 a.m. on a Monday morning and interview people on the pavement. Will you have a random sample?
    (d) 'Last night $3\frac{1}{4}$ million people watched the big fight on television.' How would this information be obtained?
    (e) A firm which manufactures dish-washing machines wants to know what percentage of the population uses their machines. They do this by selecting people at random from a telephone directory. Have they introduced bias into their sample?
    (f) 'In a random sample of 10 housewives, 9 preferred Whoosh to any other detergent.' What questions would you want to ask the advertisers about the randomness of their sample and about their method of obtaining this information?

SUMMARY

If, in N trials, an event has occurred r times, then the relative frequency of that event is $\frac{r}{N}$.

If the experiment referred to is conducted in a fair (random) manner then it is a matter of experimental fact that the relative frequency, $\frac{r}{N}$, tends (settles down) to a limit. It is this limit which is called the probability of the event.

(Sections 1, 2)

It is often possible, because of some sort of symmetry, to give simple explanations for some probabilities. For example,

$P(\text{head on coin}) = \frac{1}{2}$ there are two equally likely outcomes, one favourable.

$P(5 \text{ or } 6 \text{ on die}) = \frac{2}{6} = \frac{1}{3}$ there are six equally likely outcomes, two favourable.

But there are cases where an appeal to symmetry is no use: for example, $P(\text{drawing-pin lands point up})$.

In general, if there is a set $\mathscr{E}$ of equally likely outcomes and a set S is associated with the event under discussion then

$$P(\text{event occurs}) = \frac{n(S)}{n(\mathscr{E})}.$$

If A is any event:

$$0 \leqslant P(A) \leqslant 1;$$
$$P(A') + P(A) = 1.$$

(Section 3)

Summary exercise

1   A card is drawn from a standard pack, its suit is recorded, the card replaced and the pack shuffled. This trial is repeated many times. Roughly what proportion of cards drawn would be
(a) red;   (b) Jacks;   (c) Hearts;   (d) the Jack of Hearts?

2   A box of Smarties contains 35 red, 45 yellow and 20 green beans. What is the probability that the first Smarty I pick is
(a) red;   (b) not green?

3   What is the probability of winning all 5 tosses in a Test Match Series?

4   If two fair dice are thrown what is the probability of a total score of 8? If one die is inspected first (the other fell on the floor) and is seen to show 5 what is now the probability of a total score of 8?

5   A married couple have three children. What is the probability that
(a) there are no girls;
(b) there are more boys than girls?

6   In the game of OWZAT (pencil cricket) the first pencil bears the scores 1, 2, 3, 4, 6 and the appeal 'OWZAT'. The second pencil, only rolled after an appeal, bears 'bowled', 'caught', 'stumped', 'run out', 'not out' and 'no ball'.
(a) In a single turn, what is the probability of
(i) an appeal against the batsman;
(ii) an odd number of runs?
(b) An appeal has been made. What is the probability of the batsman not being out?

7   If the probability of being colour blind is $\frac{1}{9}$, how many people in a crowd of 500 would you expect to have normal colour vision?

8   A red die and a blue die are thrown together. What is the probability that
(a) the score on the red die is greater than 4;
(b) the score on the blue die is less than 3;
(c) both events (a) and (b) occur?

Miscellaneous exercise

1   What is the probability of drawing from a standard pack of 52 cards:
(*a*) a red Queen;   (*b*) a Queen;   (*c*) a red Diamond?

2   James glanced at the second hand of his old-fashioned watch. What is the probability that it was showing 17 or more, but less than 29, seconds past the minute?

3   Elizabeth has a digital watch. She glances at the seconds display. What is the probability that the digit 4 is showing?

4   For an examination a group of candidates were given 'index numbers' 631–670. If a candidate is chosen at random, what is the probability that his, or her, index number contains:
(*a*) the digit 5;   (*b*) the digit 6;   (*c*) the digit 6 just twice?

5   A pair of fair dice are thrown once. What is the probability that:
(*a*) there will be a least one 6;
(*b*) there will be either a double or a 6;
(*c*) there will be neither a double nor a 6;
(*d*) the total score will be at least 9;
(*e*) the total score is 10, given that one die came down showing 2?

6   Three dice are thrown. In how many different ways can they fall? (Think of them as three different colours). What is the probability of a triple 3? What is the probability of a total score of 4 or less?

7   Make a list of all possible combinations of boys and girls in a family of four children. Use a 'binary code' where, for example, 1000 stands for boy, girl, girl, girl showing a boy as eldest child followed by three younger sisters.
(*a*) What is the probability of the family being all boys?
(*b*) What is the probability of 'two of each'?
(*c*) If the eldest two are boys what is the probability that there is exactly one girl?

8   Two people each draw a card from a standard pack. Assume first that the first card is replaced and the pack shuffled before the second is drawn. What is the probability that each person draws a card from the same suit? What is the answer if the first card is not replaced?

9   On a 'one-armed bandit' there are three reels with five different fruits plus a star on each reel. After inserting a coin and pulling a handle, the player sees that the three reels revolve independently before stopping. What is the probability that:
(*a*) three lemons will appear;
(*b*) any three of a kind will appear;
(*c*) two lemons and a star will appear?

10   Two dice are thrown. Three events are given as follows:
A = the total score is 9,
B = the total score is 7,
C = at least one of the dice shows a five.
(*a*) Show all the possible outcomes, and these events, on a suitable diagram.
(*b*) Write down the following probabilities:
(i) $P(A)$;   (ii) $P(B)$;   (iii) $P(A \text{ and } B)$;   (iv) $P(A \text{ or } B)$.
(*c*) Write down the following probabilities:
(i) $P(C)$;   (ii) $P(A \text{ and } C)$;   (iii) $P(A \text{ or } C)$.
(*d*) If X and Y are any events, what is the relation between $P(X)$, $P(Y)$, $P(X \text{ and } Y)$ and $P(X \text{ or } Y)$?

11 In a form of 30, 22 like pop music, 12 like classical music and 2 like neither.
    (a) Draw a Venn diagram to illustrate this information.
    (b) How many of the form like both pop and classical music?
    (c) What are the probabilities that a member of the form, chosen at random, likes:
        (i) pop music, but not classical music;
        (ii) both pop and classical music?

12 A coin is tossed and it lands heads up five times in succession. Anne claims that the probability of a tail on the next toss is greater than $\frac{1}{2}$; Brian claims that it is less than $\frac{1}{2}$.
    (a) Do you agree with either of them?
    (b) Would you change your mind if there had been 50 successive heads?

REVISION EXERCISE 18

1 Find the value of $3 - 2x^2 - x^3$ when $x = {}^-3$.

2 Write without brackets and simplify:
  (a) $8a - 2a(a + 3) + 2a(5 - 2a)$;
  (b) $(5a - 3b)^2$.

3 Solve the inequality $3(2x - 7) + 2(5 - 4x) > 6$.

4 Calculate the angle θ shown in Figure 1.

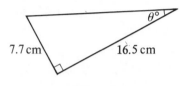

Figure 1

5 Draw the network given by the route matrix
$$\begin{array}{c} \\ K \\ L \\ M \\ N \end{array} \overset{\displaystyle \begin{array}{cccc} K & L & M & N \end{array}}{\begin{bmatrix} 0 & 0 & 0 & 1 \\ 1 & 1 & 0 & 1 \\ 0 & 1 & 0 & 2 \\ 1 & 1 & 1 & 2 \end{bmatrix}}$$

6 A sheet of metal is to have a hole drilled through it so that the area remaining is half the original area. Calculate the diameter of the hole if:
  (a) the original sheet is square, with sides of length 40.0 cm;
  (b) the original sheet is circular, with diameter 40.0 cm.

7 In the 1980 Winter Olympics the women's downhill run started at an altitude of 1181 m and finished at an altitude of 481 m above sea-level. The length of the slope was 2694 m. Find the average angle of slope of the run.

8 A car uses 18.0 litres in travelling 156 km.
  (a) Find the average rate of petrol consumption in litres per 100 km.
  (b) How much petrol would you expect the car to use for a journey of 215 km?

REVISION EXERCISE 19

1 Calculate:
  (a) $\frac{1}{4} + \frac{3}{8} + \frac{5}{16}$; (b) $\frac{8}{9} \div \frac{1}{3}$.

2 If $a = \dfrac{15}{c}$ calculate a when c is
  (a) $\frac{1}{2}$; (b) 0.0003.

3 What is the diameter of a circle of area 1.00 m²?

4 The top of a tree has an elevation of 25° when viewed from a distance of 80 m from the foot of the tree. Calculate the height of the tree.

5 The ages of a group of children are given in the table below. Calculate their mean age.

Age in years and months	13.0–13.4	13.4–13.8	13.8–14.0	14.0–14.4
Frequency	3	6	12	7

6 Find the coordinates of the images of the points with coordinates $({}^-3, 4)$, $(2, 1)$ and

($^-$2, $^-$3) under reflection in the line $x + y = 0$. Write down the matrix representing this transformation.

7   A souvenir from the Plas Aur gold-mine costs £276, which includes VAT at 15%. What would it cost for export, without the VAT?

8   The material for a wigwam is cut in the form of a 210° sector of a circle radius 3.0 m. What is the area of the material used? What is the height of the wigwam?

REVISION EXERCISE 20

1   Find the gradient and the equation of the line joining the points (4, 0) and (10, 2).

2   Solve the equation $\frac{2}{3}z - \frac{1}{2}z = \frac{4}{5}$.

3   Make W the subject of the formula $t = 15W + 10$.

4   Calculate the distance between the points with coordinates ($^-$4, 6) and (20, 1).

5   If $\mathbf{M} = \begin{bmatrix} 6 & ^-4 \\ 9 & ^-6 \end{bmatrix}$ calculate $\mathbf{M}^2$.

6   Write without brackets and simplify:
   (a) $(2a - 3)(3a + 2)$;   (b) $(2a + 3b)^2 + (3a - 2b)^2$.

7   Calculate the interior angle of a regular twenty-sided polygon.

8   Atlas' girl-friend, Mercatrix, decided to take a photograph of him carrying the world on his shoulders. She thought it would improve the picture if she wrapped a piece of tinsel round the equator. If the diameter of the earth is 68 847 stadia, calculate the least length of tinsel needed.

   How much extra tinsel would be needed if the diameter of the earth is actually 1 stadium greater than the figure given?

Answers

CHAPTER 11 CIRCLES

Exercise A (p. 2)

1 (*a*) 70 cm; (*c*) 6 m. **3** (*a*) 20 cm; (*c*) 0.6 km

Exercise B (p. 5)

1 (*a*) 38 cm; (*c*) 117.1 m. **3** (*a*) 651 km; (*c*) 1 cm. **5** False; 3.
7 21 m. **9** 8 times. **11** 1700 km/h; no. **13** (*a*) 92.9 m.

Exercise C (p. 7)

1 (*a*) 50 cm^2; (*c*) 1200 m^2. **3** (*a*) 10 km; (*c*) 7 cm. **5** 5200 m^2.
7 (*a*) 11.3 m^2. **9** (*a*) 35.9 cm; (*c*) 0.95 m. **11** 13.
13 10.4 cm.

Exercise D (p. 10)

1 25.6 cm. **3** (*a*) 50.8 cm^2; (*c*) 203 cm^2. **4** 90°. **6** 40°.

Exercise E (p. 13)

1 (*a*) 70 m^2. **3** 8.5 cm^2, 2.3 cm^3. **5** (*b*) 3.4 cm; (*c*) 7.15 cm.
7 30 cm. **11** 31 minutes.

Exercise F (p. 17)

1 3900 cm^2. **3** (*a*) 25 cm; (*c*) 19 cm.
5 (*a*) 2.1 m. **7** (*a*) 7.5 cm.

CHAPTER 12 PROPORTION AND GRAPHS

Exercise A (p. 24)

1 (*a*) (i) 28p; (ii) 68p; (*b*) (i) 8; (ii) 11; (*c*) $C = 4n$.

3

P	1	2	7	16	30	
B	6.30	12.60	44.10	100.80	189.00	$B = 6.3P.$

5 0.28 A.
7 (*a*) 1.36×10^4 kg/m^3; (*b*) 0.42 kg; (*c*) 7.4×10^{-5} m^3.

Exercise B (p. 25)

1 (*a*)

t	2	4	8	12	24
d	7	14	28	42	84

(*c*)

x	15	30	60	10	1
y	9	18	36	6	0.6

3 (*a*) 28.5 litres.
5 (*a*) 7980 ruples.

7 (*b*) 83 km/h.

9 (*a*) DM4.76/£.

11 (*a*) (i) 160 mm ;   (*b*) (i) 24 N.

Exercise C (p. 29)

1 (*a*) 3;   (*c*) $\frac{-1}{3}$.

2 (*a*) $y = 3x$;   (*c*) $y = \frac{-1}{3}x$

5 (*a*) 3;   (*c*) $^-3$.

7 (*a*) $\frac{1}{2}$;   (*c*) 1.1.

9 (*a*) 1;   (*c*) $\dfrac{p+1}{4p}$.

11 (*a*) 3;   (*c*) $\frac{-1}{2}$.

13 (*a*) No;   (*b*) 0.3; $E = 0.3L$.

15 (*c*) 41 litres;   (*d*) (i) 0.41.

Exercise D (p. 32)

1 (*a*)

x	0	2	4	6	8
$\frac{1}{2}x$	0	1	2	3	5
$\frac{1}{2}x + 3$	3	4	5	6	7

(*c*) $\frac{1}{2}$.

3 (*a*) See Figure A;   (*b*) $^-2$;   (*c*) (0, 5).

5 (*a*) See Figure B;   (*b*) 2;   (*c*) (3, 0) and ($^-1$, 0).

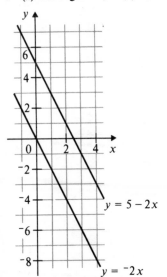

Figure A

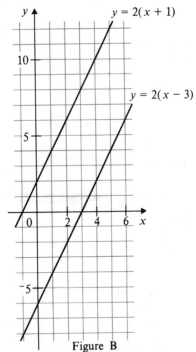

Figure B

Exercise E (p. 34)

1 $y = 2x - 2.$ **3** $x = 20 - 2t.$ **5** $y = x + 2.$ **7** $d = \frac{1}{20}t - 2.$

Exercise F (p. 35)

1 (*a*) 0.058.

3 0.17.

5 (*a*) (i) 180 km;   (ii) 60 km/h;   (*c*) (i) 60 km/h;   (ii) 0 km/h.

7 (*a*) 3.33; average speed of 3.33 m/s;
     (*c*) 1.88; acceleration of 1.88 m/s^2;
     (*e*) 0.3; average gradient of mountain slope.

CHAPTER 13   THE RIGHT-ANGLED TRIANGLE

Exercise B (p. 47)

1 $a = 5.8$; $c = 5.6$.   **2** 170 m.

Exercise C (p. 48)

1 $a = 106$; $c = 34$.   **2** 260 m.

Exercise D (p. 51)

1 $a = 74$; $c = 26$; $e = 18$; $g = 2.1$.
3 19.9 km.   **5** 0.93 m.   **7** 31 cm.   **9** (*a*) 40.2 km.

Exercise E (p. 55)

1 $a = 3.5$; $c = 0.66$; $e = 20$.
2 6.9 m.   **4** 88 m.

Exercise F (p. 58)

4 $a = 17$; $c = 23$; $e = 26$.   **6** 29 m.

Exercise G (p. 61)

1 $a = 33$; $c = 58$.   **2** 20.3°.
4 (*a*) 9.6°;   (*c*) 3.4°.   **5** 015°.

Exercise H (p. 64)

1 $a = 2.8$; $c = 0.28$.   **3** 3.5 m.   **5** 220 m.

CHAPTER 14   MATRICES

Exercise A (p. 69)

1 (*a*) 12.

Exercise B (p. 72)

1 (*a*) 4;   (*c*) $\begin{bmatrix} 27 & 56 & 16 & 63 \\ 11 & 15 & 9 & 36 \end{bmatrix}$.

4 (*a*) $\begin{bmatrix} 21 \\ 1 \end{bmatrix}$;   (*c*) $[6 \quad 22]$;   (*e*) $\begin{bmatrix} 16 \\ 6 \end{bmatrix}$;   (*g*) $\begin{bmatrix} 4 & 7 \\ ^-4 & 3 \\ 8 & 2 \end{bmatrix}$.

6 (a) $\begin{bmatrix} 22 & 38 \\ 16 & 25 \end{bmatrix}$; (c) $\begin{bmatrix} 44 & 10 \\ 32 & 6 \end{bmatrix}$; (e) $\begin{bmatrix} 17 & 32 \\ 15 & 76 \end{bmatrix}$.

8 $x = 1\frac{1}{2}$.

Exercise C (p. 74)

1 (a) £1.84.

3 3050 transistors, 7420 resistors, 3850 capacitors.

6 (a) Throfar won; (b) Runfast would have won.

Exercise D (p. 77)

1 $\begin{bmatrix} 0 & 0 & 1 \\ 1 & 0 & 1 \\ 0 & 1 & 0 \end{bmatrix}$; Matrix for two-stage journeys: $\begin{bmatrix} 0 & 1 & 0 \\ 0 & 1 & 1 \\ 1 & 0 & 1 \end{bmatrix}$.

3 $S = \begin{bmatrix} 0 & 1 & 0 & 0 \\ 0 & 0 & 1 & 0 \\ 0 & 0 & 0 & 1 \\ 0 & 1 & 0 & 0 \end{bmatrix}$ $S^2 = \begin{bmatrix} 0 & 0 & 1 & 0 \\ 0 & 0 & 0 & 1 \\ 0 & 1 & 0 & 0 \\ 0 & 0 & 1 & 0 \end{bmatrix}$.

5 $T = \begin{bmatrix} 0 & 1 & 0 & 1 \\ 0 & 0 & 1 & 1 \\ 1 & 0 & 0 & 0 \\ 0 & 0 & 1 & 0 \end{bmatrix}$; $T^2 = \begin{bmatrix} 0 & 0 & 2 & 1 \\ 1 & 0 & 1 & 0 \\ 0 & 1 & 0 & 1 \\ 1 & 0 & 0 & 0 \end{bmatrix}$.

9 (a) R^2 represents 'is a grandparent of'.

(b) R' represents 'is a child of'.

Exercise E (p. 81)

1 $\begin{bmatrix} 3 & ^-1 & ^-7 \\ 4 & 5 & 3 \end{bmatrix}$. **3** (a) $\begin{bmatrix} 2 & 3 \\ ^-4 & 5 \end{bmatrix}$; (b) $\begin{bmatrix} ^-2 & ^-3 \\ 4 & ^-5 \end{bmatrix}$.

CHAPTER 15 STATISTICS

Exercise B (p. 90)

1

Height in cm	5	6	7	8	9	10	11	12	13	14
Frequency	1	1	0	6	4	5	6	1	5	1

See Figure A.

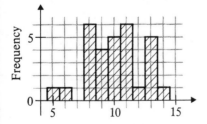

Height in centimetres

Figure A

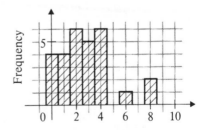

Goals per match

Figure B

3 (a)

Number of goals	0	1	2	3	4	5	6	7	8
Frequency	4	4	6	5	6	0	1	0	2

See Figure B.

5

Mass in grams	70–75	75–80	80–85	85–90	90–95	95–100	100–105	105–110
Frequency	2	5	8	11	11	7	5	1

See Figure C; 26% have a mass greater than 95 g.

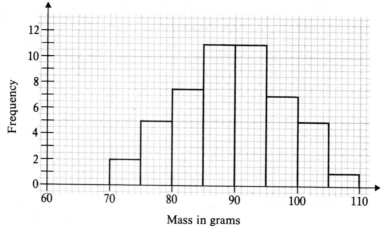

Figure C

7

Number of beats/min	50–54	55–59	60–64	65–69	70–74	75–79	80–84	85–89	90–94
Frequency	1	4	6	10	18	9	7	3	2

See Figure D.

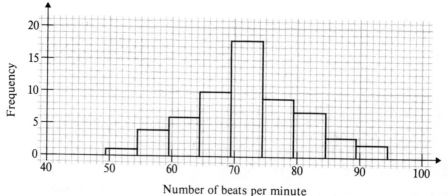

Figure D

Exercise C (p. 93)

1   Mean height $= \dfrac{302}{30} \approx 10.1$ cm.

3   Cup matches: mean number of goals per match $= \dfrac{77}{28} \approx 2.8$;

     League matches: mean number of goals per match $= \dfrac{108}{44} \approx 2.5$.

5   Total number of eggs $= 469$;   Mean number per nest ≈ 4.7.

7   0.66 misprints per page.

9   4.2 letters per word.

Exercise D (p. 96)

1   (*a*) Mean mass $= \dfrac{4475}{50} \approx 90$ g;   (*b*) 10.7 kg.

3   Mean mass $= \dfrac{375.5}{45} \approx 8.3$ kg.

5   Mean $= \dfrac{4330}{60} \approx 72$ beats per minute.

CHAPTER 16   CAN YOU CONVINCE ME?

Exercise C (p. 106)

2   (*a*) True;   (*c*) False.   3   (*a*) True;   (*c*) True.   6   (*a*) False;   (*c*) False.

Exercise D (p. 107)

1   (*a*) $2n + 2$;   (*b*) $4n + 2$.

3   Any two even numbers can be written as $2p$ and $2q$. Their difference is $2p - 2q = 2(p - q)$, which is even.

5   Any even number can be written as $2m$. Its square is $(2m)^2 = 4m^2$, which is divisible by 4.

Exercise E (p. 111)

 1   (*a*) $2x - 8$;   (*c*) $2ax - 8a$;   (*e*) $4xy - 15xz$.
 3   (*a*) $2a^2 + 3a + 1$;   (*c*) $6p^2 - 5p - 6$;   (*e*) $2a^2 + 9a - 35$.
 5   (*a*) $a^2 - 9$;   (*c*) $4b^2 - 25$;   (*e*) $r^2 - 49t^2$.
 7   (*a*) $x^2 + 6x + 9$;   (*c*) $a^2 - 10a + 25$;   (*e*) $9a^2 + 12ab + 4b^2$.
 9   (*a*) $112\,600\,000$.
11   (*a*) $(a + b)^2$;   (*c*) $(a + b)^2 - 2ab$.

Exercise F (p. 113)

 1   (*a*) $2^2 \times 3 \times 11^2$;   (*c*) $2 \times 3^4 \times 11$.
 6   $N = 100n + 10c + d = 98n + 2n + 10c + d = 7 \times 14n + 2n + 10c + d$,
      so N is divisible by $7 \Leftrightarrow 2n + 10c + d$ is divisible by 7.
 8   (*a*) $3^2 \times 5 \times 7$;   (*c*) $3^2 \times 5 \times 7 \times 11$.
10   (*a*) 3×37;   (*b*) (i) $2 \times 3 \times 37$.

CHAPTER 17   TRANSFORMATIONS AND MATRICES

Exercise A (p. 123)

1 $\begin{aligned} x' &= x \\ y' &= {}^-y \end{aligned}$.   **3** $\begin{aligned} x' &= {}^-x \\ y' &= {}^-y \end{aligned}$ **5** $\begin{aligned} x' &= y \\ y' &= x \end{aligned}$.   **7** $\begin{aligned} x' &= {}^-y \\ y' &= {}^-x \end{aligned}$.

Exercise B (p. 124)

1 $\begin{bmatrix} 1 & 0 \\ 0 & {}^-1 \end{bmatrix}$.   **3** $\begin{bmatrix} {}^-1 & 0 \\ 0 & {}^-1 \end{bmatrix}$.   **5** $\begin{bmatrix} 0 & 1 \\ 1 & 0 \end{bmatrix}$.   **7** $\begin{bmatrix} 0 & {}^-1 \\ {}^-1 & 0 \end{bmatrix}$.

Exercise C (p. 125)

1 S(*D*): (6, 17);   S(*F*):   ($^-$11, 10).

3 (*a*) $\begin{bmatrix} {}^-6 & {}^-3 & 0 & 3 & 6 \\ 9 & 11 & 13 & 15 & 17 \end{bmatrix}$

(*b*) (i) See Figure A;   (ii) yes;   yes;   (iii) $y = \frac{2}{3}x + 13$.

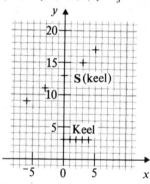

Figure A

5 (0, 0).

7 (*a*) N(*A*): ($^-$1, 3);   N(*C*): (2, 9);   N(*E*): ($^-$3, 4).
(*c*) (0, 0).

9 (*a*) $\begin{bmatrix} 6 & 7 & 8 & 9 \\ {}^-6 & {}^-7 & 2 & 6 \end{bmatrix}$.

Exercise D (p. 128)

1 (*a*) A(*P*): (0, 2);   **BA**(*P*): (0, 2);   A(*R*): (3, 4);   **BA**(*R*): ($^-$3, 4).

(*c*) $\begin{bmatrix} 0 & {}^-1 \\ 1 & 0 \end{bmatrix}$.

3 (*a*) (i) $\begin{bmatrix} {}^-1 & 0 \\ 0 & 1 \end{bmatrix}$;   (*c*) **M**: reflection in $y = x$;   **MN**: reflection in y-axis.

5

	I	X	Y	H
I	I	X	Y	H
X	X	I	H	Y
Y	Y	H	I	X
H	H	Y	X	I

I:identity
Y:reflection in y-axis

Exercise E (p. 130)

2 $\begin{bmatrix} 3 \\ 6 \end{bmatrix}$. **4** $\begin{bmatrix} -8 \\ -1 \end{bmatrix}$. **8** $\begin{bmatrix} 9 \\ 3 \end{bmatrix}$. **10** $\begin{bmatrix} -3 \\ 4 \end{bmatrix}$.

Exercise F (p. 132)

1 (a) $\begin{bmatrix} -3 \\ 2 \end{bmatrix}$ and $\begin{bmatrix} 2 \\ 0 \end{bmatrix}$.

3 (a) $\begin{bmatrix} -4 \\ 3 \end{bmatrix}$; (c) $\underset{\sim}{p}' = \begin{bmatrix} 5 \\ 2 \end{bmatrix}$, $\underset{\sim}{q}' = \begin{bmatrix} 0 \\ 2 \end{bmatrix}$, $\underset{\sim}{r}' = \begin{bmatrix} 5 \\ 6 \end{bmatrix}$; see Figure B.

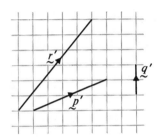

Figure B

CHAPTER 18 GRAPHS AND INEQUALITIES

Exercise A (p. 139)

1 (a)

x	1	3	5	7	9
y	12	36	60	84	108

(b) gradient = 12; (c) $C = 12n$.

3 (a) See Figure A; (b) £1; 50p;
(c) $C = \frac{1}{2}t + 1$.

5 (a) See Figure B; (b) £12; (c) 4p;
(d) $C = 0.04n + 12$.

7 $l = 20M + 30$; 4.5 kg.

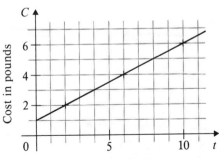

Figure A

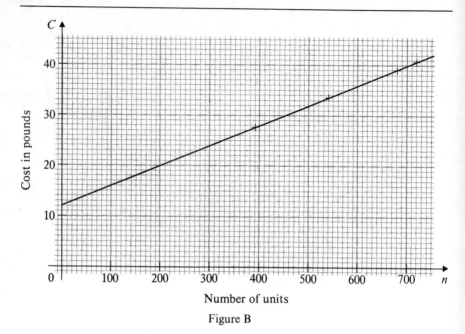

Figure B

Exercise B (p. 143)

1   (*c*) (ii) $3x + 2y = 96$;   (*d*) see Figure C;   gradient $= -\frac{3}{2}$.

3   (*b*) See Figure D;   (*c*) $12w + 16k = 96$;   (*d*) (i) 2.3 ha;   (ii) 1.3 ha.

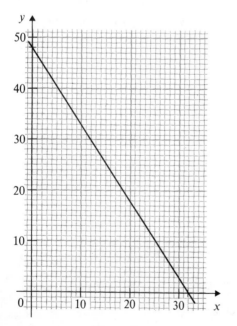

Figure C

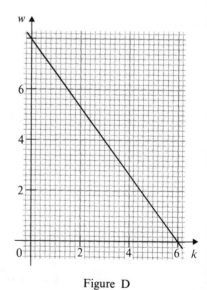

Figure D

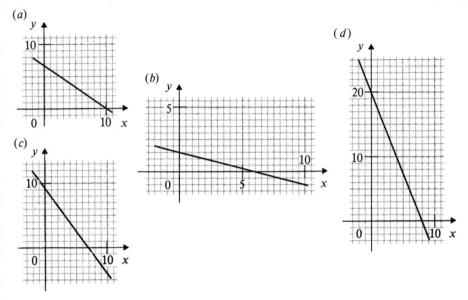

Figure E

5 See Figure E.

6 (a) $y = -\frac{2}{3}x + 6\frac{2}{3}$;   (b) $y = -\frac{1}{4}x + 1\frac{1}{2}$;   (c) $y = -\frac{4}{3}x + 9\frac{1}{3}$;   (d) $y = -\frac{5}{2}x + 20$.

9 See Figure F; $x = 2$, $y = 6$.

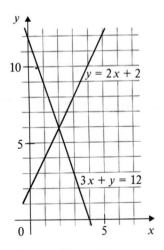

Figure F

Exercise C (p. 146)

1 See Figure G.

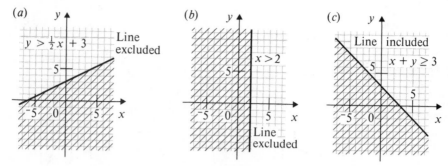

(a) $y > \frac{1}{2}x + 3$ Line excluded

(b) $x > 2$ Line excluded

(c) Line included $x + y \geq 3$

Figure G

5 (c) $5x + 4y < 44$;   (d) see Figure H;   (e) (i) 9;   (ii) 6.

7 (a) $2x + y \leqslant 24$;   (d) (i) £1;   (ii) 20 children and 2 adults.

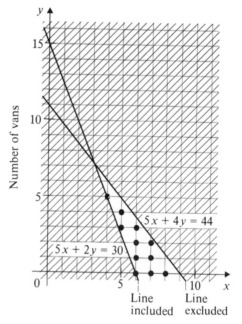

Number of vans

$5x + 4y = 44$

$5x + 2y = 30$

Line included   Line excluded

Number of lorries

Figure H

CHAPTER 19   CONFIGURATIONS

Exercise A (p. 151)

1 $p = 35$, (A); $q = 35$, (B) or $q = p = 35$ (A); $r = q = 35$ (A) or $r = p = 35$ (B).

3 $\theta = 75$; (A) and (B), or (A), (C) and (A)

5 $a = 40$ (B); $\theta + 2a = 180$ ((A) and (D)) so $\theta = 100$.

Exercise B (p. 153)

1 $a + 100 + 30 = 180$, $a = 50$; $b = 130$.

3 $e + e + 110 = 180$, $e = 35$.

5 $3h = h + 80$, $h = 40$; $i = 60$.

7 $k = 42$.

9 $n = 60$.

11 $r = 27$.

Exercise C (p. 154)

1 $a = 40$; $b = 70$.

3 $e = f = 80$; $g = 20$.

5 $j = 40$.

7 $l = 60 + 80 = 140$.

9 (*a*) 40 and 100, or 70 and 70.

11 $x = 90$.

Exercise D (p. 157)

1 $360°$; (*a*) $137°$; (*c*) $x = 36$.

3 (*a*) $S = 1440$; $144°$; (*b*) Exterior angle $= \dfrac{360°}{10} = 36°$.

5 18.

7 12.

Exercise E (p. 159)

1 See Figure A; isosceles; no.

3 See Figure B; parallelogram.

5 See Figure C.

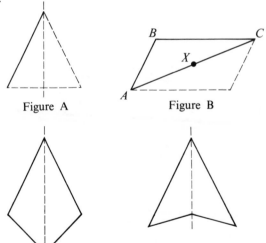

Figure A   Figure B

Figure C

Exercise F (p. 162)

3 Rhombuses and squares.

5 Parallelograms which are not rhombuses.

7 Rhombuses.

9 (*a*) S.

CHAPTER 20   PROBABILITY

Exercise A (p. 170)

1 $\frac{1}{4}$.   **3** 0; 1; $r \leqslant N$ so $\dfrac{r}{N} \leqslant 1$.

Exercise B (p. 172)

1 (*a*) $\frac{7}{10}$;   (*b*) $\frac{3}{10}$.   **3** (*a*) $\frac{1}{2}$;   (*b*) $\frac{3}{10}$.

5 (*a*) $\frac{2}{5}$;   (*c*) $\frac{1}{5}$.   **7** $\frac{19}{20}$.

Exercise C (p. 174)

1 (*a*) $\frac{1}{4}$;   (*c*) $\frac{1}{4}$.   **3** $\{(B, B), (B, G), (G, B), (G, G)\}$; $\frac{1}{2}$.

5 (*a*) $\frac{1}{6}$;   (*c*) $\frac{1}{2}$.   **7** (*a*) 216.

9 (*a*) $\frac{1}{13}$;   (*c*) $\frac{1}{52}$.

Index

addition of matrices   80–1
angles
  and parallel lines   150, 163
  of a polygon   156, 164
  of a triangle   151–2, 164
area
  bounded by a circle   6–7, 20
  of curved surface of a cylinder   12, 20
  of a sector   10
arrowhead   160

Bhāskara   112
Big Ben   5
brackets   108–10

Chevalier de Méré   168
chord   1, 19
circles   1–22
circumference of a circle   2–4, 20
combination
  of matrices   70–2
  of transformations   127
compatible matrices   72, 81
cones   14–17
  surface area of   16–17, 20
configurations   150–67
conjectures   103
constant of proportionality   23
converse   106
cosine   45, 46–7, 50, 65
counter-example   104
cylinder
  area of curved surface of   12, 20
  volume of   12, 20

data storage   69
diameter of circle   1
difference of two squares   109, 116
distributive rule   108–9
divisibility, tests for   112–13
dominances   78–9, 83

equations, graphs of   27–9, 32–3, 141–2
ERNIE   175
Euclid   150, 152

fallacies   120–1
frequency   86–9
frequency diagram   87–9
frequency table   86
  finding mean from   92–3

gradient
  average   35
  of straight lines   27, 39
  surveyor's   62
graphs
  equations of   27–9, 33
  gradients of   27–8
  of inequalities   144–6
  straight line   27, 32, 138–42
grid references   46–7
grouped frequency tables   88–90
  finding mean from   95–6

implication signs   105
inequalities   144–6
inverse functions   60
isosceles triangle   154

kite   160

linear equations   141–2

matrices
  addition of   80–1
  for dominances   78–9, 83
  multiplication of   70–2
  relations and   79
  route   76–7
  transpose of   79, 82
mean   92–6
mid-interval value   95
Montagne de Lure   36
multipliers   24, 39

Pappus   22
parallax   68
parallel lines   150, 163
parallelogram   161
Pascal, Blaise   168
π (pi)   2–4

195

polygons 156–7
position vectors 131–2
proof 107
proportion 23–9
Pythagoras' theorem 63–4, 65, 108, 111–12, 117

radius of a circle 1–2
random choice 175
rates 25, 40
refractive index 68
relative frequency 169–70
rhombus 160, 161–2
route matrices 76–7

sector of a circle 9–10, 19, 20
sine 45, 48, 50, 65
squares 110, 162
Staten Island ferry 59
statistics 84–100
symmetry
    of quadrilaterals 164–5

of triangles 164
types of 159

tangent (tan) 56–58, 65
transformations 122–35
    combining 127
    matrices representing 123–5
    rules for 122–3
    of vectors 130
transpose of a matrix 79, 82
trapezium, isosceles 161
triangles 151–4
    equilateral 155
    isosceles 154
trigonometric functions 45
Tsu Chung Chieh 4

vectors
    position 131–2
    transformations of 130
volume of a cylinder 12, 20

World Trade Center 59